Practice Education
in Social Work

OTHER TITLES IN THIS SERIES

The Approved Mental Health Professional's Guide to Mental Health Law	ISBN 978 1 84445 115 9
Critical Thinking for Social Work 2nd edition	ISBN 978 1 84445 157 9
Law and the Social Work Practitioner	ISBN 978 1 84445 059 6
Vulnerable Adults and Community Care	ISBN 978 1 84445 061 9
The Social Worker's Guide to the Mental Capacity Act 2005	ISBN 978 1 84445 129 6
The Approved Social Worker's Guide to Psychiatry and Medication	ISBN 978 1 84445 089 3
Practising Quality Assurance in Social Care	ISBN 978 1 84445 084 8
Managing with Plans and Budgets in Health and Social Care	ISBN 978 1 84445 134 0
Social Work Practice with Older Lesbians and Gay Men	ISBN 978 1 84445 182 1
The Integration of Mental Health Social Work and the NHS	ISBN 978 1 84445 150 0
Evidence-based Policy and Practice in Mental Health Social Work	ISBN 978 1 84445 149 4

To order, please contact our distributor: BEBC Distribution, Albion Close, Parkstone, Poole, BH12 3LL. Telephone: 0845 230 9000, email: learningmatters@bebc.co.uk. You can also find more information on each of these titles and our other learning resources at www.learningmatters.co.uk.

Practice Education in Social Work: A Handbook for Practice Teachers, Assessors and Educators

JANET WALKER

KARIN CRAWFORD

JONATHAN PARKER

Series Editor: Keith Brown

LearningMatters

First published in 2008 by Learning Matters Ltd

British Library Cataloguing in Publication Data
A CIP record for this book is available from the British Library.

ISBN: 978 1 84445 105 0

Cover and text design by Code 5 Design Associates Ltd
Project Management by Swales & Willis
Typeset by Swales & Willis Ltd, Exeter, Devon
Printed and bound in Great Britain by TJ International Ltd, Padstow, Cornwall

Learning Matters Ltd
33 Southernhay East
Exeter EX1 1 NX
Tel: 01392 215560
info@learningmatters.co.uk
www.learningmatters.co.uk

FSC
Mixed Sources
Product group from well-managed
forests and other controlled sources

Cert no. SGS-COC-2482
www.fsc.org
© 1996 Forest Stewardship Council

Contents

List of Figures ix

List of Tables x

List of Boxes xi

Foreword from the Series Editor xii

About the authors xiii

Introduction 1
Practice learning for social work educators 1
The development of the role of the practice educator 3
The post-qualifying framework for social work 4
Book structure 10
Summary 14
Professional development and reflective practice 14

1 **What is education in practice?** 15
Introduction 15
Defining social work 16
The context for social work practice 17
The practice of social work 18
Qualifying for social work 23
Practice education and learning 28
Critical reflection: making sense of practice 32

2 **What is learning?** 36
Introduction 37
How does the individual student learn? 37
Behaviourist theories 42
Social cognitive learning theories 42
Humanist theories 43
Experiential learning 43
Whole brian learning 47
Other aspects of learning 47

V

Learning to learn 48
How do I, as a practice educator, facilitate and enable
   student learning? 50
Conclusion 51

3 What is teaching? 53

Introduction 54
Learning and teaching in practice 54
Supporting the transfer of learning to practice 57
Developing your role as a 'teacher' 60
Developing teaching strategies 63
Teaching strategies 66
Recognising diversity in learners 72
Reflections on self 75

4 What is assessment? 77

Introduction 78
Meanings of assessment 79
What does the research say? 82
Assessment in practice learning/practice education 86
Continuing development and self-assessment as a
   practice educator 87
The assessment of students 87
The process of assessment as a practice educator 89
A self-efficacy model for assessing practice learning 93
Conclusion 97

5 What is supervision? 99

Introduction 100
Defining supervision 100
Functions of supervision 102
Models of supervision 105
The process of supervision through the 'life' of the placement 108
Issues of power in the supervisory relationship 114
Conclusion 117

6 Managing and developing practice learning experiences 118

Introduction 119
Planning before the placement 121
Induction 126
The development of learning agreements 128
Practice curriculum 129
Writing the report 133
Evaluating your plans and the managed process 135
Conclusion 136

7 What about me? 137

Introduction 137
Why do I need to think about my support and development
    needs? 138
What is the place of reflective and reflexive practice for
    me as a practice educator? 141
How do I continue to develop as a knowledge-informed
    practice educator? 146
What strategies and support processes are available to
    support me in managing my role and responsibilities as a
    practice educator? 148
How can my needs for support and learning be met within
    my networks of colleagues and other practice educators? 151
Where do I go from here? 153
Conclusion 154

Summary 156

**Appendix: Guidance on the Assessment of
Practice in the Workplace** 159

References 175

Index 185

List of Figures

2.1	The continuous spiral of professional development and learning	38
2.2	Three groups of learning theories	42
2.3	Kolb's experiential learning cycle	44
2.4	The experiential learning cycle in practice learning	45
3.1	The practice educator: roles as 'teacher'	61
3.2	Reflecting on your teaching	75
4.1	The complex directions of assessment in practice learning	79
4.2	Practice Learning Self-Efficacy Scale	95
4.3	A task-centred model for facilitating assessment in practice learning	97
6.1	A simple GANTT chart to develop a project plan for a placement	125
6.2	A simple critical path analysis for a placement	127
6.3	An exemplar learning agreement form	130
6.4	A SWOT analysis as an aid to evaluating placement management	135
7.1	Examples of practical reflective practice activities associated with Kolb's experiential learning cycle	144
7.2	Strategies and skills for managing time and workload	150

List of Tables

0.1	GSCC Post-Qualifying Framework for Social Work (England)	5
0.2	GSCC requirements for practice education for post-qualifying education and training	6
0.3	The three domains framework of generic statements	7
1.1	Two views of professional practice	33
2.1	Pedagogy and andragogy	38
2.2	The VAK model	46
2.3	Adapting teaching and learning to students' characteristics	50
3.1	Four positions on learning	55
3.2	The three-way relationship: the student, the practice educator and the university tutor	58
3.3	Some teaching methods	67
4.1	Areas of assessment and models	81
6.1	Mapping the needs and requirements when providing learning experiences	122
6.2	Induction planner	128

List of Boxes

0.1	Terminology	2
1.1	The roles and tasks of social work	20
1.2	Characteristics of good social work	21
1.3	Regulating and supporting organisations for social care in England	23
1.4	Summary of *The Requirements for Social Work Training*	25
1.5	Preparation of the social work student for practice learning opportunities	26
1.6	*National Occupational Standards for Social Work*	27
1.7	Values and ethics	28
1.8	Domains and requirements	32
1.9	Some questions to support critical reflection	34
3.1	Self-directed learning	65
3.2	Supporting the reflective process	70
4.1	Judging the evidence	92
5.1	Definitions of supervision	101
5.2	Anti-oppressive practice	103
5.3	Types of power	116
6.1	Action and learning plans	132
7.1	Extract from GSCC requirements for post-registration training	140
7.2	Literature summary – extracts from Moon (2004)	142
7.3	Literature summary – extract from D'Cruz et al. (2007)	143
7.4	Literature summary – Clutterbuck (2001)	149

Foreword from the Series Editor

All the texts in the Post-Qualifying Social Work Practice series have been written by people with a passion for excellence in social work practice. They are primarily written for social workers who are undertaking post-qualifying social work awards, but will also be useful to any social worker who wants to consider up-to-date practice issues.

The books in this series are also of value to social work students as they are written to inform, inspire and develop social work practice.

Keith Brown
Series Editor
Centre for Post-Qualifying Social Work, Bournemouth

About the authors

Janet Walker is a Principal Lecturer in Social Work at the University of Lincoln. Her academic responsibilities include supporting learners, teaching, programme and curriculum development of postgraduate interprofessional programmes. She also has experience of working with other countries in undertaking joint research projects and in developing teaching and learning in social care.

Karin Crawford is a Senior Lecturer in Social Work at the University of Lincoln where she has responsibility for supporting learners, teaching and curriculum development in the area of health, social care and management.

Professor Jonathan Parker is Head of Social Work and Learning Disability at Bournemouth University and, with colleagues, has developed the Centre of Social Work and Social Care Research. He is past chair of the Association of Teachers in Social Work Education and currently vice-chair of the Joint University Council Social Work Education Committee.

Introduction

This book is about teaching and learning in practice, specifically for students undertaking professional programmes of study. Learning in practice is an essential feature in supporting the development of a competent practitioner, and plays a central role in professional formation. Placements provide a learning environment for students and the student's experiences in practice stimulate that learning. For students on placement there is not only the opportunity to 'carry out' practice but critically to improve and extend their professional knowledge and process skills (Eraut, 1994).

This book is primarily aimed at practice educators, those people, based in practice who carry out practice learning, teaching, supervision and assessment of students undertaking learning in practice as part of their qualifying programme. The term 'practice educator' will be used throughout the book, but this will be interspersed with references to practice teachers, supervisors and practice assessors, recognising that these terms are used in a range of documents to denote the roles of individuals undertaking the support and assessment of individuals in practice. The term Practice Educator has been chosen to reflect the changing context of practice learning, particularly in social work education.

The focus in this book will be on social work education specifically for those individuals who act as practice assessors for students studying for qualification as social workers. It is primarily intended to support experienced and qualified social workers undertaking their own professional development within the General Social Care Council (GSCC) post-qualifying framework for England. It will also be relevant to post-qualifying practice education awards in Wales, Scotland and Northern Ireland. The book will also appeal to other professionals supporting students undertaking a period of assessed learning in practice as part of their award; for example nurses, occupational therapists and other allied professionals will be able to gain insight into the different theories, processes and skills which support students in their learning in practice settings.

Practice learning for social work educators

The content of practice learning for social work arises from expectations of government, employers and regulator, as well as from those who practise social work and those who use it. There have been many changes to the structure of both qualifying and post-qualifying education for social work. The changes in relation to qualifying as a professional social worker are identified in Chapter 1. The changes for post-qualifying education are discussed within this introduction.

Box 0.1: Terminology

- 'Student' is taken to mean the individual who is undertaking a programme of study leading to a professional qualification. Their programme of study will contain a significant assessed placement in practice.

- 'Practice assessor' is taken to mean the person who assesses the competence, or otherwise, of social work students. The task of a practice assessor is to enable the student to integrate theory and evidence-based practice into day-to-day work, to help the student to explore their values, and to address issues of anti-oppressive and anti-discriminatory practice. They will provide 'formal' supervision of the student. This person may not be based in the placement in which the student is undertaking their assessed practice; for example they may be an off-site ('long-arm') practice assessor. If this is the case then the agency will identify a work-based supervisor to support the student and work alongside the practice assessor.

- 'Work-based supervisor'/'practice supervisor assessor' is used to mean a person who is on-site who will provide day-to-day support and supervision to the student. They work alongside the practice assessor and will inform the assessment of the student.

- 'Practice teacher' is taken to mean those who specifically hold the Practice Teaching Award. This award was available through programmes approved by the GSCC under the previous post-qualifying framework for social work (CCETSW, 1995); these awards are therefore no longer available as there are new requirements in relation to the new post-qualifying framework (GSCC, 2005a).

- 'Practice educator' is used to mean those people, based in practice, who undertake the teaching, supervision and assessment of students undertaking learning in practice as part of their qualifying programme.

- 'Practitioner' is taken to mean individuals working in a range of occupations in social work or in other 'enabling' roles, for example, health and education.

- 'University tutor' is taken to mean the person who evaluates the teaching and learning on placement and supports the student and practice assessor in the placement. The link is realised through phone contact and 'three-way' meetings during the placement.

- 'Practice learning' is taken to mean the learning that takes place whilst a student is on placement in a practice setting. It is designed to help students apply knowledge, skills and values into practice.

- 'Programme provider' is taken to mean the university which provides educational programmes.

- GSCC refers to the General Social Care Council, the professional regulation and registration body for social work in England. This was previously the Central Council for Education and Training in Social Work (CCETSW). www.gscc.org.uk

- SfC refers to Skills for Care. SfC is concerned with workforce planning and development of the social care workforce for adults, including the development of national standards and a national development strategy and qualification framework. www.skillsforcare.org.uk

- CWDC refers to the Children's Workforce Development Council which provides similar functions to SfC in relation to the children's workforce. www.cwdcouncil.org.uk

The development of the role of the practice educator

Opinion has varied over the past forty years as to the need for the person who acts as a Practice Educator during the placement of a student social worker to hold a professional qualification. One view was that 'the only qualification necessary [is that they should be] reasonably competent and knowledgeable in her own field of practice' (Young, 1967: 12). For the student social worker, it seemed that merely 'sitting alongside' a practitioner would ensure that they would learn to do the 'job'. The Central Council for Education and Training in Social Work (CCETSW) published Paper 26.3 in 1989 (further revised in 1991) (CCETSW 1991 [1989]), setting out a new, competency-based requirements for practice teachers who supervise student social workers. The learning outcomes for the Practice Teaching Award was developed to provide an opportunity for individuals to achieve a qualification to support them in their roles and responsibilities in providing learning and teaching, assessment and support of students in practice. Competences to achieve the award were prescribed through the national Post-Qualifying Education and Training Award framework (CCETSW, 1995), with achievement of all the PQ competencies ultimately leading to the Post-Qualifying Award in Social Work (PQSW). The PQSW was achieved by meeting six general and two core requirements. The Practice Teaching Award provides two of the general requirements for the PQSW (PQ5 and PQ6).

The Practice Teaching Award was seen as a means of ensuring quality and standards for students on placement with a recommendation that all practitioners who play a key role in the learning and assessment of students on practice placements should be Practice Teaching Award holders. Whilst this was the aspiration, in practice this has been hard to achieve, with a continuing concern about the lack of high- quality practice placements supported by trained, qualified practice teachers. Kearney (2003) acknowledges that during the latter years of the Diploma in Social Work the numbers of placements available were being reduced due to high turnover of social workers and high levels of vacancies. In addition, social workers who gained the Practice Teaching Award were subsequently moving into management positions.

Following the major reforms by the Department of Health (DoH, 2002b) to the qualification to practice as a registered social worker, with an honours degree replacing the two-year Diploma in Social Work, the 'solution' to increasing the number of people available to support and assess students in practice from the key national bodies, GSCC

and Skills for Care (SfC) had been to abandon the concept of the practice teacher in favour of the concept of the practice assessor. The development of the role of the practice assessors was seen to reflect the 'new environment', requiring a 'shift in perception from individual assessors of individual students to a workplace where every social care worker sees practice learning as their business' (Kearney, 2003: 2). 'Critical mass' (Kearney, 2003:5) was seen as the key to providing and sustaining practice placements over a period of time.

The post-qualifying framework for social work

With changes to the routes to qualifying as a social worker, significant changes have also been made to the framework for post-qualifying education. The routes to achieving post-qualifying awards for social work are complex.

The previous framework and standards for awards was develop by the Central Council for Education and Training in Social Work (CCETSW, the predecessor organisation of the GSCC), with development, accreditation and assessment of programmes 'managed' by regional consortia, made up of employers, colleges and universities. Some programmes were 'centrally credit rated' by CCETSW/GSCC. One of these awards was the Practice Teaching Programme, providing a qualification for those individuals supervising and managing social work students whilst on practice placements as part of their progress towards achieving their social work qualification. With the changes to the qualifying routes for social work, the GSCC has undertaken a major reform of the post-qualifying awards.

The *Post-Qualifying (PQ) Framework for Social Work Education and Training* (GSCC, 2005a) defines the general requirements for all new national post-qualifying programmes. These are provided through universities in partnership with local stakeholders (including the statutory and independent sectors, and service users and carers). Universities providing programmes of study linked to PQ requirements must be approved by the GSCC; in addition Regional Planning Networks (supported by SfC and on behalf of the Children's Workforce Development Council [CWDC]) made up of employers, service users and academic institutions) are responsible for identifying need in the region and verifying specific programmes to be provided by universities. It should be noted that post-qualifying requirements differ between the different countries of the UK.

General requirements include:

- Programmes are intended to be flexible and modular, making them accessible for potential students;

- The focus is on application and assessment of learning in practice;

- Programmes must be linked to:

  - the specific requirements for each specialism. The specialisms and the specialist 'pathways' are outlined in Table 1;

  - *National Occupational Standards for Social Work* (Topss/SfC, 2002);

  - the GSCC *Codes of Practice* (GSCC, 2002a);

Table 0.1: GSCC Post-Qualifying Framework for Social Work (England)

Level	Potential route	Intended to	Level of qualification	Comments
Specialist	• Working with Children and Young People their Families and Carers • Social Work with Adults • Social Work in Mental Health Services • Leadership and Management (for residential mangers only)	Consolidate, deepen and extend initial professional competence in a specialist context	Graduate Diploma/Honours degree (top up)/Postgraduate Certificate	Consolidation of competence must be successfully completed before the start of any other module can be started Core Practice education (Enabling Others) must be included
Higher Specialist	• Professional Practice (with pathways in Children and Families; Adults; Mental health) • Leadership and Management • Applied Professional Research • Practice Education	Focus on the knowledge and skills needed to make complex judgements and decisions	Postgraduate Diploma (Masters level)	Qualification for the role of Approved Mental Health Practitioner (AMHP) is at this level Aspects of practice education are integral to the roles expected of practitioners
Advanced	• Professional Practice (with pathways in Children and Families; Adults; Mental health) • Leadership and Management • Applied Professional Research • Practice Education	Focus on the knowledge and skills required for professional leadership and the improvement of services (professional leadership/advanced practice skills)	Masters level	Aspects of practice education are integral to the roles

- *Guidance on the Assessment of Practice in the Workplace* (Topss/GSCC, 2002). These are outlined in Table 3.

- Programmes must have a strong interprofessional element.

- Consolidation of Practice must be demonstrated against generic and specific award requirements at Specialist Social Work Award level as a first module.

In addition, the significant increase in practice days within the new qualifying social work degree means that there is a need to develop and sustain a greater number of individuals to support and assess students in the workplace. This has been recognised within the PQ

Table 0.2: GSCC requirements for practice education for post-qualifying education and training

Level	For whom	Content and competencies
Specialist	No specific stand-alone award but a specific Core Education module must underpin all PQ specialist awards as an integral aspect of the process of acquiring in-depth competence.	The three core domains outlined in *Guidance on the Assessment of Practice in the Workplace* (Topss/ GSCC, 2002) (see Table 0.3). The generic PQ criterion related to: teaching and assessing the practice of student social workers and mentoring and supporting students or colleagues (GSCC, 2005a: para 49). Contribute to the learning organisation primarily through engagement with individual pre-qualifying learners and unqualified staff on a one-to-one basis.
Higher Specialist and Advanced	A practitioner who may begin to be recognised as an expert and may lead groups of colleagues, teams, other communities, and/or represent their employer, in local, regional and national training networks.	Develops learning from the three core domains and includes: supporting, mentoring, supervising or managing others, enabling them to identify and explore issues and improve their practice (GSCC, 2005a: para 51); and supporting, mentoring or managing others, exercising practice, research, management or educational leadership to identify and explore issues and improve their own practice (GSCC, 2005a: para 52). A more in-depth understanding of the discipline of teaching and assessment and a growing awareness of the student learning experience, involving directing teaching and assessment to focus on the needs, perceptions and experiences of students and learners and the relationship between students, learners and the subject matter. Using knowledge, experience and awareness, the practice educator may then lead others in the design, direction and development of teaching and assessment. They should seek to become champions of the learning organisation.

Table 0.3: The three domains framework of generic statements which define and describe the core activities involved in assessing the practice of others (Topss/GSCC, Guidance on the Assessment of Practice in the Workplace, 2002b)

Domain	A. Organise opportunities for the demonstration of assessed competence in practice	B. Enable learning and professional development in practice	C. Manage assessment of learners in practice
	A and B must be assessed before a full and final assessment of their competence in all the domains, including domain C		
	1. Take responsibility for creating a physical and learning environment conducive to the demonstration of assessed competence.	1. Establish the basis of an effective working relationship by identifying learners' expectations, the outcomes which they have to meet in order to demonstrate competence, and their readiness for assessment. Agree the available learning opportunities, methods, resources, and timescales to enable them to succeed.	1. Engage learners in the design, planning and implementation of the assessment tasks.
	2. Negotiate with all participants in the workplace, including service users and carers, appropriate learning opportunities and the necessary resources to enable the demonstration of practice competence.	2. Discuss, identify, plan to address and review the particular needs and capabilities of learners, and the support available to them. Identify any matters which may impact on their ability to manage their own learning.	2. Agree and review a plan and methods for assessing learners' performance against agreed criteria.
	3. Work openly and cooperatively with learners and their line managers, workplace colleagues other professionals, and service users and carers, in the planning of key activities at all stages of learning and assessment.	3. Discuss and take into account individuals' learning styles, learning needs, prior learning achievements, knowledge and skills. Devise an appropriate, cost-effective assessment programme which promotes their ability to learn and succeed.	3. Ensure that assessment decisions are the outcomes of informed, evidence-based judgements and clearly explain them to learners.
	4. Coordinate the work of all contributors. Ensure they are fully briefed, understand their roles and provide them with feedback.		4. Evaluate evidence for its relevance, validity, reliability, sufficiency and authenticity according to the agreed standard.
	5. Monitor, critically evaluate and report on the continuing suitability of the work environment,		5. Use direct observation of learners in practice to assess performance.
			6. Base assessment decisions on all relevant evidence and from a range of sources,

Table 0.3: Continued

Domain	A. Organise opportunities for the demonstration of assessed competence in practice	B. Enable learning and professional development in practice	C. Manage assessment of learners in practice
	learning opportunities, and resources. Take appropriate action to address any shortcomings and optimise learning and assessment. 6 Contribute to the learning and development of the agency as a training organisation. Help to review and improve its provision, policies and procedures and identify barriers for learners.	4. Make professional educational judgements about meeting learners' needs within the available resources, ensuring the required learning outcomes can be demonstrated in accordance with adult learning models. 5. Identify which aspects of the management of the learning and assessment programme learners are responsible for in order to achieve their objectives. Describe and agree the roles of the work-based assessor in mentoring, coaching, modelling, teaching and supervision. 6. Establish how the learning and assessment programme is to be reviewed. Encourage learners to express their views, identify and agree any changes and how disagreements on any aspects of it are resolved. 7. Advise learners how to develop their ability to manage their learning. Deal with any difficulties encountered by them.	resolving any inconsistencies in the evidence available. 7. Encourage learners to self-evaluate and seek service users, carers and peer group feedback on their performance. 8. Provide timely, honest and constructive feedback on learners' performance in an appropriate format. Review their progress through the assessment process, distinguishing between formative and summative assessment. 9. Make clear to learners how they may improve their performance. Identify any specific learning outcomes not yet demonstrated and the next steps. If necessary, arrange appropriate additional assessment activity to enable them to meet the standard. 10. Ensure that all assessment decisions, and

the supporting evidence, are documented and recorded according to the required standard. Produce assessment reports which provide clear evidence for decisions.

11. Ensure that disagreements about assessment judgments and complaints made about the assessment process are managed in accordance with agreed procedures.

12. Seek feedback from learners on their experience of being assessed, and the consequences of the assessment programme for them. Incorporate the feedback into future assessment activity.

13. Contribute to standardisation arrangements and the agreed quality-assurance processes which monitor the organisation's training strategy.

framework by specifying that all individuals undertaking awards at Specialist level must undertake a specific core education module. For those undertaking other pathways of learning at Higher Specialist and Advanced levels of the framework must include aspects of practice education. Specific awards in practice education are at Higher Specialist and Advanced levels within the framework and are intended to be aimed at experienced mentors, practice assessors and practice educators.

Central to this is a movement away from a position of one student with one practice teacher to a more integrated approach that makes practice learning 'everybody's business' (Practice Learning Taskforce, 2003). This is more likely to be achieved, it is argued, within a culture of 'learning organisations' with a 'team approach' to students on placement. Practice learning and practice assessors are seen as having a key role in the growth of a learning culture within social care. The advantages to an organisation and team in providing practice learning opportunities for students has long been recognised as contributing to the work of the team, stimulating the learning environment and supporting recruitment (Davies and Connolly , 1994).

Book structure

This book will examine contemporary theories and knowledge in practice learning, teaching and education, with a clear emphasis on developing the theoretical and creative skills and knowledge of the individual. A key focus will be to support readers to reflect on the implications of this for their role as a practice educator.

Meeting relevant standards

All chapters have drawn on the standards outlined in three key documents:

- GSCC (2005a) *Post-Qualifying Framework for Social Work Education and Training*.
- GSCC (2005b) *Specialist Standards and Requirements for Post-Qualifying Education and Training*.
- Topss/GSCC (2002) *Guidance on Assessment of Practice in the Workplace*.

These standards reflect learning up to a Master's level of qualification. All of these documents are available on the GSCC's website: www.gscc.org.uk

All of the chapters will help to meet the following standards from the GSCC (2005a) *Post-Qualifying Framework for Social Work Education and Training* at *Specialist* level:

5. At this level, the aim is to develop well-rounded practitioners . . . who have demonstrated competence in a range of key areas including . . . self-management and use of supervision and mentoring and practice education.

49. In order to satisfy approval requirements, specialist programmes must show how they enable qualified social workers to . . .

viii. teach and assess the practice of student social workers and mentor and support students or colleagues.

For practitioners undertaking the *Higher Specialist* award it will enable you to meet the demands of complex decision-making and high levels of professional decision-making (Standard 51).

For practitioners undertaking the *Advanced* award it will enable you to demonstrate the requirement for you to take a leadership role in developing your own practice and in promoting good practice (Standard 52).

All the chapters will draw on the GSCC (2005b) *Specialist Standards and Requirements for Post-qualifying Education and Training*, recognising that there is an expectation that everyone undertaking awards that draw on post-qualifying standards will support the learning of others in practice.

Specifically at *Specialist* level the general principle is:

> 10. *Practice education specific training at the specialist PQ level draws on the belief that irrespective of location and employment mode, from the point of qualification onwards, all social workers should commence the transition from one who has been enabled by others to one who now enables others.*

> 11. *At the specialist level, practice education is conceived of as an integral aspect of the process of acquiring in-depth competence. The capacity to enable and nurture others and then recognise and confirm their achievements is evidence of professional self-development. The appropriate standards for this at the specialist PQ level are contained in the three domains outlined in Guidance on the Assessment of Practice in the Workplace.*

(Topss/GSCC, 2002).

For *Higher Specialist* and *Advanced* levels the general principle is:

> 19. *In relation to practice education at the higher specialist and advanced levels, these principles of pedagogy, designed to promote and enhance the adult learning experience, must be located within the workplace and aligned to the needs of the organisation. The linkage with the assessment of practice in the workplace remains paramount.*

In addition Standard 37 identifies twelve specific principles of pedagogy and adult learning. All chapters will support learners in meeting these standards.

Topss/GSCC (2002: 10–11) *Guidance on Assessment of Practice in the Workplace* document outlines seven specific value requirements for work-based assessors in order to promote anti-oppressive and anti-discriminatory practices, and three domains of activity 'in which the applied value and professional development base for work-based assessors should be integrated but which may be thought to be sets of activities carried through in all work-based assessment' (Topss/GSCC, 2002: 8).

- Domain A: Organise opportunities for the demonstration of assessed competence in practice
- B: Enable learning and professional development in practice and
- C: Manage the assessment of learners in practice.

11

Each chapter will identify the relevant individual standards identified under each domain, and will also identify the relevant value requirement. All chapters will draw on and identify the relevant domain specific knowledge and value requirement identified in the document.

The content of the book

There are seven core chapters to this book.

Chapter 1 What is education in practice?

This chapter will focus on the changing context of contemporary social work practice education and its centrality for the role of practice educator. It will examine the changing context of practice, particularly for social work, specifically the organisation and management of organisations in providing services through collaborative working. The reader will be invited to identify and reflect on their understanding of their professional identity and role. This will support them in considering the importance and emphasis of their role in developing and supporting students as practice educators.

It will provide an overview of the social work degree and the development of the practice educator's role in social work. Definitions and explanations of the various roles and responsibilities associated with practice education will be provided. It will develop the readers' understanding of current expectations and the challenges for the practice educator, emphasising the partnership aspect as a relationship between the practice educator, academic institution and the student.

Chapter 2 What is learning?

This chapter invites the reader to consider and evaluate their overall approach and perspective on learning in practice education. It will consider what is student-centred learning, examine the concept of knowledge, and the various 'ingredients' available in the development of the learning process: this will include the personal 'sensors' (communication through the senses, emotions in learning), the learning environment, activities that promote learning and the internal environment (understanding ways of learning and stimulating intelligence). The relationship between the learning of 'theory' (academic context of learning) and work-based learning as an applied and holistic process will be explored as a critical theme for effective learning, with critical reflection as the key capability of the practitioner in enabling this process. Models and theories will be examined to support the reader's understanding.

Chapter 3 What is teaching?

Moving on from an exploration of learning, this chapter invites the reader to consider and evaluate their overall approach and perspective on teaching in practice education. Definitions of teaching will be offered and the role of the practice educator as a 'teacher' will be examined. Different methods of teaching will be outlined, particularly those that support the development of skills and values and address the issues of anti-oppressive practice. Models and theories will be examined to support the readers understanding.

Chapter 4 What is assessment?

This chapter invites the reader to consider and evaluate their overall approach and perspective on assessment in practice education. It will define the concept of assessment and examine the purpose and principles of assessment. The concept of formative and summative assessment will be explored. The chapter will consider how the practice educator gathers evidence to support assessment. Self-efficacy beliefs will be examined and explained. This chapter will necessarily deal with power issues and relations that inevitably arise in respect of this element of the practice education process.

Chapter 5 What is supervision?

This chapter will examine the concept of 'supervision' as one of the most important factors in supporting and determining the quality of the service to service users, and the outcome of the practice education experience of the student and practice educator. It will examine the theory and practice of supervision, with a focus on the specific supervision needs of students. It will examine the functions of supervision. The power issues between the practice educator and student will be explored. Stages, strategies and skills of supervision will be discussed. Direct practice in supervision will be considered, that is to say the format and structure of supervision. The practice educator will be invited to consider their own needs in relation to supervision and support in relation to the learning, teaching and assessment of the student.

Chapter 6 Managing and developing practice learning experiences

Preparing and planning the placement will be considered, including developing a practice curriculum, the construction of the learning contract and negotiating within and outside the agency to develop creative and novel experiences, including networked practice learning opportunities. The context of different practice learning settings will be examined, for example the statutory, private, independent or voluntary sector. The different stages of a placement will be considered and the role and responsibility of the practice educator and student at these stages. The necessary partnerships and collaboration with the academic institution will be examined. Consideration will be given to identifying others who may be involved in the practice placement at individual (e.g. another colleague), team, agency and organisational levels, and how this may take place.

Chapter 7 What about 'me'?

This chapter will examine the development of self, considering the personal strategies that could support the practice educator in managing their role and responsibilities. It will consider issues of professional development. It will develop the reader's understanding of the potential of a wider network of practice educators through an examination of the concept of 'communities of practice'.

Summary

This chapter will provide a summary of the key learning points from the book. It will highlight the key themes of the 'learning organisation' as a key concept to embed student learning in practice.

This book is interactive. However you choose to use this book, you are encouraged to be an active participant in your own learning, taking responsibility for your own learning, identifying your knowledge and skills as a practitioner and as a practice educator, and especially in reflecting on and applying your learning to practice. Throughout the book there will be:

- Activities to develop, support and reinforce the readers' learning, reflections and understanding;

- Use of summaries of contemporary research evidence and key journal articles to extend the reader's understanding;

- Reflective opportunities within the text to develop and reinforce the reader's learning;

- Clear guidance to further reading to develop and extend the reader's understanding.

Professional development and reflective practice

This book places great emphasis on skills of analysis and reflection in and about practice. As a professional working in practice, you will be engaged in a continual process of life-long learning as a way of keeping up to date, ensuring that knowledge and research inform your practice as a way of developing and improving your skills and honing values and ethics for practice. The concept of reflective practice will be familiar to you: you recognise the importance of engaging in reflexive and reflective practice in all your interactions. Reflection about, in and on your practice is considered as the underpinning principle of the post-qualifying framework.

As a practice educator you will recognise the value and critical importance of supporting and developing the skills of the student in reflecting on and analysing their own practice, and in using the processes involved in reflection both within and in talking about their practice with you. The processes involved in reflection are reviewed in Chapter 3.

Chapter 1
What is education in practice?

Introduction

This chapter is intended to provide you with an overview of the context in which practice education takes place and the implications for education for practice, particularly for social work. We begin this chapter by examining definitions of 'social work'. This will provide a basis for the next section, which explores the rapidly changing context of practice and where social work 'fits' within this environment, especially in engaging service users and carers. You will be invited to identify and reflect on the implications and impact of these changes both in practice and for your professional identity and role. We then turn to look at education for practice through an examination of the processes involved in qualifying for social work. Critically we will then seek to support you in identifying the roles and responsibilities of the practice educator and reflecting on the implications for you and your practice as an educator.

Defining social work

Definitions provide us with a degree of certainty about the profession in which we work; they have the potential to provide clarity, a sense of identity and purpose in a demanding professional environment in which the profession is practised, especially in the face of challenges and ambivalence to the profession of social work. Defining what 'social work' is could be said to be complex especially in attempting to acknowledge the breadth and depth of social work operating within complex human situations. Nevertheless we present two definitions of social work which seek to capture these complexities. Before you begin this section reflect on your own definition and understanding of social work.

ACTIVITY

How would you define 'social work'? What do you see as it key tasks and functions? What do you see as the challenges for the profession now? Into the future?

The widely accepted definition of social work has been developed by the International Federation of Social Work (IFSW).

> *The social work profession promotes social change, problem solving in human relationships and the empowerment and liberation of people to enhance well-being. Utilising theories of human behaviour and social systems, social work intervenes at the point where people interact with their environments. Principles of human rights and social justice are fundamental to social work.*

> (IFSW, 2006 cited in Cox and Pawar, 2006: 22)

The most recent definition of social work in England has been outlined in *Options for Excellence*:

> *Social work is a problem-solving activity, carried out by the worker through relationships with the individual, family and community. Social work is usually needed when individuals, families or groups are facing a major and often life changing problem or challenge. Social workers help individuals and families to achieve the outcomes they want in the ways they prefer.*

> *Social work has a specific focus on:*

> * *promoting people's ability to maximize their own capabilities and life options, including participation in education, training, employment, social and leisure activities;*

> * *developing people's ability to form positive relationships within their family and their social network;*

> * *helping people to create and maintain independence, and, when this is not possible, to benefit from alternative forms of support that protect their dignity, rights and choices; and*

- *protecting people's human rights, and promoting the exercise of their rights and responsibilities as citizens.*

(DoH and DfES, 2006: 49)

How do these definitions compare to your own definition? The first definition is intended to encompass the global dimensions of social work; it therefore could be said to conceptualise social work in a broad sense. For everyday practice these themes may seem a little remote; nevertheless they can be identified within governance and law, such as the UN Convention on the Rights of the Child and the Human Rights Act 1998. The challenges of these for social workers are evident in the professional responsibilities undertaken by individual social workers: for example, for Approved Mental Health Professionals (AMPHs) in making decisions about orders for treatment. Additionally, the IFSW definition reflects the importance of relationships with the individual, for example through the empower-ment of the individual, at the level of direct practice, but also acknowledges the wider political and social issues through the issue of social justice, for example structural disadvantage; issues in social exclusion. Whilst understanding of social work and the application of knowledge and skills may vary at a global level, what appears to be common to all is the acceptance of its value base and commitment to social change (Healey, 2001). The second definition identifies social work's concern with working with individuals, families and communities; for example, the importance of relationships and face-to-face practice. It also acknowledges the importance of the context in which individuals, families and communities interact and in which social work practice takes place. However, this definition could be criticised as merely reflecting the current expecta-tions of social work, particularly as outlined in policy documents, rather than seeking to reflect the dynamic contribution and potential of social work and social work practice.

Potentially a more workable definition for 'everyday practice' is offered by O'Connor et al. (2006: 9), who provide a definition based on the focus and purpose of social work practice.

The focus of social work practice is the interaction between people and social arrangements. The purpose of practice is to promote the development of equitable relationships and the development of people's power and control over their lives, and hence to improve the interaction between people and social arrangements.

The context for social work practice

In the UK we are living through a period of radical reform of the public sector, especially that part of it that is concerned with the welfare of citizens.

(Jordan and Jordan, 2006: 13)

There has been rapid and continuous change within the social welfare sector over a number of years. This has had a significant impact on the role of those working in the social welfare system, including social workers. This can be evidenced, for example, through the impact of legislative and policy changes throughout the sector.

As Blewitt (2008) suggests, the interrelationship between policy and practice is complex and often messy; there can exist a tension for the practitioner and the organisations between all the different messages outlined in a whole number of different policy initiatives and political messages. In addition 'social welfare organisations are complex systems and a range of unintended consequences can arise from different factors' (2008: 239). Pressures in one service could, for example, mean that resources may be 'channelled' from other service areas. The 'modernisation' agenda has led to a rationalisation of services and a mixed economy of care in which the market-led model has been extended into all aspects of service delivery. Service delivery has been increasingly in organisations that have seen the integration of services between education and children's services; and for adults through integration with health services. This has been underpinned by regulation and inspection regimes; internal and external performance management and quality assurance systems; and national star ratings and league tables (Hafford-Letchfield, 2006).

The growth of bureaucracy and managerialism, especially under New Labour, has been criticised for tilting the balance between organisational criteria and professional judgement (Martin et al., 2004) and for making organisations focus on administrative, procedural and organisational aspects of their role (Lymbery and Butler, 2004). However Senior and Lodes (2008) remind us that the attempt to develop criteria of risk and need has been about the equitable focus of resources. The endeavour has been to deal with individuals fairly and to ensure equitable meeting of need within the community; in addition, clear policy and procedure are seen as essential in safeguarding individuals.

The relevance of these changes for service users and carers (and citizens in general) has been an approach to wanting to empower them to be involved in the development of services: terminology such as 'consultation', 'involvement', 'empowerment' and 'participation' has been increasingly evident in the language of organisations. Policy directives (for example, *Every Child Matters*, DfES, 2004, and *Our Health, Our Care, Our Say*, DoH, 2006) have been based on substantial consultation with users and carers. The nature of practice is also changing: there is an expectation that agencies will encourage choice, promote independence and consultation, and provide cost-effective services with increasing number of service users becoming employers, through direct payments (DoH, 1996). In completing a qualification to become a social worker or undertaking post-qualifying training there is a requirement to involve service users and carers in all aspects of development and delivery of the programme of learning.

The practice of social work

It has been suggested that social work is 'socially constructed' (Parton and O'Byrne, 2000; Payne, 2005). This perspective proposes that there is no fixed state within social work; social work is the consequence of changing expectations of the social conditions in which social work is practised. Social work is historically and culturally determined. This is reflected in the relationship that social work has with the state; Parton (1996) suggests that it is the interrelationship with the state that determined social work rationale and legitimacy.

Within the profession there has been concern about the increasing bureaucratisation and trend towards greater regulation, surveillance and inspection (Adams et al., 2005b). This is seen as an attempt to reduce the potential of risk and harm to users of service; it can also be seen as monitoring and controlling the actions of the professional. As Harris (2003) suggests, every aspect of social work has been profoundly affected, in the last fifteen years, by the culture of competition and the increase of managerialism. For many there is the feeling of being overwhelmed and restricted to working with rigid frameworks and dispensing scarce resources. Cooper and Lousada (2005) argue that practitioners and managers have been colonised by organised procedures and rules and have no concept of doing other than directed by the growing rule-book. It is important to acknowledge that these views and feelings about practice are not peculiar to social work but also reflect the concerns of other professionals and professional groups, such as those in health and education.

Social workers have had to adjust to periods of immense change in terms of their roles and responsibilities; in the organisational and managerial structures in which they work, for example through working in multi-disciplinary teams, and in the complex, and often harsh, environments in which they practice. Social workers are accountable to a wide range of institutions and individuals: the law, their employers, their professional ethics and standards, colleagues, service users and carers. As we have identified, social work is governed by laws and bureaucratic rules and procedures, which confer power but can also be said to restrict professional autonomy.

There is no escaping the profound influence of political and economic factors upon the focus and nature of the social work task. There has been a dominance of 'procedures' over reflective practice. Systems to ensure agency accountability have led to the development of detailed procedures as a response. While these have conferred powers on practitioners, they have also restricted professional autonomy (Adams et al., 2005a). This can lead to tensions between government and those paid by the state to tend to vulnerable people.

As a social worker you will certainly recognise the many challenges for social work and social work practice. O'Connor et al. (2006) suggest social work practice is bound by the domain of social welfare and the social, economic and cultural structures in which it is embedded. As professional workers there is a need to maintain a balance between the technical skills, for example in working within procedural guidelines, and the professional agenda of working with the complexity and working creatively. Complexity arises from the situations in which practitioners engage; creativity arises from the need to work innovatively in responding to the challenges and in the judgements and decisions that need to be made (Adams, 2007). Sheppard (2006) suggests that that there is a need to distinguish between the surface characteristics of social work (those that are subject to changes in context and emphasis, such as changes directed by procedures and policy) and those characteristics that are enduring and at a deeper level.

In seeking to identify the enduring and deeper-level characteristics, there is a need to remind ourselves of the legitimacy of social work. Cree and Davis (2007) provide insights into very positive views from service users and carers in defining what they want from social workers. Service users and carers want practitioners who will listen to them, treat them with respect and who see them in the context of their families and the communities in which they live. Practitioners come into social work from a desire to help others and to bring about social justice. The enjoyment of social work is in building relationships, working creatively with others and making a difference in their lives and in society as a whole.

Box 1.1: *The roles and tasks of social work*

In *The Changing Roles and Tasks of Social Work: A Literature Informed Discussion Paper* (2007), Blewitt et al. have sought to provide an overview of current and recent understanding to the roles and tasks of social work from professional and policy literature to provide a context for discussion.

The report is organised into five sections:

1. Towards an understanding of social work policy and practice:

   - ore components: This section identifies seven core components:

   (a)   Understanding the dynamic between the individual and the social

   (b)   Social work and social justice

   (c)   The transformatory significance of the relationship

   (d)   The enabling role of social work

   (e)   The therapeutic role of social work

   (f)   The management of risk to both the community and the individual

   (g)   The evidence base for social work practice

2. The contexts of social work

   - Structural factors

   - A policy context for social work with adults

   - A policy context for child and family social work

3. Roles and tasks in social work practice with adults

4. Roles and tasks in social work practice with children and families

5. Towards 2020: the challenge for social work

As Blewitt et al. suggest:

> the paper is based on a conviction that social work as a profession is well placed to meet the challenges of a complex and rapidly changing policy context and to make an important and unique contribution to all of the new service configurations in respect of children and adult services.

> (2007: 2)

Accessed from: www.gscc.org.uk News and Events\Consultation

Box 1.2: Characteristics of good social work

Cree and Davis (2007) draw together characteristics of good social work from the perspectives of 59 people from across the UK about how and why social work came into their lives.

Good social work is:

- Responsive – this means providing immediate and timely help. This also means services that are accessible – in terms of language (for example, the lack of jargon) and geographical setting. Social work response must be respectful of the service user.

About relationship building:

> In order to build relationships with others, social workers must be prepared to reflect on who they are and what they bring to their social work practice; they must be aware of the impact of themselves on others.
>
> (2007: 151)

- Person-centred – this means seeing service users as a whole person. This means providing a flexible range of services.

- About support which is both emotional and practical.

- Holistic – this means such things as being committed to working with others and bringing together different services to support people. It also means a commitment to improving communities, therefore reducing the need for social work in people's lives.

- About balancing rights, risks and protection.

- Knowledgeable and evidence-based.

- Future orientated – this means helping service users to look to the future, set goals and make realistic goals.

- There for the long term. This means not only continuity in terms of who is the social worker but also in acknowledging that some people are likely to have social work contact for the rest of their lives.

The importance of the processes we engage in and the relationships that we build with service users and carers is a critical element that distinguishes social work. In addition, as Lymbery and Postle (2007) suggest, social workers can be distinguished from other professions in their ability to appreciate and work at a wider macro level. This acknowledges the wider political and social context in which individuals, groups and communities live, and the potential for inequality and injustice to impact on the lives of the people. For Beresford and Wilson (1998) this involves not only ensuring that service users are able to present that perspective, but also incorporating that knowledge and analysis in the debates about inclusion and exclusion.

The social work profession is concerned with the notion of relationships within care and caring for others and this can most readily be understood through the profession's value base and commitment to social justice at micro and macro levels . . . The social work profession is most able to differentiate itself from others within the broad field of the helping professions by asserting the need for the profession to engage directly with others in a service user's network and engage directly with people's relationships, not only with individuals.

(Burt and Worsley, 2008: 38)

ACTIVITY

Reflect on the environment in which you are practising and identify the challenges and opportunities for your practice.

- *Key legislation, policy and guidance that inform and guide services in your practice area*

- *The organisational context in which you practice*

- *The team in which you practice*

- *Working with other professionals*

- *Working with service users and carers*

- *The implications on you as a professional social worker*

- *What are the implications for:*

  - *your role as a practice educator?*

  - *the student?*

In order to prepare yourself for supporting a student in a practice placement it is important to consider the environment in which social care practice takes place. You will have no doubt identified a significant range of challenges and opportunities for practice, for social work practice and for your own practice. In turn these will have implications for you in working as a practice educator and for the student you will be working with. This will help you in 'defining' the context in which the placement will take place; the learning opportunities and challenges available within the placement; the professional environment in which the student will undertake their practice; and it will help you identify your own position as a practitioner and the professional and the personal values and beliefs that guide your own practice. In doing this, we hope you will be able to reflect on your professional identity and role. This will support you further in critically reflecting on your practice and the implications for your role as a practice educator in developing and supporting students.

In this next section we move to examine qualifying for practice as a professional in social work. We examine the role and responsibilities of the practice educator with this and reflect on what this will mean for you as the practice educator.

Qualifying for social work

Social work education has, in recent years, undergone major changes, with a shift in increasing the level of qualification from diploma to degree level. There has been a rigorous overhaul of the academic and practice element of social work degree programmes. This is in recognition of the increasing complexity of the nature of professional social work practise; to raise the status of the profession and to increase recruitment and the standard of those recruited. The task faced for education in social work is one of managing a complex array of factors, which impinge on its design and delivery, to produce a programme that is coherent but is also flexible and open to innovation.

For social work in England, contextual forces include concerns to enhance the nature and quality of practice with service users and carers through reforms within and regulation of the social care workforce. A critical factor in this has been reforms to ensure better-trained social work professionals, to improve competence and confidence in the workforce, with the establishment of key national organisations (DoH, 2002a) and, critically, the reform of qualifying and post-qualifying education.

Box 1.3: *Regulating and supporting organisations for social care in England*

The General Social Care Council (GSCC) has been established as the regulatory, registration and inspection body for social workers and for those institutions providing qualifying training in social work to promote 'the highest standards of social care in England for the benefit and protection of people who use services and the wider public' (GSCC, 2002a: 1). The GSCC is the statutory registering body for social care workers in England (with other councils in other parts of the UK), maintaining a register of social care staff, including social work students, fit to practise. The GSCC takes action if there are breaches of the ethics and standards required for registration. As part of this process the title of 'social worker' is protected by law since 1 April 2005 (Care Standards Act, section 63) so that only those who are properly qualified, registered and accountable will be able to use this title. *Codes of Practice* (GSCC, 2002a) are a critical part of regulating the workforce, providing guidance for practice and on standards of conduct which workers have to meet. (www.gscc.org.uk)

Previously known as the Training Organisation for the Personal Social Services (Topss), Skills for Care (SfC) for adults and the Children's Workforce Development Confederation (CWDC) for child care have been established to develop a national workforce development strategy, and standards and qualifications for the social care workforce. This includes the development of national occupation standards within a training and qualifications framework. (www.skillsforcare.org.uk and www.cwdcouncil.org.uk)

The Social Care Institute for Excellence (SCIE) aims to develop and promote knowledge about good practice in the sector. It was established to 'develop and promote knowledge about what works best in social care' (Department of Health, 2002a: 3), through the identification of 'best practice' and assisting on embedding these in practice. (www.scie.org.uk)

Since September 2003, following major reforms by the Department of Health (DoH, 2002b), the qualification to practise as a registered social worker has been a three-year full-time (or equivalent) honours degree, replacing the two-year full-time Diploma in Social Work. The first students from these revised programmes graduated in summer 2006. The honours degree level qualification for practice as a social worker emphasises the centrality of learning for and in practice, and learning to practise.

> *The new social work qualification has been introduced to ensure that the training of social work students will result in higher standards of service delivery to the people who rely on them in times of need, and ensure that graduates are confident and competent to practice on qualification. We have always made it clear that the emphasis of training must be on practice and the practical relevance of theory. This means that students need a plentiful and varied supply of good opportunities to practise and learn safely, the success of the new qualification depends on this.*
>
> (Ladyman, Parliamentary Under Secretary of State for Community, 2004: iii)

All social work courses follow a 'prescribed curriculum' combined from the Department of Health *Requirements* (2002b); the Quality Assurance Agency *Subject Benchmarks* for social work (QAA, 2000) and the *National Occupational Standards* for social workers (Topss/SfC, 2002).

The Department of Health (2002b) requirements for the degree clearly state that all students must undertake at least 200 days gaining the required experience and learning in practice settings. These 200 days must be taken in at least two separate practice agencies and include experience of working with two different service user groups. There is a commitment to practice learning opportunities that include the primacy of users' experiences, and understanding and experience of collaborative working with other professionals. The preparedness of the student for the experience of practice begins before the placement starts with a stipulation that students are assessed by their university as 'fit' for undertaking practice prior to the practice learning experience.

> *. . . the responsibility of universities is to ensure that all students undergo assessed preparation for direct practice to ensure their safety to undertake practice learning in a service delivery setting. This preparation must include the opportunity to develop a greater understanding of the experience of service users and the opportunity to shadow an experienced social worker.*
>
> (DoH, 2002b: 3)

Decisions about 'fitness to practise' are necessary, not only to comply with the requirements of the professional bodies but also to ensure the protection of those individuals the student will have contact with during professional training and to ensure students are appropriately prepared for entry to the profession, i.e. that they demonstrate professional attitudes and clearly understand and demonstrate professional behaviour.

The proportion of days spent by the student in practice learning opportunities represents a major proportion of the study time on social work programmes; the importance of the practice learning experience should not be underestimated for social work students, the practice educator (named as practice assessor within the degree), the agency in which practice is be undertaken and for academic staff involved in social work education. The

Box 1.4: *Summary of The Requirements for Social Work Training (DoH, 2002b)*

At the *point of entry* to the programme, providers must ensure that individuals possess the appropriate personal and intellectual qualities to be social workers and should undertake an individual or group interview as part of the selection process. Candidates must have English and Maths at least at Key Stage Level 2; be able to understand and make use of written materials and to communicate effectively and accurately in written and spoken English. Providers must ensure that stakeholder representatives and service users and carers are involved in the selection process.

For *teaching, learning and assessment* on the programme – the content, structure and delivery of the programme should enable social work students to demonstrate that they have met the national occupational standards for social work and the social work benchmark statement, to ensure they are suitable for admission to the GSCC register of social workers; this includes valuing diversity and equalities awareness.

In addition all students must undertake specific learning and assessment in:

- Human growth and development, mental health and disability;
- Assessment, planning, intervention and review;
- Communication skills with children adults and those with particular communication needs;
- Law; and
- Partnership working and information sharing across professional disciplines and agencies.

Regular and accurate assessment should ensure that students have met all the standards before being awarded the degree of social work. Programme providers must ensure that the teaching of theoretical knowledge, skills and values is based on their application in practice.

Providers should ensure that all students undergo assessed preparation for direct practice to ensure their safety to undertake practice learning in a service delivery setting. This must include the opportunity to develop a greater understanding of the experience of service users and the opportunity to shadow an experienced social worker. All social work students must spend *at least* 200 days gaining required experience and learning in practice settings.

Each student must have experience:

- in *at least* two practice settings
- of statutory social work tasks involving legal interventions
- of providing services to *at least* two user groups (e.g. child care and mental health).

Box 1.5: Preparation of the social work student for practice learning opportunities

Universities will prepare students for practice and make an assessment of the suitability of a student for practice in different ways; however it may include the following:

- Self-declaration: at the beginning of the social work programme students will be required to complete a self-declaration form confirming their fitness to study for a social work programme. This will include a declaration about health and any criminal convictions.

- Registration of the social student on the General Social Care Council (GSCC) register. Registration criteria for student social workers cover three main areas: good character, physical and mental fitness, and good conduct.

- Shadowing a qualified and experienced social worker prior to undertaking practice learning. This may include producing written evidence; for example, a brief report by the social worker on the student's experience, and their judgement of the preparedness of the student, and a reflective account of the experience by the student.

- Academic preparedness will include successful completion of academic modules; academic modules may include specific modules linked to preparedness for practice and/or integration of criteria for preparedness for practice integrated into modules; for example, communication and interpersonal skills, understanding of legal frameworks, theoretical frameworks and so on.

- Understanding the experiences of service users is central to practice and therefore to the preparation for practice. This may include direct input by service users into preparing for practice and supporting the student in developing their understanding of the views and experiences of service users, especially as experts on their unique experiences.

- Support and supervision from an academic tutor. This will include support for academic work but also support in judging the progress of the student and their readiness to practice.

centrality of practice learning to the degree, and in the development of the student as a confident and competent qualified social worker, is clearly recognised within the degree. Practice educators have a central role in the student experience of practice learning (Cartney, 2000) and in support of the formation of professional skills and identity.

National Occupational Standards (NOS) for social work (Topss/SfC, 2002) provide the criteria for the assessment of competence in practice. They outline the range of knowledge, skills and values that the student must demonstrate, evaluate critically and apply to their practice. They consist of broad statements of six key functions ('roles') within social work, as practised in all service settings. The key roles are split into twenty-one units which are further sub-divided into seventy-seven elements of competence. Each element is expanded

Box 1.6: National Occupational Standards for Social Work (Topss/SfC, 2002)

1 Key Role 1: Prepare for and work with individuals, families, carers, groups and communities to assess their needs and circumstances

   • Prepare for social work contact and involvement

   • Work with individuals, families, carers, groups and communities to help them make informed decisions

   • Assess needs and options to recommend a course of action

2 Key Role 2: Plan, carry out, review and evaluate social work practice, with individuals, families, carers, groups and communities and other professionals

   • Respond to crisis situations

   • Interact with individuals, families, carers, groups and communities to achieve change and development to improve life opportunities

   • Prepare, produce, implement and evaluate plans with individuals, families, carers, groups and communities and professional colleagues

   • Support the development of networks to meet assessed needs and planned outcomes

   • Work with groups to promote individual growth, development and independence

   • Address behaviour which present a risk to individuals families, carers, groups and communities

3 Key Role 3: Support individuals to represent their needs, views and circumstances

   • Advocate with and on behalf of individuals, families, carers, groups and communities

   • Prepare for and participate in decision-making forums

4 Key Role 4: Manage risk to individuals, families, carers, groups and communities, self and colleagues

   • Assess and manage risk to individuals, families, carers, groups and communities

   • Assess, minimise and manage risk to self and colleagues

5 Key Role 5: Manage and be accountable, with supervision and support, for your own social work practice with your organisation

   • Manage and be accountable for your own work

   • Contribute to the management of resources and services

into performance criteria. To achieve the level of competence the student must demonstrate within their practice the achievement of the performance criteria.

In addition there are six value and ethical requirements (each with a number of criteria), summarising the expectation of social workers from the perspective of service users, carers and organisations, following a number of consultations with them.

Box 1.7: Values and ethics

The 'Value and Ethics: Statement of Expectations' has six key headings, each with a number of expectations.

1. Communications skills and information sharing: there are twelve expectations

2. Good social work practice: there are thirteen expectations

3. Advocacy: there are four expectations

4. Working with other professionals: there are three expectations

5. Knowledge: there are three expectations

6. Values: there are five expectations

Full details can be found at: www.skillsforcare.org.uk

Practice education and learning

Education in practice is a core element of educational programmes that prepare professionals for academic awards (such as social work and nursing) and registration to practise as a professional. Practice education is the development and delivery of high-quality practice, learning and teaching opportunities in a relevant practice setting. Learning in practice has a central role in professional formation of the student.

Students learn from being engaged in practice. Placement experiences will constitute a significant part of education programmes and are a vital factor in promoting understanding, development and application of professional knowledge and practice. They help students become fit for practice, fit for purpose and fit for award by the time they complete their programme. Crucially, the student learns from being involved in practice and through the guidance and support of the practice educator.

Each placement provides students with educational and learning opportunities to develop their professional knowledge and practice through observation and experience of good practice and being able to engage in good practice alongside a practice educator. Learning professional practice knowledge is not achieved through observation and practice alone: students must also develop their own practice knowledge and skills through engagement in their own learning – for example, through direct practice with service users and carers or discussion with experienced colleagues and other professionals. The practice educator has a central role in this process.

Being a practice educator

Social work education has always been located at the intersection of a perennial tension between the need to establish academic credibility for the discipline – to be seen to be theoretical, rigorous and analytical – and the need to provide soundly based, practically applied learning experiences that will enable the student to work effectively with people. The structure of learning within the social work degree could be seen as an attempt to balance these two demands.

ACTIVITY

Reflect on your own motivation for being a practice educator. What qualities and skills do you feel you bring to this role?

What do you see as the challenges within a placement for you as a practice educator; the team; service users and carers; the student?

What do you see as the benefits within a placement for you as a practice educator; the team; service users and carers; the student?

There are many reasons which motivate people to work with and support students in the role of the practice educator: you may have been motivated by your own positive experiences as a student; possibly, if you have had a negative experience, you recognise the learning from this and have a commitment to improving the experience of any student you will be supporting. You will recognise and be able to articulate how your own use of knowledge, use of theories, application of skills, demonstration of values in practice and experience has been developed to a competent professional standard that would benefit and support the learning of others. It may be that you are interested in extending and developing your own knowledge and skills through supporting a student. Intrinsically it will be that you feel you have something to offer and are committed to supporting the learning and development of a student to becoming a professional, competent social worker. As a practice educator you should be prepared to be a positive role model for the students; being confident and competent in your own practice is essential. You should be able to demonstrate that you are aware of current practice. Being able to articulate and demonstrate your value base and a commitment to anti-oppressive practice is critical; for example, recognising working in partnership with service users and carers as being central to social work practice. You will recognise the importance of working with others; as part of team, with other professionals and agencies and especially working with service users and carers. Being reflective and evaluating your practice should form part of your own learning and development as a professional worker. Some of the qualities and skills you may have thought about are: approachable; friendly; organised; supportive; honest/open; enthusiastic; reliable; knowledgeable; good listener; professional – can demonstrate 'leadership'; show respect to service users; work as part of a team and with others; committed; non-judgemental; interested in students and supporting their learning and development; objective ('fair but firm') – the list could go on!

The challenges you identified in working with a student may have included: balancing your own work commitments whilst supporting and supervising a student; gaining support from other for your role and responsibilities as a practice educator (for example, within the team, from your manager, from your organisation); having and developing the necessary knowledge and skills in learning and teaching to support the students professional development; 'getting on' with the student ('What if the student has problems in practice?'; 'What happens if I should need to fail a student?'); knowing how to work alongside the academic institution; understanding the paperwork and the requirements for practice in order to support the student but also in being able to prepare your own report; the willingness to share with and be honest about your own practice, including weaknesses.

The benefits for you in being a practice educator are in being able to develop new skills and knowledge to facilitate learning in the workplace. Through working with a student you will be you will be consolidating and developing your own practice, gaining further insight into your own knowledge and skills as a practitioner, and your own professional identity and the values, beliefs and attitudes that inform and guide your own practice.

You may have been feeling by this stage, 'What am I taking on?'! However we hope that you recognise that the benefits are plentiful; the value of supporting a student to the successful conclusion of a placement is enormous. In addition, you are not alone in this process.

Students will not arrive at the placement as a 'blank canvas': they will have had an opportunity in the university to explore the knowledge, theories and skills that inform practice; to examine issues of anti-oppressive practice and the values, beliefs and attitudes that impact and inform practice as a professional activity and for them personally. In addition, students will have had an opportunity to undertake a 'shadowing' placement. Some students will have had experience of working in social care – some to a limited extent, and some with more substantial experience. Some students may have had experiences as users of services or as carers of users of services.

The student should be prepared for placement and committed to their own learning and development with the placement. This includes such things as:

- coming to the placement prepared and informed;
- taking responsibility for their learning;
- being prepared to make good use of learning opportunities and demonstrating a commitment to their own professional development;
- being prepared to engage in reflection on their performance and behaviour, and be open to constructive criticism and guidance;
- understanding and working in accordance with the *Codes of Practice* (GSCC, 2002a) and understanding and working with the *National Occupational Standards for Social Work* (Topss/SfC, 2002) and the academic standards and expectations of the university;
- taking responsibility according to his/her stage of development and training, whilst being able to articulate and acknowledge the limits of his/her knowledge, experience and responsibility so as not to endanger him/herself or other people;

- preparing for supervision, taking responsibility for any actions agreed in supervision;
- providing feedback throughout the placement and at the end of their placement experience.

You will have the support of the university in the arrangements for the placement and through documentation to assist you in the process involved in the placement and in the assessment of the student; the university should maintain close links with you and the student to provide support, and, if there are problems, should respond promptly and work with you and the student to seek a resolution.

ACTIVITY

You may wish to consider developing this exercise further to consider the challenges within a placement for your team; service users and carers; the student? . . . the benefits within a placement for your team; service users and carers; the student?

Cameron-Jones and O'Hara (1997) emphasise the fundamental importance of the practice placement as these placements take place in the 'real world'. They suggest that all placements have a common purpose – to help people to understand and carry out real and difficult tasks, in real environments, in touch with real clients, in a culture of real deadlines in the company of actual jobholders. Whilst this definition offers an insight into the context in which practice learning takes place, Waters (2001) proposes that practice has a more intrinsic function. She suggests that the purpose of placements is to allow for the acquisition of professional knowledge, skills and attitudes; the 'theorising of practice' and 'practising of theory' (Schön, 1983); and to allow for professional identity formation and enculturation, described as the process by which students are inducted and adopt the professional culture. These views suggest that there may be a creative tension between the academic/theoretical learning and practical learning in social work education. Learning, and the acquisition of knowledge, can be viewed as individual enrichment; it is about what goes on in your head – how you make sense of the world around you and your place within it. However, learning is also said to exist within a 'community' – knowledge is socially mediated within the real world in a community of professional practice and in the wider community.

The complexity of the human interaction that social work engages in means that the 'notions of ambiguity, indeterminacy and uncertainty are at the heart of social work' (Parton and O'Byrne, 2000: 44). Students of social work will need guidance and support to 'cope' with the challenges of working within the context of fluid, uncertain situations and environments and rapid changes. In order to withstand these pressures and maintain professional integrity, values and beliefs, students need to be equipped to be know-ledgeable; skilful; resilient; able to 'self-manage'; and able to operate in complex uncertain situations and environments. Barnett and Hallam (1999) suggest 'supercomplexity' (multiple standards, multiple purposes, multiple knowledges and multiple consumers) requires a pedagogy that is operative in three domains – knowledge, action and self. Thus they argue that a pedagogy for supercomplexity needs to be based on a view of learning

---

Box 1.8: Domains and requirements

Domain	Requirements
Knowledge	Knowledge of theories, policies and practice
	Recognition of multiple perspectives
	Different levels of analysis
	Ongoing enquiry
Action	Skills-based with awareness of context
	Operating to challenge structural disadvantage
	Working with difference to empowerments
Self	Questioning personal assumptions and values
	Engaged self
	Negotiating understanding and interventions.

---

construed 'as the acquisition of those human capabilities appropriate for adaptation to conditions of radical and enduring uncertainty, unpredictability, challengeability and contestability' (1999: 142).

They point out that doing so will attend to students' development of knowledge and the enactment of skills within the 'pedagogical space to develop their own ideas, to inject something of themselves into their learning and to make and to substantiate . . . their own truth claims' (1999: 148). The claim here is that the domain of 'self' is central to development of those purposeful orientations needed for advancement in the world.

Lymbery and Butler (2004) describe the professional elements of social work as a balance between technicality and indeterminacy. Whilst there must be tangible proof of competency (being equipped with the 'tools for the job'), there is also a requirement to be able to exercise judgement and values, drawing on theories and research learned and continually reflected upon. An examination of Fish's (1995) two views of professional practice should support you to consider the different views involved in professional practice.

Critical reflection: making sense of practice

Working with uncertainty and complexity and working creatively with others requires us to think about our position as professionals and provide 'meaning' to our practice. As a practice educator you will need to support students not only in making 'sense' of the context in which they will be currently practising, but also in using the learning in a variety of other contexts. In addition:

Table 1.1: Two views of professional practice (Fish, 1995: 43)

The technical rational view	The professional artistry view
Follows rules, laws, routines and prescriptions	Starts where rules fade, sees patterns, frameworks
Uses diagnosis, analysis	Uses interpretation/appreciation
Wants efficient systems	Wants creativity and room to be wrong
Sees knowledge as permanent	Knowledge is temporary, dynamic, and problematic
Theory is applied to practice	Theory emerges from practice
Visible performance is central	There is more to it than surface features
Technical expertise is all	Professional judgement counts
Sees professional activities as masterable	Sees mystery at the heart of professional activities
Emphasises the known	Embraces uncertainty
Standards must be fixed; standards are measurable and must be controlled	That which is fixed and measurable is often trivial and should be set alongside professional accountability
Emphasises assessment, inspection	Emphasises investigation, reflection, deliberation
Change must be managed from the outside	Professionals can develop from inside
Quality is really about the quality of that which is easily measurable	Quality comes from deepening insight into one's own values, priorities and actions
Technical accountability	Professional answerability
This is training	This is education
Instrumental view	Education is intrinsically worthwhile

. . . ways of teaching and learning need to be scrutinised for their capacity to foster ability to learn from practice experience, to formulate contextual knowledge, to be open to differences and to reaffirm the broader values and missions of the social work profession.

(Fook, 2007: 38)

Your ability to critically reflect on your practice is an essential feature of this; this will be an essential skill to support students to develop and apply within their own practice. Throughout this book you will find exercises to support your reflection on your practice as a practice educator, and to support the student in developing their skills in critical reflection.

Just as the student should be keeping a Reflective Journal we would strongly encourage you do the same. If you are undertaking a programme study in order to achieve a qualification as a practice educator this will be a critical part of your study in supporting and providing evidence of your learning and development. As professionals we cannot learn from our own practice unless we position ourselves to constantly learn from it. A Reflective Journal can be used as a practical tool – to outline events, to describe circum-stances, to vent feelings – but its prime use is to reflect on the experience, identify the learning to support and enhance our professional practice.

Charles and Butler (2004) provide a comparison between 'accommodating' and 'reflective' practice. In the former a sense of control is achieved by adopting the language and

---

Box 1.9: *Some questions to support critical reflection*

- What happened?

- Why am I choosing to write about this particular incident/experience?

- What went well? Why? Is there anything from this experience I can use again?

- What went not so well? Could I have done anything to prevent this?

- How do I feel about it?

- Can I identify how I demonstrated my professional (and personal) value base?

- Am I able to recognise appropriate and potentially inappropriate use of power as a practice educator in working with this student?

- What would I change and why?

- Are there any gaps in my professional knowledge? If so how can I go about changing this?

- Are there gaps in my professional practice? If so how can I go about changing this?

- What have I learned: about myself; my knowledge on the subject; my professional skill; the student?

- Are there any general principles that I can use again?

- Did I enjoy this teaching session? If so, why? If not, why not?

- Did I achieve the intended learning outcomes? How do I know this? Is there anything I would/could do differently?

- Did the student appear to enjoy the teaching experience? If so, why? If not, why not?

---

standardised practice of the agency – 'they respond to the workplace's emotional intensity by bureaucratising difficulties'. Reflective practitioners 'relish the uncertainties inherent in working in the swamp', using these to increase their professionalism through drawing on the knowledge, theory and value base of social work to carefully select methods and to make considered decisions that ensure that service users and carers are central within their practice. As Bolton (2005: 2) states:

The structures in which our professional and personal roles, values and everyday lives are embedded are complex and volatile. Power is subtle and slippery, its location is often different from how it appears. Deep reflection and reflexivity for development involve:

- *authority and responsibility for personal and professional identity, values, action, feelings;*
- *contestation;*
- *willingness to stay with uncertainty, unpredictability, questioning.*

(Author's own italics)

It is essential for practitioners to feed their critical and self-critical awareness by keeping up to date with other people's research and also to engage in their own evaluation of their practice. Evaluation should be with users, not practised in isolation from them. Fook (1999: 207) suggests that the integration of theory with practice does not happen when knowledge is applied mechanistically to practice. Critical reflection is a process, 'a way in which we engage with our contexts in order to deconstruct and critically reconstruct'.

Acting as professional social workers touches upon our personal values and makes it critical that we examine these whilst in training and in our chosen careers. We have to understand our beliefs and assumptions and make them explicit. We have to be prepared to question them self-critically and have them challenged by others; we have to adopt this self-critical, self-questioning approach as a way of work. This forms part of our commitment to continuing professional development. Post-qualifying study is an essential part of the commitment you demonstrate to your lifelong learning.

FURTHER READING

Lymbery, M. and Postle, K. (eds) *Social Work: A Companion to Learning*. London: SAGE.

O'Connor, I., Hughes, M., Turney, D., Wilson, J. and Setterlund, J. (2006) *Social Work and Social Care Practice*. London: SAGE.

Both these books provide excellent coverage of the contemporary debates about practice and the key themes, issues and concepts underpinning social work practice

Cree, V. and Davis, A. (2007) *Social Work: Voices from the Inside*. London: Routledge.

Cree and Davis draw together characteristics of good social work from the perspectives of 59 people from across the UK on how and why social work came into their lives.

McDonald, C. (2006) *Challenging Social Work*. Basingstoke: Palgrave Macmillan.

A more challenging book, exploring the challenges and realities of practice and examining the future path of the profession.

Chapter 2
What is learning?

MEETING THE POST-QUALIFYING SOCIAL WORK STANDARDS

The material in this chapter links to the following Domain standards:

Domain A: Organise opportunities for the demonstration of assessed competence in practice

1. Take responsibility for creating a physical and learning environment conducive to the demonstration of assesses competence.

2. Negotiate with all participants in the workplace, including service users and carers, the appropriate learning opportunities and the necessary resources to enable the demonstration of practice competence.

3. Work openly and co-operatively with learners, their line managers, workplace colleagues, other professionals and service users and carers, in the planning of key activities at all stages of learning and assessment.

4. Co-ordinate the work of all contributors. Ensure they are fully briefed, understand their roles and provide them with feedback.

5. Monitor, critically evaluate and report on the continuing suitability of the work environment, learning opportunities, and resources. Take appropriate action to address any shortcoming and optimise learning and assessment.

Domain B: Evaluate critically the methodologies and techniques that enable learning and professional development in practice

1. Establish the basis of an effective working relationship by identifying learners' expectations, the outcomes which they have to meet in order to demonstrate competence and readiness for assessment. Agree the available learning opportunities, methods, resources, and timescales to enable them to succeed.

3. Discuss and take into account individuals' learning styles, learning needs, prior learning achievements, knowledge and skills.

4. Make professional educational judgements about meeting learners' needs within the available resources, ensuring the required learning outcomes can be demonstrated in accordance with adult learning models.

7. Advise learners how to develop their ability to manage their learning. Deal with any difficulties encountered by them.

Introduction

In the previous chapter you have considered the changing context of contemporary practice education and looked at what this means for you as an educator and the students that you work with. Having framed the context of your learning and teaching practice, in this second chapter you will consider and evaluate your overall approach and perspective on learning in professional practice education.

With two main sections, your reading in this chapter will start by considering how individual students learn in the practice education context. Thus, for example, this section will include exploration of adult learning theories, different approaches to learning and consideration of the concepts of student-centred learning and the development of knowledge, skills and professional values. The second section of the chapter moves on to look at your role, as a practice educator, in facilitating and enabling student learning. In this part of the chapter your learning from the earlier part of the chapter will be built upon to consider ways in which you can stimulate the development of the learning process, through for example planning learning, agreeing learning opportunities and activities, and monitoring the progression of learning. As is reflective of all professional practice, the student and practice educator do not, cannot and should not work or learn in isolation. Therefore, the discussion will widen to consider how other factors influence and can support learning; for example, the physical environment, the organisational context and the involvement of others, including service users, other practitioners and inter-professional, multi-agency working. Throughout the chapter, the relationship between the learning of 'theory' (academic context of learning) and work-based learning as a holistic process will be explored as a critical theme for effective learning, with critical reflection as the key capability of the practitioner in enabling this process.

How does the individual student learn?

The answer to this question, if indeed there is one answer, could take a whole book or perhaps a series of books to address. So in this small part of this one chapter, we intend to introduce you to some key ideas, theories and principles that might prompt and direct your further studies on learning in practice.

Learning takes place in many different ways and at different levels. So for example, you might *learn* your mobile telephone number, which is really memorising. Or you may have some new ideas, reflections or thoughts about an event or incident which then changes the way you perceive it or they way you might tackle something similar again. In this way you are fitting your new *learning* with existing ideas to deepen your *knowledge* and *understanding*. There are some significant terms in this paragraph, all of which may reveal contested or complex definitions. We shall explore knowledge and understanding further as the chapter progresses. What is clear, though, is that in the context of enhancing ourselves as professionals, studying formally and informally, our pattern of learning, skills and knowledge acquisition most commonly takes place in a continuous spiral of further development. This is illustrated in Figure 2.1; does this pattern reflect your own learning over time?

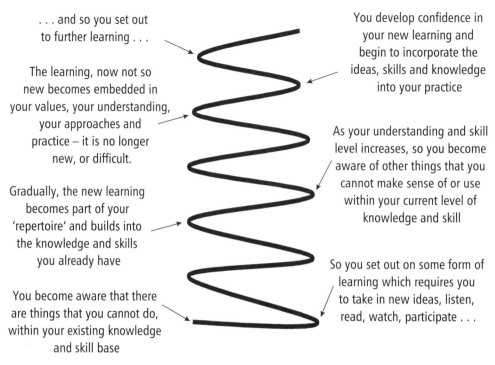

... and so you set out to further learning ...

The learning, now not so new becomes embedded in your values, your understanding, your approaches and practice – it is no longer new, or difficult.

Gradually, the new learning becomes part of your 'repertoire' and builds into the knowledge and skills you already have

You become aware that there are things that you cannot do, within your existing knowledge and skill base

You develop confidence in your new learning and begin to incorporate the ideas, skills and knowledge into your practice

As your understanding and skill level increases, so you become aware of other things that you cannot make sense of or use within your current level of knowledge and skill

So you set out on some form of learning which requires you to take in new ideas, listen, read, watch, participate ...

Figure 2.1: The continuous spiral of professional development and learning

Whilst the development of adult learning theories arises from a relatively new area of study we are aware that, compared to children and young people, adults have special learning needs and requirements as learners. The theories of adult learning were pioneered by Malcolm Knowles (1980) with his theory of *Andragogy* (childhood learning being known as pedagogy). Before exploring Knowles' approach in more depth, Table 2.1 is provided to give you, very broadly, a brief comparison of the different perspectives and assumptions inherent in theories of children's learning and theories of adult learning.

Thus, effectively andragogy is a set of assumptions about how adults learn. Knowles' ideas can be seen to link back to the early 1900s, when the specialist nature of learning and

Table 2.1: Pedagogy and andragogy

	Pedagogy	Andragogy
The *student* is perceived as being . . .	dependent	self-directing
The student's *prior experience* is to be . . .	built upon	used as a resource for self and others
The student's *'point of entry'* into learning . . .	can be standardised by age	develops from life issues, experiences and problems
The student's *motivation and approach to learning* is fostered through . . .	external rewards and punishments	internal incentives and curiosity

teaching adults was first being considered. Despite others both before and after him, Knowles is considered to be the principal expert on andragogy. Knowles explains how adults learn by exploring some significant concepts about the nature of the adult learner.

Adult learners are autonomous and self-directed

Adults are seen as independent learners with the role of the educator being one of facilitating and enabling learning to take place. Within this, the theory of andragogy tells us that adults should be actively involved in the learning process; they should be able to influence the curriculum, being given responsibility within it. However, despite the assumption that adults are autonomous and self-directed learners, many adults have been through previous educational experiences which have left them as dependent learners, or sometimes passive learners, so as practice educators you may need to enable students to develop new patterns of learning, where they become self-directed and become motivated by taking responsibility for their own learning.

Adult learners set out with an accumulation of life experiences and knowledge

Andragogy acknowledges and gives value to the life, and possibly work, experiences that adults bring to learning. In social work practice education, all students will bring a range of life and learning experiences with them, some may have relevant previous employment experience, others may have had extensive educational experience before coming to the university (e.g. previous degrees). Some learners may bring the experience of being a service user or carer to their new learning. All experiences and prior knowledge are seen as a resource to reflect upon, build upon, share and develop.

Adult learners are goal-orientated

Adults are seen to know where they want to be or get to! Educators need, therefore, to be explicit about the aims of the activities and teaching in relation to learning, so that learners know exactly what they need to do to get to where they want to be! Under the more standard pedagogical model, it is assumed that the student will simply learn what they are told to learn. Perhaps you remember as a child having to memorise things at school, maybe reciting your 'times-tables' for mathematics or the 'period table' in chemistry; did you ever question why? Working with adults, in practice education, you can pre-empt learners' needs to know, by asking them questions such as; *What will you achieve by doing this*? and *How can I, as your teacher, help you attain your goals?* Furthermore you can utilise the social work key roles, units and values to direct students to why they need to undertake certain activities or learning opportunities, and to reinforce the importance of the learning.

Adults are relevancy-orientated

Similarly to the assumptions laid out above, adults are seen as needing to appreciate a clear reason and relevance for the particular aspect of learning. It must be applicable to their course or their goals, having a clear and apparent connection to moving them forward. As a practice educator you will be helping learners to identify the objectives and planned outcomes of their learning. The process of social work supervision clearly has a role to play in helping you to work with the student so that they see the value and relevancy of their learning. Thus for example, prior to practice, you could ask the student to reflect on what they expect to learn, how will it help them to meet their goals and how they envisage bringing the learning into their future practice.

Adults are practical

Again, in a similar vein to the foregoing, adults are seen to focus on what is most useful to their goals and purpose, making decisions about what they actually need. Thus adult learners could be described as being pragmatic or practical in their approach. This approach is often most starkly evident where the student's focus is very explicitly on what they need to do for the assessment/s; this is also referred to as being a *strategic learner* or taking an *achieving approach* (Biggs, 1987; Tait et al., 1998; both cited in Biggs, 2003: 14).

Surface learning and deep learning

So far we are beginning to build up a picture of the adult learner and their approach to learning. Marton and Saljo (1997) undertook research to look into whether students approached learning in different ways; they were interested to find out whether students were doing different things which resulted in different levels of learning. Their findings led to the notions of *surface* and *deep* learning.

Surface learning is where students take a superficial approach. For example, this can refer to memorising, as opposed to understanding; 'skating the surface' rather than engaging and attempting to meaningfully grasp the concepts. Biggs (2003: 14) offers this description:

> The concept of the surface approach may be applied to any area, not only to learning. The phrases 'cutting corners' and 'sweeping under the carpet' convey the idea: the job appears to have been done properly when it hasn't.

Deep learning or a deep approach to learning, on the other hand, is one where the learner attempts to look within and beyond the initial task, text or learning opportunity. The learner tries to understand the message, searches for meaning, the teacher or author's intention, the conclusions to be drawn, the implications for practice, integrating theory/practice, making critical, reasoned judgements, often questioning and coming up with further ideas. Biggs (2003: 15) offers this description

> The deep approach arises from a felt need to engage the task appropriately and meaningfully, so the student tries to use the most appropriate cognitive activities for handling it.

> When students feel this need to know, they automatically try to focus on underlying meaning, on main ideas, themes, principles or successful applications.

Chris

Chris is a social work student on first practice placement within a youth offending team. The practice assessor works diligently to ensure that goals, activities and strategies are in place for Chris's practice learning at all times, using supervision both formal and informal to set out and confirm these learning plans. Likewise Chris is able to evidence achievement, meeting key roles and targets set along the way. However, whilst it is clear that Chris intends to achieve a 'pass' through this placement, it is also clear that Chris does not intend to do any more work than is absolutely necessary. Thus, for example, the practice assessor can see that Chris's reflective journal entries are often no more than a few sentences long, they seldom include reference to theory or to further reading and they offer little depth of insight into Chris's developing practice.

Akira

Akira is a social work student working on the early part of the second practice learning opportunity, in a busy Adult Care Management team. Sometimes the team and the practice assessor become frustrated with Akira, who seldom does anything without asking questions, looking for additional information and spending time researching through files. For example, Akira was allocated some work with a service user who was considering the option of an Individual Budget to fund care. Akira's first action was to scour the Internet and to search for books and journals in the university library to read about Individual Budgets, the background to them and any research evidence related to their implementation.

It is not difficult to see which of these learners may be taking a *surface* and which is taking a *deep* approach in these case examples. However, the approach taken is not like a fixed style of learning for each learner, but is more about a relationship between the learner and the context in which the learning takes place. There is a real danger if we start to 'label' learners, but as practice educators, understanding different approaches to learning can enable us to think carefully about how the learning is structured so that a deep approach to learning is facilitated. Later in this chapter the learning environment is considered further.

Within this broader understanding of how adults approach learning, learning in social work practice can be seen as a dynamic triangular interaction, between the practice educator, the practice of professional social work, including others involved in that experience, and the social work student. Here we give you an outline of three groups of learning theories where each can be seen to stress the significance of one element of that triangle (see Figure 2.2). It is important to be aware, though, that each of these groups of theories work represents a continuum of models and approaches with extremes at each end. For example, the behavioural theories range from a simple model of reinforcement to models that enable exploration of a range of options or possible responses.

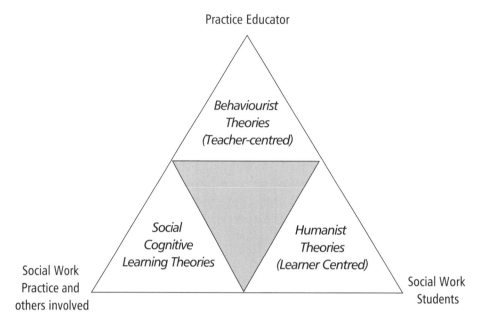

Figure 2.2: Three groups of learning theories

Behaviourist theories

Theories that fit in this group suggest that individuals learn by receiving stimuli and then responding to those stimuli, hence these theories give a clear cause and effect explanation of teaching. As a teacher you have an active role as you lead the learning by selecting the stimuli (or learning opportunity), by reinforcing the approved responses and by discouraging the 'wrong' responses. In other words, reward and punishment follow success and failure. B.F. Skinner (1904–90), in early work on behaviourism, proposed that the shaping of learning and the control of the process lay with the teacher. Behaviourist approaches, which are applied across a wide range of different levels, subject and skill areas, view knowledge or behaviours as either right or wrong. The role of the learner is a passive one, from this perspective.

Social cognitive learning theories

Bandura (1965) developed this further and suggested that the learner has choice and some control, and that the learner does not simply respond automatically, but makes conscious decisions in the process. In this way, Bandura, it could be argued, began to consider the centrality of the learner in the process – the learner as being active in the process – and to recognise the possibility for creativity and individualisation. This group of theories is called *cognitive* because they emphasise the role of conscious thought processes in behaviour, and *social* because they stress the significance of learning with others and from others. With the perspective of the mind and brain being actively engaged in the learning process, these approaches also explain development of insight, different perspectives, levels of understanding and perception. Cognitive theories acknowledge gradual development of understanding, application, analysis and perception through learning, and consider that feedback and learner–other learners–teacher interactions are essential components of the learning process. Furthermore, as shown in Figure 2.2, whilst, from these approaches, the learner is active in the process, the learning is dominated by the subject matter, in this case, social work practice itself.

Humanist theories

Humanist theories, also sometimes known as *facilitation theories*, are based on psychosocial analytical approaches. Carl Rogers (1902–87), a name you are likely to associate with the development of person-centred psychotherapy and counselling, has been a key contributor to the development of humanistic approaches to understanding learning.

This area offers potentially a more complex set of theories, which stress the uniqueness of individual learning, the complexity of learning and the centrality of the learner – or student-centred learning. However, humanistic interpretations can be seen as being more akin to recommendations of how effective learning can be enabled, rather than strictly theoretical approaches that describe and explain how learning actually takes place. As might be expected by the term *facilitation theories*, the underpinning principle of humanist approaches is the focus on the active role of the empowered, autonomous, goal-setting learner, with the educator role being one of facilitation, establishing the right environment and offering a wide range of learning opportunities. There is an inherent belief that learners have a natural enthusiasm for learning and will bring their experiences and ideas into play as they take responsibility for their own learning. The educator, or facilitative teacher, is attentive, listens to the learners, attends to emotional aspects of learning and interacts constructively with the learners throughout. From the perspective of these theories, the role of the teacher therefore is to increase the range of experiences so that the student can use these in any way they please to achieve their own desired learning. Some academics believe that this range of theories will influence adult education more and more in future years.

In this chapter so far, as we have considered different explanations about how individual students learn we have not within all of this encountered a model that effectively and clearly makes the connection between learning and the development of practice in the workplace. However, David A. Kolb in a seminal text *Experiential Learning* (1984) developed the concept of the learning process through *Kolb's experiential learning cycle*.

Experiential learning

With experience and learning-by-doing seen, from this perspective, as the basis of all learning, this approach can be particularly useful in helping us to understand social work practice learning. It describes a process of learning that shows how people generate, from their own experiences, the concepts, rules and principles that guide their behaviour in new situations, and how they modify these concepts to enhance their development and improve their effectiveness. In other words, how they continue to learn and develop through reflection on experience.

The learning cycle is conceived as a dynamic, continuously recurring cycle, in that all learning is re-learning and learning is based on critical reflection upon experience. It is acknowledged, however, that it may take several cycles to develop expertise, as there is always more learning possible. It is conceived as a four-stage cycle (see Figure 2.3).

Kolb's model, at its most effective ensures critical and reflective goal-directed action, and evaluation of the consequences of that action. Its main contribution, for our purposes, is that it provides a way of understanding active learning for the development of knowledge, skills and abilities through social work practice.

ACTIVITY

As a practice assessor, consider how you might use Kolb's learning cycle when working with a student in practice. How might the experiential learning cycle inform your practice as an educator and, more specifically, how could you use it, for example in supervision with a student, or to work with a student to identify evidence of their learning?

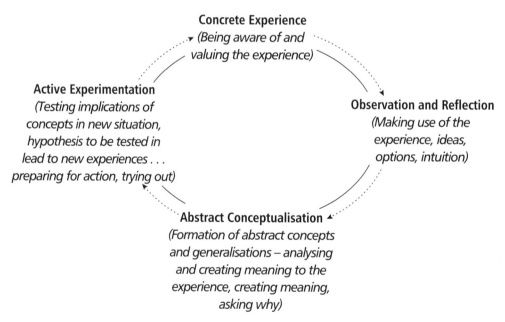

Figure 2.3: Kolb's experiential learning cycle

Source: Adapted from Kolb (1984)

The learning cycle offers a very structured and useful way of working openly with students. Students can use this to frame some of their reflective writing for example and you could assist them with this process. It could also be used to guide some of your supervision discussions. Taylor et al. (1999) present Kolb's cycle as a model for presenting evidence that demonstrates student learning. We have added to their model and reproduced it as Figure 2.4. You may find it helpful to use the figure and work around the cycle with one specific 'concrete experience' learning opportunity, for example, 'undertaking an assessment'.

Building on Kolb's work, Peter Honey and Alan Mumford developed the notion of 'learning styles', suggesting that adults tend to use a range of styles of learning at different times for different learning and that they tend to have a preference for one or two modes above the others. The learning styles offer a typology of preferred modes of learning, with learners being active learners, reflective learners, theorising learners or experimental learners. Honey and Mumford's work led to the development of the *Learning Styles Inventory* (Honey and Mumford, 2000) which is a personal test instrument using a 'tick-box' approach to identifying your own preferred learning style. The inventory has been subjected to much critique both positive and negative – you can find many versions both free and purchasable on the Internet, so if you have not explored this for yourself, you can do so. The learning styles are all modes of 'active' learning, which have been criticised for 'putting people into categories' or 'labelling'. Perhaps, though, as educators, this approach may be useful in helping to explain how people might be learning and how you can more effectively enable that learning.

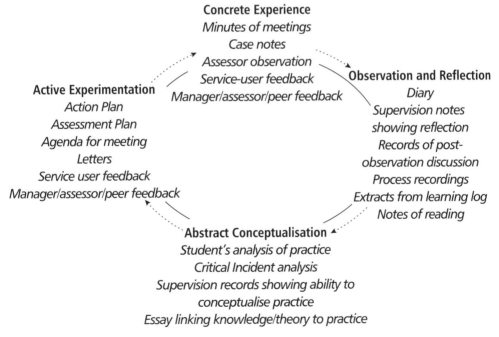

Figure 2.4: The experiential learning cycle in practice learning

Source: Adapted from Taylor et al. (1999: 158)

You are advised to take some time and explore Internet sites that offer access to the Learning Styles Inventory – there are many, but if you are a practice assessor working with a higher education institution, it is very likely that you can access the inventory through that institution. Consider the following:

- *Do you know your own preferred learning style and the implications of it? If not, work through the questionnaire and consider what it tells you.*

- *How might you use this approach with students?*

Essentially, we cannot make assumptions about how students prefer to learn and thus it is necessary for practice assessors to adopt a wide range of teaching–learning activities in order to meet the range of students needs. One of the critiques of the learning styles approach is that it may be culturally specific and that there may be an age-related dimension that has not been fully explored. However, you might find it useful to discuss with your students who may, themselves, have undertaken the *Learning Styles Inventory*. It may be possible for you, with your students, to consider ways in which they could develop their approach to become more balanced in their style of learning. Of course, exactly the same applies to you as a learner.

Another established learning styles model is known as the Visual-Auditory-Kinesthetic learning styles model or 'inventory', usually abbreviated to VAK. It would be useful for you to consider how this differs from those you have read about so far in this chapter. The VAK concept and theory has connections to children's education, the Montessori school of thought, and was originally developed to support teaching and learning with dyslexic children. The VAK theory has since moved on to become more applicable across education of young people and adults, as it provides a clear perspective for understanding individuals' preferred ways of learning, which are easily linked to the development of appropriate modes of teaching. Additionally, the VAK model, whilst stating that most

Table 2.2: The VAK model

VAK learning style	Outline	Description
Visual	Seeing and reading	Prefer to learn through seeing. Develop understanding through pictures, visual displays, graphs, charts, diagrams, colour and illustrations.
Auditory	Listening and speaking	Prefer to learn through listening, taking in verbal input and developing understanding through interpretation of speech, its tone, speed, pitch and approach to oral presentation.
Kinesthetic	Touching and doing	Prefer to learn through contact, touch, direct involvement and a 'hands-on' approach – developing understanding by 'having a go' and testing out.

people possess a dominant or preferred learning style, acknowledges that many people have a mixed and evenly balanced blend of the three styles.

Whole brain learning

The brain is an extremely complex organ, but it has been suggested that two different parts of the brain are responsible for particular areas of learning (right and left brain) (Armstrong, 2003). This learning is linked to two types of thinking: analytical and creative. As you might expect, these claims are controversial, but suggest that left-brain activity is responsible for the logical, or analytical side of thinking, whilst right-brain activity is responsible for creative, lateral thinking. People are thought to have dominance or preference for one or the other. Engaging in activities suited to your preference is said to lead to high motivation, in which case it could be useful to know whether you, or those you are working with, are 'lefty' or 'righty'! It is suggested that the most effective 'brain' orientation, is that which is balanced and to support this exercises have been developed that purport to assist individuals to develop in this way.

Other aspects of learning

In this chapter we have only been able to offer a brief introduction to some of the principles of adult learning and some of the key theories and models. However, what is most important to remember when considering any theoretical explanation is that students are individuals and they will all differ as learners in:

- the emotions and feelings they bring to, or that are invoked in their learning;
- their study skills, their intentions or approach and understanding;
- their preferred way of learning and the habits they have developed through previous learning;
- their approach to studying and learning;
- their own objectives and reasons for learning.

ACTIVITY

Consider the different models and principles of adult learning outlined in the chapter and develop a SWOT (strengths, weaknesses, opportunities and threats) analysis of the approaches, theories or models in respect of their implications for practice learning in your workplace setting. You could start by looking at each of the following:

- *Knowles' theory of andragogy*
- *Kolb's experiential model of the learning process*
- *Honey and Mumford's learning styles*
- *behaviourist theories*

For this activity we have listed only four approaches, thus not including cognitive and humanist approaches, this has been purely to make the activity 'manageable'. If you find the activity useful, you could extend and develop it to include a wider range of models. You may have found that you need to extend your reading and study in order to undertake the exercise meaningfully, but by looking at strengths, weaknesses, opportunities and threats, you will be starting to analyse and critique the approaches and their applicability for your own practice. You may have identified some important influences on learning that are not considered by different models, which are then weaknesses. For example, approaches like VAK, Kolb's model and consequently Honey and Mumford's too, have been criticised for being too prescriptive and leaving out some of the complexities of the learning process, for example emotions and feelings that impact on and influence learning.

Emotions and feelings

There is little doubt that learning involves thinking, feeling and doing. We are learning all of the time, but often at a pre-conscious level and hence we may not always be actively aware of our learning. Being conscious and recognising our own learning is sometimes referred to as *learning to learn*, it is also the basis of the reflective practitioner.

Learning to learn

Understanding the learning process, your own preferred approach to learning, as well as having insight and awareness of progress in learning, is a defining component of high performance. Sometimes called *metacognition* this is effectively about 'knowing about knowing' (Cree, 2005: 57). The skills and knowledge needed to meaningfully adopt this approach are a significant element of personal development and becoming a truly reflective practitioner. Understanding how you learn is important to self-development because it does the following things:

- It puts you in charge of your own learning;

- It maximises the likelihood of real learning taking place;

- It reduces the learner's dependency on the teacher; and

- It develops skills which can improve the efficiency and effectiveness of learning over time.

We have seen, however, in this chapter, how all learners are individual and differ in their approach to learning. Learners may also exhibit different, and sometimes unexpected, attitudes and approaches to learning at different times and in different environments. Those learners who have developed awareness of their own learning will be able to articulate how these different contexts impact upon their approaches. However, for others it will be your responsibility, as a practice educator, to facilitate an exploration of these differences, so that you and the learner can explore what lies beneath them, with a particular focus on ensuring that there are as few barriers to learning as possible.

Barriers to learning

Obstacles and barriers that impede learning can sometimes be easily identified and remedied, but can also at times be complex and challenging to bring to the surface. A severe headache, for example, will certainly hinder learning, but is commonly short term and occasional. However, a student who lacks confidence and perhaps has experience of previous 'failed' studies may present more of a challenge for the facilitator, being potentially significantly hampered in their learning over a longer period.

ACTIVITY

Consider the following learner behaviours and the barriers to learning that might be presented in this way. For each bullet point, write down your ideas about actions you might take as a practice educator in order to assist the student to progress their learning in these circumstances.

Then add in other barriers to learning that you may have experience of and again, note your practice in those circumstances, alongside.

- *The student appears to learn in episodic bursts. Their ability to concentrate appears to be sporadic and their learning is not continuous.*

- *The student appears to be satisfying the immediate goals only and is not curriculum-orientated – for example, the student undertakes the practice activities required, but does not reflect upon the wider learning, linking theory to practice – they are very 'short termist' in their approach and do not consider future application of the learning.*

- *Learning styles – the student appears to have a strong preference for one or other learning style;*

  (a) They always use their existing knowledge or experience and seem reluctant to take on new concepts;

  (b) They always take a trial-and-error approach;

  (c) Rather than use their learning, skills and knowledge, they appear to only copy the approaches of other workers.

It is always difficult to respond to an activity of this type, as in reality it would be necessary to know and understand the learner before making a judgement about how to work with them in the most effective way. However, in Table 2.3 we give some suggestions of actions that the educator may take in the specific circumstances given.

Table 2.3: Adapting teaching and learning to students' characteristics

Student learning characteristics	Ways to adapt the teaching and learning to enable learning to take place
The student appears to learn in episodic bursts. Their ability to concentrate appears to be sporadic and their learning is not continuous.	*Rely on short burst of learning activity, breaking material into manageable units, but attaching each one onto other items of learning to try and increase the sum of learning.*
The student appears to be satisfying the immediate goals only and is not curriculum-orientated – for example, the student undertakes the practice activities required but does not reflect upon the wider learning, linking theory to practice – they are very 'short-termist' in their approach and do not consider future application of the learning.	*Make all of the learning relevant to the student's apparent need for immediate satisfaction.* *Set the student some clear goals and discuss the issues with them. Start where the student feels comfortable, doing activities and learning opportunities immediately, not allowing for planning to result in the student losing interest.* *It may be possible to turn the situation around prior to setting (or letting the student know the detail of) the learning opportunity, by asking the student to think about areas of practice that might enable them to practice certain theoretical applications.*
Learning styles – the student appears to have a strong preference for one or other learning style; (a) They always use their existing knowledge or experience and seem reluctant to take on new concepts (b) They always take a trial and error approach (c) Rather than use their learning, skills nd knowledge, they appear to only copy the approaches of other workers	*Be aware of the different learning styles –* *First, enable learners to relate materials to existing knowledge, but then make the links for them to new materials and encourage them to be active in making the links to new learning with lots of reinforcement and feedback;* *Use supervision to move the student towards a more reflective and thoughtful approach to practice. Always question their thinking constructively;* *Value the importance of a 'demonstration' model, but then question the student on the strengths and weaknesses of other worker's approaches, thus starting to move the student to be an independent thinker who is active in their learning.*

How do I, as a practice educator, facilitate and enable student learning?

Your role as a practice educator is multi-faceted, but in the context of this chapter a significant activity will be finding ways to effectively support learning through facilitation and communication. This will include, planning learning with the learner and others involved in a structured, logical and coherent manner so that the learning outcomes are addressed. Through this you would set objectives for learning and ensure confidence and readiness for assessment. Planning learning requires that you take account of the learner's needs and individual learning style, as discussed throughout this chapter, and that you, as far as possible, enable the learner to take advantage of suitable practice learning opportunities, methods and resources within appropriate timescales, so that they can achieve the required learning. In negotiation with the learner and others involved, you will be making a range of professional judgements about the progress of learning and subsequent additional learning needs, which will lead to further planning for learning, enabling the learner to advance on the continuous spiral of learning described at the outset of this chapter. Your aim should be to empower the student to take control of their own learning and to be aware of their own approach to learning; in this way you will be enabling self-development and 'learning to learn'.

Within this, it is important that you pay due attention to all the influences on learning, such as the environment, the organisational context and the involvement of others. Thus the importance of the physical and learning environment and the context of practice can be significant in supporting effective learning, but can also be the cause of considerable barriers to progress. As a practice educator, you will need to consider how you create and sustain an appropriate learning environment, and ensure that the resources and support are available to those with whom you are working.

Further to considering the physical environment, you will need to plan for the involvement of others in the learning process. So, for example, considering how colleagues, both other students and qualified social workers, but also professionals from across the multi-disciplinary settings of practice, will be able to support you in enabling learning. Additionally, a valuable opportunity for learning is afforded by the participation of service users and carers in the learning process; however, this needs to be carefully and sensitively planned so that all those who contribute feel valued and safe in doing so.

Conclusion

The General Social Care Council (2005b: 6) states that the 'principles of pedagogy', which have been 'designed to promote and enhance the adult learning experience, must be located within the workplace and aligned to the needs of the organisation'. This clearly underlines the significance of the interdependent relationships between different locations, forms and approaches to the learning of theory and learning practice. This holistic, dynamic association has been an underpinning principle of this chapter; it will also underpin your approach and your developing understanding of learning in practice education.

This chapter started by exploring how individual students learn; then encouraged you to consider how your practice as an educator can assist that learning process; and finally broadened the analysis to consider the influence of the learning environment, service users and other professionals in the course of the learning. It has been necessary to construct the chapter in sections, to organise your reading, to give it meaning and to build the learning, much as you will need to structure, build and contextualise learning for the students that you work with. However, in reality, learning in the workplace, teaching, mentoring and supporting the development of others, does not take place across neat silos, compartments or sections like those in this chapter. Learning is 'multi-dimensional' being influenced by 'the social context, its character, development and practice' all of which are 'shaped by the nature of the learning dialogue offered to the student' (Light and Cox, 2001: 63).

In the next chapter you will take your own development further to consider how your understanding of learning influences your approach and role as a teacher in practice education.

FURTHER READING

Burgess, H. and Taylor, I. (eds) (2005) *Effective Learning and Teaching Social Policy and Social Work*. Abingdon: RoutledgeFalmer.

Whilst the whole of this book is relevant and useful to the professional practice educator, Chapter 5 'Students Learning to Learn' would prove particularly supportive to your reading of this chapter.

Chapter 3
What is teaching?

MEETING THE POST-QUALIFYING SOCIAL WORK STANDARDS

The material in this chapter links to the following Domain standards:

Domain A: Organise opportunities for the demonstration of assessed competence in practice

1. Take responsibility for creating a physical and learning environment conducive to the demonstration of assessed competence.

2. Negotiate with all participants in the workplace, including service users and carers, the appropriate learning opportunities and the necessary resources to enable the demonstration of practice competence.

Domain B: Enable learning and professional development in practice

1. Establish the basis of an effective working relationship by identifying learners' expectations, the outcomes which they have to meet in order to demonstrate competence, and their readiness for assessment. Agree the available learning opportunities, methods, resources, and timescales to enable them to succeed.

2. Discuss, identify, plan to address and review the particular needs and capabilities of learners, and the support available to them. Identify any matters which may impact on their ability to manage their own learning.

3. Discuss and take into account individual learning styles, learning needs, prior learning achievements, knowledge and skills. Devise an appropriate, cost-effective assessment programme which promotes their ability to learn and succeed.

4. Make professional judgements about meeting learners' needs within the available resources, ensuring the required learning outcomes can be demonstrate in accordance with adult learning models.

5. Identify which aspects of the management of the learning and assessment programme learners are responsible for in order to achieve their objectives. Describe and agree the roles of the work-based assessor in mentoring, coaching, modelling, teaching and supervision.

7. Advise learners how to develop their ability to manage their own learning. Deal with difficulties encountered by them.

Domain C: Manage the assessment of learners in practice

5. Use direct observation of learners in practice to assess performance.

7. Encourage learners to self evaluate and seek service users, carers and peer group feedback on their performance.

Introduction

In this chapter we will build on and develop your learning from the previous chapter through developing and extending your understanding of learning and your role and responsibilities as a 'teacher' in supporting learning within the practice setting. We will particularly examine the relationship between you as the practice educator and the student, and working with the academic institution. The intention of this chapter is to examine your role as a 'teacher' and consider teaching strategies that will support this process. We will invite you to reflect on your approach to teaching of the student.

Learning and teaching in practice

In the previous chapter we examined the different theories that support learning in practice. As we have seen, the processes by which we learn are far more complex than merely acquiring knowledge from an 'expert'; to encourage learning we need to design teaching activities that recognise the implications of different ways (theories) of learning. Without recognising and facilitating the process of learning, the integration of knowledge and theory and the development of skills will be severely hampered. As practice educators we need to recognise our own approaches to teaching others and how this impacts on the students' learning experience. Ramsden (1992: 12) suggests: 'The aim of teaching is simple: it is to make student learning possible . . . To teach is to make an assumption about what and how the student learns; therefore, to teach well implies learning about students' learning.' Whilst Ramsden is writing about the process of teaching in higher education, he does remind us of the importance of the interrelationship between theories of learning and the ways in which they impact on our approach to teaching. Your views on learning and the ways in which students learn are inextricably linked to your approach to teaching. Cowan's (1998: 47) description of teaching focuses on the 'activity' of teaching: '[teaching is] the purposeful creating of situations from which motivated learners should not be able to escape learning or developing'.

In Table 3.1 we have provided a brief summary of approaches; in addition we have referred to another position on learning, that of 'Situational Learning'. Situational learning emphasises the importance of the work context in learning, stressing the participation of the individual in a whole community of learning. Learning that takes place within the culture of the working environment is claimed to be comprehensive, according to Lave and Wenger (1991), as it incorporates development of professional identity and social relations. The perspective argued by Lave and Wenger is one that suggests that the socio-cultural context, through the influence of 'communities of practice', is the most important determinant of learning. Lave and Wenger (1998: 45) describe a community of practice as 'the property of a kind of community created over time by the sustained pursuit of a shared enterprise. It makes sense, therefore to call these kinds of communities *communities of practice*' (authors' italics). For those new to the community (of practice), Lave and Wenger (1991: 108–9) comment: 'the purpose is not to learn *from* talk as a substitute for legitimate peripheral participation; it is to learn *to* talk as a key to legitimate peripheral participation'. This orientation has the definite advantage of drawing attention to the need to understand knowledge and learning in context. Eraut et al. (2002) also

Table 3.1: Four positions on learning

Theoretical framework	Behaviourist	Cognitivist	Humanist	Situational
Examples of theorists	Pavlov, Watson, Skinner	Lewin, Piaget, Ausubel, Bruner, Gagne	Maslow, Rogers	Bandura, Lave and Wenger, Salomon
Learning process	Change in the student's behaviour	Located in internal mental process	A personal act to fulfil potential	Interaction/observation in social contexts. Movement from the periphery to the centre of a community of practice
Place where learning occurs	Stimuli in the external environment	Within the internal cognitive structuring of the individual learner	Related to affective and cognitive needs	Learning is in the relationship between people and environment
Purpose in education	To produce a behavioural change in the learner in the desired direction	To develop the individual's capacity and skills to learn better	To support the learner to become self-actualised, autonomous	To enable the full participation of the learner in communities of practice
Educator's role	To arrange the environment to produce the desired effect	To provide the structures of the content of learning activity	To facilitate the development of the whole person	To work to establish communities of practice in which conversation and participation can occur
Relevance to adult learning	Behavioural objectives Competency-based education Skill development and training	Cognitive development Intelligence, learning and memory as function of age Learning how to learn	Andragogy Self-directed learning	Socialisation Social participation Associationalism (a connection of ideas, memories, or feelings with each other, or with events) Conversation

Source: Adapted from Merriam and Caffarella (1998)

challenge prevailing views about the superiority of formal education for effective workplace learning. However, in an earlier text Eraut (1994) offers a connection between these two potentially opposing forms of learning, stating: 'in practice contexts theoretical knowledge has to be adapted to suit the particular demands of each situation' (2002: 27). Thus, before knowledge can be used, a connection between knowledge and the situation under consideration needs to be made. Schön (1983: 48), in describing professional practice, contrasts 'the high, hard ground', based on theory, science and research, with the messy 'swampy lowland', where complex human problems raise challenges to be grappled with. The bringing together of these two things – formal learning and work practice – is seen by Barnett (2002) as a contemporary challenge. He argues that 'effective work' requires both formal and informal learning.

ACTIVITY

Reflect on the 'community of practice' in which you are engaged. What opportunities are there for the student to learn from others in the team? Or to learn from others within the organisation? And others 'outside' the immediate team in which you work? How could they contribute to the student's learning?

In this activity we are inviting you to consider the student learning within the wider context of the team, organisation and the environment in which social work is practised. It is important for a student to have experience of teamwork; your role will be to support and monitor these experiences. Student experience will be developed and enriched through learning from working in and as part of a team. However, we also need to recognise that there are many challenges, and that students will need opportunities to learn and reflect on the experiences of working as part of a team and with others.

There are critiques of the notion of the 'community of practice'; first, this notion implies that learning can only take place within a community of practice. In additional, there are inherent issues in communities in relation to 'power' and 'power relationships', which may be difficult for students to understand and transcend in order to participate fully. However, the notion of community of practice and the broader conceptualisation of situated learning provides significant pointers for practice.

- Learning is the relationship between people: it is not just what goes on in people's heads but takes place through the involvement of the individual in the wider community of their practice;

- As practice educators, you have a critical role to play in working with the student to become a participant within that community of practice;

- Problem-solving and learning from experience are central processes, and they take place through co-participation in situations of activity, context and culture.

In Chapter 7 we explore the concepts of 'communities of practice' in relation to your own development.

Supporting the transfer of learning to practice

Transfer of learning underpins education and, indeed, is a fundamental part of life.
(Cree and Macaulay, 2000: xiii)

Placement in a practice setting provides the opportunity for learning to be transferred from the learning environment and developed and applied to practice. As we have seen in the previous chapter, the adult student brings with them a range of prior learning experiences from their personal and occupational lives, which will influence their approach to learning. In addition, the student on placement will have acquired knowledge, skills and experiences learned in the context of the academic environment. Placements in practice allow for learning to be applied, developed and used creatively in practice with service users and carers; professional knowledge should be derived through practice and the systematic analysis of that experience (Fook, 2002; Gould and Taylor, 1996). For Macaulay (2000: 21), transfer of learning provides an answer to 'how the ideals of the profession can be maintained . . . while enabling budding practitioners to deal with messy, chaotic and contradictory reality that they will encounter'. As a subconscious process, transfer of learning happens continually as we reconstruct our knowledge on the basis of new information and new experiences. When we are working with students, we are inviting them to make this a conscious process – not only to articulate those connections but to make appropriate and relevant connections. In this way we are seeking to encourage deep, as opposed to surface, learning (see Chapter 2).

The three-way relationship: the student, the practice educator and the university tutor

The three-way relationship between the student, the practice educator and the university tutor is essential to ensure that the appropriate learning, teaching and support is in place to enable the student to develop and apply this learning to their professional practice and in support of their personal learning and development.

ACTIVITY

Reflect on the different roles and responsibilities of those involved in the three-way relationship. What are your expectations of each of these roles?

In Chapter 6 we examine the management and development of the learning experiences on placement. You may have your own personal expectations and requirements in relation to your expectations of the student and your expectations of the university tutor; you will need to articulate these clearly at the beginning of any placement. Table 3.2 seeks to identify some of the specific ways in which the student, the practice educator and university tutor can support and work together within the practice placement.

Table 3.2: The three-way relationship: the student, the practice educator and the university tutor

	Student	University tutor	Practice educator
Expectations, roles and responsibilities	• Demonstrate a commitment to the placement and their learning and development throughout the placement. • Provide a detailed analysis of their previous learning and learning undertaken within the academic setting, including access to previous assessed work, identifying and articulating areas of strength and areas for development. • Have an in-depth understanding of the processes and paperwork it is necessary to complete to form the assessment of learning whilst undertaking the placement in practice. • Prepare for and attend all supervision sessions with the practice educator and any learning, teaching and development opportunities. • Prepare for and attend all relevant meetings with the practice educator, with the tutor, and with the practice educator and tutor. • Ensure that they monitor, with the support of the practice educator and tutor, their own learning pathway and keep the tutor and	• Collaborate with the student and practice educator in the development and support of learning and teaching within the practice setting to support the student's professional learning and development. • Provide information and advice in relation to the student's previous (and future) learning within the academic setting. • Provide information and advice in relation to the academic award, and professional and academic standards and expectations. • Provide support and guidance within the practice setting. • Provide detailed guidance and support in relation to the university's expectations for the practice placement, including relevant academic work and paperwork to be completed. • Review and monitor the practice placement to ensure that there are relevant learning and development opportunities to support the student. • Support the practice educator and support and encourage the student with learning skills,	• Ensure they are aware of the programme structure and content, relevant professional standards, and the learning and teaching associated with the placement and the award. • Liaise with tutor to ensure the student is maintaining progress. • Provide regular and timely supervision to support the student. • Communicate and engage with the student as a professional support and 'critical friend' in support of their learning and development. • Support the student in applying and reflecting on their learning to professional practice. • Observe the student's practice. • Provide relevant teaching and learning opportunities in consultation with the student and (where appropriate) the tutor. • Work with and ensure that service users and carers inform and contribute to the student's learning and assessment of the student's practice. • Promote regular contact with the tutor and prepare for and attend appropriate three-way meetings.

- practice educator informed on their progress, seeking appropriate guidance and support when they require it.
- Prepare for and attend all relevant university teaching days held during the practice learning opportunity.
- Inform the tutor and their practice educator of any specific circumstance that might impact on or inhibit their learning and/or progress towards their award.

including critical evaluation of their practice, relating theory to practice and transfer of learning.
- Act as the point of contact for any specific problems or difficulties encountered within the placement, especially at an early stage, if there are concerns about the student's practice or a student who may be failing their placement.
- Provide individual guidance and academic support to the student.
- Communicate and engage with the student and practice educator in supporting their academic progress towards successful completion of the placement.
- Coordinate and attend relevant three-way meetings between the student, mentor and themselves.
- Provide guidance on academic work.

- Monitor, evaluate and assess the student's learning and development and progress throughout the placement, providing relevant reports when required.

Developing your role as a 'teacher'

Approaches to teaching

Teaching approaches that facilitate adult learning are critical in supporting students to transfer their learning into practice and in developing their learning in practice. Ramsden (2004: 59) outlines three different approaches to teaching of students:

Approach 1: *Teaching as telling or transmitting*. This is similar to the 'Didactic' approach (Griffin, 2006) where the student is seen as an 'empty vessel' to be 'filled' by information from the teacher.

Approach 2: *Teaching as organising student activity*. This is similar to the socratic approach (Jarvis, 2006) The student is seen as having some knowledge and the teacher's role is to 'question' the learner, to bring out and develop their knowledge and understanding.

Approach 3: *Teaching as making learning possible*. This is similar to the 'facilitative' approach (Gregory, 2006), where the teacher sets the conditions for learning and acts as a resource for the student; the student is supported in directing their own learning.

ACTIVITY

Consider each of these approaches. Under what circumstances might you adopt each of these approaches?

There are times when we may need to adopt a didactic or Socratic approach to enabling, for example at the beginning of a placement or when the student has to deal with 'new' situations. In these cases it may be appropriate for practice educators to impart information and the student has to listen. Here the emphasis is on content and information. Within a practice placement there are many opportunities for a student to learn from well-designed activities, for example from shadowing others in the team and shadowing in other agencies; from direct teaching. Using a questioning approach can help students to move more quickly from one stage to another. However, what we may not have control of is what the student does with the content of the teaching; for example the student's ability to transfer and apply the teaching learned in these contexts to other situations, and in work with different service users. A facilitative style of teaching can be linked to the humanist and experiential learning approaches that we outlined in Chapter 2. As a facilitator you 'help others develop from the inside out, meaning from a values and feeling domain to their expression in behaviour . . . facilitation can be explored in terms of both being and doing' (Gregory, 2006: 102).

As students undertake placements as part of their academic programme of study, we hope that they will provide their own motivation to learn from practice and have developed their own discipline to do so. In addition, they should bring their own, already developed cognitive abilities to bear on the subject matter. Nevertheless, the practice educator still has a crucial and demanding role to play in the process of student learning, by creating a context in which the student's desire and ability to learn can work most effectively. What we are suggesting is that ultimately 'teaching' is less about what the teacher does than about what the teacher gets the students to do. As a practice educator you are well placed to arrange for the student to think with and about the ideas they are learning for an extended period of time, so that they learn their way around a topic. Unless students are thinking with and about the ideas they are learning for a while, they are not likely to build up a flexible repertoire of performances of understanding.

> *Transfer of learning will thus be facilitated by a learning experience that is well taught and well integrated with previous knowledge, teaching methods which seek to enhance the ability of the students to make connections and ample scope for putting learning into practice.*

(Macaulay, 2000: 17)

Your role as a teacher

A good teacher helps the student to learn by contributing to their development in a number of ways. Figure 3.1 seeks to outline the different ways in which you can contribute to that learning.

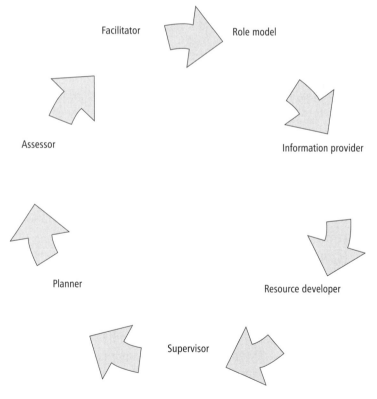

Figure 3.1: The practice educator: roles as 'teacher'

Source: Adapted and developed from Harden and Crosby (2000)

In acting as a *role-model*, there are two specific areas. First, this relates to your own approach to practice on the job – acting as a role-model within your own practice. This means being able to explain your own practice, the knowledge, theories and skills you draw on in working with particular service users and carers, and explaining what you have learned. This also relates to your learning from practice and the values you demonstrate in your own practice and in your role as practice educator. Modelling critical reflection on your own practice is central to this. As Payne (2002: 123) states: 'If we are to practise from knowledge and theory, we must have ways of thinking which turn thinking into practice action. Reflection is a way of doing this.' Second, you will demonstrate this in your approach as a 'teacher' – in your approach to the subject, the knowledge that you demonstrate, and in outlining and exploring the range of possibilities and choices available in engaging and working with service users. This offers you a unique opportunity to share some of your own enthusiasm for the social work profession and for working with service users and carers.

As an *information provider* you will be able to provide the student with the information, knowledge and understanding of the discipline and subject of social work. This includes:

- working with individuals and groups of service users and carers;

- day-to-day practice;

- organisational knowledge; and

- sources of local, regional and national knowledge, information and resources.

Critically you will be able to share your thoughts (and in support of the students thoughts) as a reflective practitioner.

As a *supervisor* you will be responsible for creating formal and informal opportunities to review and assess the student's work. Supervision is seen as a key process in supporting students in placement and is discussed in Chapter 5.

As a *resource developer* you will act as a provider in selecting, adapting or producing materials for learning; for example, case studies; undertaking role-play and so on. You will also be providing guides for practice. This will include:

- Practice curriculum as a guide for learning, the learning opportunities available (see Chapter 6);

- Legislation, guidance, policy and procedures that inform and guide the practice within your agency, within your service area and within your specific discipline;

- Direction and teaching on models and theories that guide practice in your service area, for example application of the processes models of practice (for example the ASPIRE model [Assessment, Planning, Intervention, Review and Evaluation] – for more details see Parker and Bradley, 2003) and those used in support of formal assessments (for example, Prochaska and DiClemente's Model of Change).

As a *planner*, you will be developing and planning the learning across the whole placement; for example, building up 'complexity' and opportunities to demonstrate practice. This will also be demonstrated through individual teaching events; individual learning events linked to learning needs and phases of the student's placement (for example, teaching more complex skills, such as court skills, later in a placement).

Throughout the placement you will be acting as an *assessor* of the student's work and practice. This is both 'formative' – i.e. ongoing throughout the placement and in support of the student's learning – and 'summative' in your final assessment of the student at the end of the placement.

As a *facilitator* you will have a role that recognises the student-centred view of learning, based on facilitation (rather than a role purely as an information provider). In addition, you will be acting as a mentor to the student through the provision of support and guidance.

Developing teaching strategies

As we have identified in Chapter 2 and further in this chapter, there are a number of personal, theoretical and contextual influences on the ways in which individuals engage in their learning. Additionally, in Chapter 2 we have identified that, in considering the learning needs of the student, we need to take into account the student's own starting point and provided you with some strategies to do this. In this section we are seeking to identify a range of different teaching methods that are intended to support the student in transferring their academic learning to practice and developing their learning from practice.

In designing teaching strategies we may be seeking to develop and extend the student's learning in a number of areas. These include development of understanding in:

- Knowledge: 'context' knowledge about the placement, such as practical issues of office systems and processes; being able to use appropriate IT systems for recording and monitoring; knowledge about the organisation, the service provided and the service users and carers with which it engages; knowledge of relevant legislation, policy and procedures within your agency; use of relevant documents and forms.

- Theories: supporting the student in recognising and applying relevant theories to their practice; developing the student's understanding of the specific theories that are relevant to the practice of your agency.

- Skills: supporting the student to recognise and apply relevant skills to their practice; developing the student's understanding of the specific skills that are relevant to the practice of your agency.

- Values: supporting the student to examine their personal and professional values; the conflicts and dilemmas of applying values in practice.

- Anti-oppressive practice: engaging with the complexity and diversity of practice; the nature of power and oppression and the impact on individual lives.

- Working with service users and carers: developing ways to involve service users and carers though partnership working and empowerment; supporting the student to recognise the position of and the complexities of engaging with vulnerable service users and their carers.

In thinking about the content and range of the teaching you will need to be drawing on the relevant standards that form the assessment for the placement; in the case of social work students this will be the *National Occupational Standards for Social Work* (Topss/SfC: 2002). In addition there will be expectations from the programme on which the student is studying about the learning required and the expectations of the student. Your thinking will be informed by discussion with the university tutor. Importantly this will be informed through discussion with the student. The preparation of the practice curriculum (see Chapter 6) will also contribute to this. A potential way of generating greater understanding of the student's learning needs is through using the principles of 'self-directed learning'.

The practice educator's role has traditionally been seen as that of practice and content expert. In this role, the practice educator knows what should be learned and how to learn it; the practice educator has responsibility for the learning. In self-directed learning, however, 'the focus of learning is on the individual and self-development, with learners expected to assume primary responsibility for their own learning' (Caffarella, 1993: 26). The interplay between the learning situation and the learner is the starting point for the development of self-directed learning strategies. One of the educator's roles is to draw upon, adapt, and create strategies and supporting resources consistent with the interplay between situation and learner.

Adult educators can best facilitate self-directed learning through:

- Helping the learner to recognise the starting point for their learning, for example, through supporting their reflection on previous learning and experience (for example through the process of supervision);

- Being familiar with a wide variety resources to support the learning, including teaching resources;

- Inspiring adult learners to view knowledge and understanding as contextual, to see value frameworks as cultural constructs, and to appreciate that they can act on their world individually or collectively to transform it;

- Recognising learner personality types and learning styles;

- Creating a partnership with the learner to set goals, strategies and evaluation criteria by using negotiation through a learning contract;

- Through the facilitation of teaching and learning experiences;

- Demonstrating skills in listening and communication;

- Encouraging the learner to set objectives that can be met in several ways and that offer a variety of options for evidence of successful performance.

As we have suggested when examining the different approaches to teaching, practice educators should understand adults as learners and accept a humanistic philosophy, seeing teaching as a human act (Freire, 1998). This means letting go of the traditional view of 'teacher control'. Despite the principles of this approach you may need to be more directive initially in supporting the learner to identify their learning needs, being prepared

Box 3.1: *Self-directed learning*

Knowles (1975: 18) describes self-directed learning (SDL) as 'a process in which individuals take the initiative, with or with out the help of other, to diagnose their learning needs, formulate learning goals, identify resources for learning, select and implement learning strategies, and evaluate learning outcomes'.

Others have described this process as self-planned learning, inquiry method, independent learning, self-education, self-instruction, self-teaching, self-study and autonomous learning. Whilst these labels seem to imply learning in isolation, Knowles pointed out that SDL usually takes place in association with various types of help – for example, practice educators; university tutors and peers.

Knowles' five-step model of self-directed learning consists of:

1. Diagnosing learning needs: estimating the current level of one's knowledge and skill or one's progress in gaining the desired knowledge and skill; deciding what detailed knowledge and skill to learn

2. Formulating learning outcomes/goals: setting specific goals, deadlines or intermediate targets; deciding on timescales – beginning, mid-point and end of the learning episode

3. Identifying human and material resources for learning: deciding the specific activities, methods, resources or equipment for learning

4. Choosing and implementing an appropriate learning strategy: including identifying any factors that have been hindering learning or inefficient aspects of the current procedures

5. Evaluation of learning outcomes/goals.

For Knowles, SDL is grounded in his conceptualisation of andragogy in that:

1. It provides a learning environment showing that the learner is accepted, respected and supported.

2. Attention is on self-diagnosis of needs for learning.

3. It involves the learner in planning a personal programme.

4. The practice educator acts as a resource person, a procedural specialist, and a co-inquirer, and not in trying to make the other person learn.

5. The practice educator helps the learner in a process of self-evaluation.

6. It places great emphasis on techniques that tap the experience of adult learners.

to build learner control slowly. An attitude of openness and trust is imperative for self-directed learning to thrive. Mutual respect, mutual trust, collaboration, a sense of support, as well as a sense of humanness, are important elements which the practice educator can affect and/or implement.

Teaching strategies

Think of as many methods of teaching as possible that could support students' learning in practice!

Having identified and negotiated the learning needs of the student we need to consider how we will meet their learning needs. No doubt you will have come up with a range of methods to support teaching: in Table 3.3 we have identified some methods of teaching that could support you.

As you will see, central to the process of learning is the process of reflective practice. Linking teaching, learning and practice in supporting 'change' in the learner can be achieved through critical analysis of the 'positioning' of the individual (and others) within the process of learning.

> *Critical reflection is the process by which adults identify the assumptions governing their actions, locate the historical and cultural origins of the assumptions, question the meaning of assumptions, and develop alternative ways of acting*
>
> (Stein, in Fook et al., 2006: 12)

As we have already indicated, reflection on practice is a critical skill. Working with people is often messy, unpredictable and not easy to understand; it is rarely open to 'off-the-shelf' remedies and outcomes are often unpredictable.

> *. . . the capacity to draw back in order to reflect on what is happening . . . enables learning to take place in a way which allows thought-less action to become thoughtful.*
>
> (Yelloly and Henkel, 1995: 8)

Critical reflection allows those working with people to identify and question assumptions about content, context, theories and process. Professional knowledge needs to be informed by an appraisal of the way in which that knowledge informs the understanding and interaction with the person's situation and how our values and beliefs shape that experience.

Table 3.3: Some teaching methods

Method	Description of technique
Discussion	This presents the opportunity for a dialogue between the student and the practice educator and/or others about a range of issues, for example, an event, a piece of practice, a piece of reading and so on.
	• Guided discussion: the practice educator or student poses a question for discussion orally or in writing;
	• Inquiry-based discussion: the practice educator poses a question/issue that requires the student to undertake research and/or investigation which informs the future discussion;
	• Reflective discussion: to promote 'internal' dialogue: through asking questions such as 'What do you think about that?', 'Could you explain that?' and 'What are your thoughts about this?'
	• Explanatory discussion: where the practice educator or student provides an explanation of a particular phenomenon or event.
Questioning	The intention is to use a range of questioning techniques to support the student's thinking about an issue or problem. The aim is to encourage critical thinking about the practice. Questions could include: What are you doing? What is the objective (of your intervention)? What are the key issues? What is the priority? What are the good things about what is going on? The bad things? What factors have been considered? Has anything been left out? Who are the relevant people with relevant views? What views do they have? What is your intuition about this (piece of work)? How does if make you feel? Are there alternative courses of action? What choices are available? What do you want to achieve? What will be/is the consequence of your intervention? What are the benefits and advantages of what is being proposed? Are there alternative ways of intervening?
Reflective diary/journal	These are often used as a means of encouraging student and practitioner reflection. The student is encouraged to keep a regular diary on their practice as a vehicle for reflection. The purpose of the journal is to record experience; facilitate learning from experience; support understanding and the representation of that understanding; develop critical thinking or a questioning attitude; increase active involvement in, and ownership of, learning; increase ability in reflection and thinking; enhance problem-solving skills; as a means of assessment in formal education; enhance reflective practice; for reasons of personal development and self-empowerment; for therapeutic purposes or as means of supporting behaviour change; enhance creativity; improve writing; improve or give 'voice'; as a means of self-expression; and to foster communication, in particular reflective and creative interaction (Moon, 1999).

Table 3.3: Continued

Method	Description of technique
Critical incident analysis	This means asking a student to write about an incident, intervention and/or conversation with a service user about an issue or problem that is central to their relationship. It provides the opportunity to enhance students' ability to recall the details of their interactive work with service users and/or colleagues; to write clearly and coherently about the complex thoughts, actions and feelings that comprise their social work practice; to reflect on their work, integrating theoretical concepts, skills and values that are being taught in the curriculum. A suggested process for learning from this is to use four columns: the intervention/conversation is written in the first column; the next column is used for the student's reactions and thoughts; the third column is used for the practice educator's comments and feedback; and the final column is used for analysis of the intervention, identification of the skills used and assessment of the learning from the intervention.
Case study	Developing case studies by the practice educator; preparation of a case study by the student for discussion; using existing material in relation to cases, for example, drawing on Inquiry Reports. Alternatively discussion could centre on an existing case (one of the practice educator's or the student's). Different approaches could be taken to examining the case: examining the theoretical framework that informs the assessment and intervention and considering alternative theories; working with the student to construct 'tools' for practice, such as genograms and family trees; examining the roles and responsibilities of the different professionals in relation to the case and the wider issues of partnership and collaboration with others; discussing the experience and impact of oppression and discrimination on the service user and wider issues of poverty and social exclusion.
Interview	'Discovery' interviews can allow students to learn from others; for example, discussions with service users about their experiences as people with specific needs, as an opportunity to learn from their 'stories'. The process could be based on the following: introduction of the reason for the interview; encouragement to talk freely about the experience; questioning to gain further information or clarity and provide explanation; analysis and reflection with the support of the practice educator.
Observation	Where the student: • Observes the practice of others: with service users and with carers; in situations with other professionals; or the practice of other professionals; others with specific expertise; or to complete a specific piece of practice (for example, assessment);

	• Observes others as 'perceptive' observation; for example the systematic, detailed and precise observation of a child to further the student's knowledge and/or to inform an assessment; or • The student's practice is observed by the practice educator and others. Observation can provide opportunities for briefing/preparation prior to the observation; debriefing the experience; discussion about learning from the experience; feedback (where appropriate and relevant) from the service user and carer; opportunities for reflection on the observation; writing about the experience;
Presentation	The student is invited to prepare a presentation on a specific topic identified by the practice educator and student. The student presents their findings to the practice educator and/or others.
Exercises	The practice educator uses pre-prepared material with the student. There are a number of texts and packages to support this. All books in the Learning Matters: Transforming Social Work Practice series have exercises and case studies to draw on (www.learningmatters.co.uk). Agency Training Sections will have materials that contain exercises; for example, materials produced by the DfES for *Every Child Matters*. In addition the university tutor can provide advice on relevant materials.
Teaching	The practice educator provides teaching on a particular themes or topics identified to develop and enhance the student's knowledge, understanding and skills.
Role-play/ skills rehearsal	This provides the opportunity for the student to 'practise' an intervention or process with the practice educator and/or with others. It is not intended to be an opportunity to act but rather an opportunity to promote discussion, enhance learning and promote reflection. It allows the student to develop an understanding of others' perspectives; encourages students to work with others in analysing situations and developing workable solutions; provides students with an opportunity to apply concepts they have learned; gives students the chance to gain insights into interpersonal challenges they are likely to face in their careers and private lives; enables students to effectively contrast problem-solving methods by role-playing a situation several times from diverse perspectives; offers a constructive channel through which feelings can be expressed and feedback processed; and presents students with a forum for building self-esteem and confidence.
Reading	The practice educator invites the student to read a particular piece of work and address questions which have been pre-prepared by the practice educator.
Research	Research can allow students to investigate a particular subject or topics to gain a greater understanding of the issue; it can develop research-mindedness in the student and a critical, evidence-based approach to developing practice and applying research to practice. Research can also be used to address specific issues, for example, within an agency; in meeting a service user or carer needs; to support developments in the community.

Box 3.2: Supporting the reflective process

Lehmann (2006) has developed a '345' model as a model of analysis in relation to narratives; it also offers a useful structure to support the reflective process.

Lehmann identifies three ways to reflect:

1. Reflection on content: what information is presented? What knowledge or theories are identifiable?

2. Reflection on meaning: what does this 'mean' to us? Do we agree with this perspective? Are there alternative points of view? What assumptions are we making? What are the values that we are drawing on? How is this impacting on our personal and professional attitudes and beliefs?

3. Critical reflection: what are the assumptions that we are making (personal, emotional, social, cultural, historical, political)? (Fook et al., 2006). What are the changes that I need to make?

Lehmann identifies four processes in reflective thinking:

1. Investigative process: seeking and finding knowledge;

2. Explanation process: reasoning and fitting together that information and knowledge: 'What happens next . . .?'; 'What will happen if . . . ?'

3. Understanding process: understanding why the person acts the way they do; personal insights into your own reactions; contemplating the possibility of change; formulating an alternative approach;

4. Transformational process: within ourselves as to the constraints and feelings and reasons why we act in this way. The realisation that there are a number of different perspectives; bringing into consciousness our choices and 'develop[ing] a sense of ownership for what lies within our repertoire of professional actions' (Lehmann, 2006: 209).

Lehmann outlines five questions for reflective thinking:

1. What is this about? What is this presenting in terms of issues/problems?

2. What more do I need to know?

3. How do I understand this? An opportunity to debate and 'compare notes' with the practice educator.

4. What other perspectives are there? What else? An investigation of the alternative perspectives.

5. How could this be different? What are my personal changes; shifts in values, attitudes and beliefs?

Rose

Rose was an experienced practitioner when she was seconded to a professional course. She undertook her first placement in her previous workplace, a centre working with children with learning disabilities, and passed with very positive comments. The university tutor has told you that she is struggling with her academic work – but generally manages to 'scrape through'. In her current placement, in a mental health setting, she is struggling to engage with service users and colleagues: she avoids engaging and communicating with people, stating that the service users are 'different' because of their mental health problems.

Joe

Joe is an amiable young man, who is easy to get on with. He is on his final placement in a voluntary agency offering community-based support to drug users. He is a popular and accepted figure with service users; staff comment that he is often indistinguishable from the service users. Although he forms good relationships with them, he rarely translates these into a basis for action to ameliorate the service users' concerns. He has a lack of professional presence and identity, and has a reluctance to move into a professional role.

Justice

Justice, a gentle, quiet black African man, is a refugee. In his home country he was a teacher. In his first placement (within a small voluntary placement providing support to parents) he did well, demonstrating good personal and interpersonal skills and a sound value base. He is currently in his final placement in a busy statutory children and family team. Justice appears to be struggling to meet the demands of the placement; for example:

- *He struggles to understand the processes and systems;*

- *He finds the forms and procedures complex and spends a lot of time reading and completing the paperwork, coming in on his study day and working late into the evening.*

Engaging with service users is difficult and he has experienced discriminatory and abusive language from them.

What issues for the student do these cases raise for you? What teaching strategies could you use that might support each student?

Clearly it is difficult to make judgements based on little information! Your starting point would be to raise your concerns with the individual student, identify their perspective on the situation and seek to negotiate with them how to overcome the difficulties.

Rose has clear previous experience of practice to build on; however, what she appears unable to do is transfer this learning from her previous setting to this setting, nor is she able to identify and apply her learning from the academic setting. She appears to lack knowledge and understanding of the needs of service users with mental health difficulties; this may contribute to her lack of skills in engaging users and carers. Rose will need support to identify transferable skills from her previous work and placement, as well as help to identify 'gaps'. Working with Rose to identify gaps in her knowledge and broaden her perspective through direct teaching will help her; this could be supplemented with reading/guided reading and the possibility of undertaking a research project could build up her knowledge and confidence. Exploring case studies and using role-play could enhance her skills.

Joe appears to have issues in relation to lack of professional boundaries and lack of professional identity. Joe will need support to examine professional boundaries and roles (see for example the exercise on 'Boundaries' in Doel and Shardlow, 2005: 35–8). Opportunities for shadowing with yourself, others in the team and other relevant professionals could provide the basis for discussion and reflection on his personal and professional identity.

For Justice, acknowledging the strengths that he has and the skills that he brings to the placement is essential; what may need to happen is the opportunity to 'step back' and create the space required for Justice to gain control of his learning with your support. This may involve reducing his workload, while offering teaching on systems and processes could support him. In addition, he may benefit from opportunities to observe others and to observe key processes, for example, case meetings. Opportunities to role-play would improve his communication skills. Clear support needs to be given to Justice in being able to challenge the discrimination he is experiencing from service users, by giving him permission (and the language) to challenge this as unacceptable, and by his being able to withdraw from the visit/intervention if the abuse becomes acceptable for him. Any extreme forms of abusive or violent behaviour from service users, carers and others needs to be challenged by the agency.

Recognising diversity in learners

All educators have a professional responsibility to accept every adult learner as of equal worth, regardless of race, gender, ability or background. Engaging all student learners as partners in the learning process requires you to reflect on your own knowledge about your approach to equality in the learning environment.

Reflect on your own assumptions, beliefs and attitudes towards, and knowledge about, the variety of students that you may engage with as a practice educator.

Think through the way you present the practice environment and experiences to the student. Do the examples and images you use reflect and acknowledge the diversity of learners and their experiences?

Analyse your expectations for the potential of learners. Are they based on a potential stereotype of a social work student based on an individual's membership in a particular community or cultural group?

As a professional working with range of people, you will be able to acknowledge diversity and difference; you will be able to recognise the personal, cultural and social (Thompson, 2006) impact of oppression and discrimination; you will be aware of the impact of poverty and issues in relation to social exclusion (Sheppard, 2006). You will be aware that your expectations, behaviour and language will impact on the way that you perceive people in general, and the student in particular. For example, students may respond differently to a male practice educator than to a woman practice educator; practice educators may respond differently to younger students than to older adults. Engaging learners in the process of extending beyond personal and professional stereotypical or narrow examples can be another means of developing partnerships. As a practice educator you will need to foster a belief that change and development are possible for all people and that your role is to assist the process in all learners. It is about how we act towards out learners and it is about how we value the learner.

CASE STUDY

Sylvia

Sylvia is a young black woman who is a refugee from Zimbabwe. Whilst living in the country her husband was subject to physical torture and she was arrested on several occasions. Sylvia has struggled with her studies, particularly as she has two jobs as a night care assistant. Her mother in Zimbabwe has serious health issues and Sylvia is saving to bring her to this country. She has concerns for her marriage – her husband is out every night. He taunts her by saying if she leaves him than she will lose her status as a refugee and be sent back to Zimbabwe. 'I cannot leave – I have nothing, only this course and the hope of a better job keep me going,' she says. Sylvia is outwardly optimistic about people; she is always smiling and very positive about the future.

Jun

Jun's first language is Chinese, as she comes from Hong Kong. She is a quiet and generally reserved; she makes copious notes. Whilst her English is very good, she finds it very difficult to make sense of some of the concepts and issues. Jun cannot make sense of the 'Western' positioning in relation to life-span development as it is so different from her own understanding and position, for example in relation to values and attitudes. Her fear is that unless she can learn the 'right answers' then she will fail the programme.

Carol

Carol has a disability which requires her to use a wheelchair on occasions; she can become fatigued, which means that she finds it difficult to concentrate. She is very concerned about how she will cope in a practice placement.

Peter

Peter has excellent verbal and inter-personal skills; he is a popular member of the programme. His academic work has been poor and, as result of the intervention of his university tutor, he has recently been diagnosed with dyslexia. He is very apprehensive about his first practice placement, especially the amount of written work and forms to be completed.

A consequence to creating an effective learning environment is providing an equitable learning environment. Many learners – for example, women; individuals from different cultural and ethnic backgrounds; people with disabilities, – have not experienced support or equality in the learning environment. As a result, they have frequently felt disconnected and disengaged from the formal learning task. The above cases represent very small examples of some of the diversity of issues that students' experience and bring to their leaning. Each student will have a unique set of circumstances that will require an individual response. Some of key points may include:

- Acknowledging your own 'immediate' views, while remaining open to the student's perspective and to identifying learning and development opportunities to support students;

- Acknowledging the limits of your own knowledge in working with diverse and complex issues and seeking help from appropriate sources;

- Supporting the student to fit in with the team by enabling them to communicate their own needs, recognising the boundaries of confidentiality in sharing personal information and/or in negotiating with the student the information that needs to be shared with managers and/or the team;

- The importance of working with the university and the student's academic tutor in identifying any specific learning 'tools' or resources that may support students; this may include specific assessments that have been undertaken with the student by support services; for example, Student Support Services;

- The importance of an open, honest, supportive and trusting relationship with the student, in order for them to feel confident to raise concerns.

Reflections on self

Reflection and self-evaluation are integral parts of professional competence. Reflecting on practice should include the process of evaluation. In the context of supporting the learning of a student, this means asking such questions as: 'How do I know if I am doing (for example, my teaching as a practice educator) well, or well enough?' Consequently this process promotes and supports both the learning and developmental needs of the student and you as a practice educator. What turns experience into learning is reflection. Just as you have used Kolb's learning cycle (1984) in your work with students, you could apply it to your own reflections on your role as a practice educator, for example in reflecting on a teaching event that you may have undertaken with a student.

Brookfield (1986) suggests five principles of effective practice as an educator. They include:

- respect for the learner's self-worth;

- a collaborative arrangement between facilitators and learners;

- praxis;

- fostering critical reflection; and

- empowering adults to become more fully self-directing in their learning.

Respect for learners is communicated through our own behaviour as practice educators and the way we manage the learning process. If we knowingly or unknowingly engage in behaviours that students find belittling or destructive, their learning is affected negatively. If we knowingly engage in behaviours that say to the student, 'I respect you as a person regardless of your past experience,' the learning is affected positively. Collaboration refers to the joint quality of deciding what is to be learned, how it will be learned, and when it has been learned: teaching and learning are a transaction between you and the student. Praxis refers to the recurring 'journey' through the process of experiential learning –

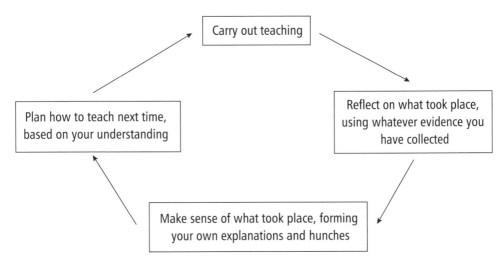

Figure 3.2: Reflecting on your teaching

activity is followed by reflection on that activity, and more activity and reflection follow. Experiencing and reflecting are built into the process. Freire (1972) was concerned with praxis; for him this includes making a difference to the world and includes a commitment to human well-being, the search for truth and respect for others. Critical reflection means helping our participants to surface and confront some of their habitual ways of looking at the world. Critical reflection involves the examination of our assumptions and developing alternative ways of looking at the world that might be more productive and healthier. Empowerment means giving power to the student so that they can continue the development of their own independence. It means that we avoid playing the 'expert' with all of the answers and set our participants on the path to thinking, searching and empowering themselves and others.

FURTHER READING

Cree, V.E. and Macaulay, C. (2000) *Transfer of Learning in Professional and Vocational Education*. London: Routledge.

The focus of this book is transfer of learning, particularly for social work. The first three chapters provide an overview of transfer of learning, placing it within contemporary educational debates. The following nine chapters describe various methods that might be used within the teaching context.

Doel, M. and Shardlow, S.M. (2005) *Modern Social Work Practice: Teaching and Learning in Practice Settings*. Aldershot: Ashgate.

This interactive book provides a range of exercises designed to provide the learner with key aspects of current social work practice.

Jones, K., Cooper, B. and Ferguson, H. (eds) (2008) *Best Practice in Social Work: Critical Perspectives*. Basingstoke: Palgrave Macmillan.

With each chapter written by different authors and taking a different service user perspective, the book seeks to apply a critical, theoretical analysis to descriptions of social work practice. It provides a lived sense of best practice and how it makes a positive difference to people's lives.

Gould, N. and Taylor, I. (eds) (1996) *Reflective Learning for Social Work*. Aldershot: Ashgate.

White, S., Fook, J. and Gardner, F. (eds) (2007) *Critical Reflection in Health and Social Care*. Maidenhead: Open University Press and McGraw-Hill Education.

Both these books provide excellent, accessible theories and practice of reflection in professional practice from the perspective of a range of authors.

Trevithick, P. (2005) *Social Work Skills: A Practice Handbook*, 2nd edn. Maidenhead: Open University Press.

This invaluable book provides accessible descriptions of methods, practice and critical skills for social work practice.

Lishman, J. (ed.) (2007) *Handbook of Practice Learning in Social Work and Social Care: Knowledge and Theory*. London: Jessica Kingsley.

This book provides a comprehensive introduction to the theory, knowledge research and evidence relevant to learning in practice.

Chapter 4
What is assessment?

MEETING THE POST-QUALIFYING SOCIAL WORK STANDARDS

The material in this chapter links to the following Domain standards:

Domain A: Organise opportunities for the demonstration of assessed competence in practice

1. Take responsibility for creating a physical and learning environment conducive to the demonstration of assessed competence.

2. Negotiate with all participants in the workplace, including service users and carers, the appropriate learning opportunities and the necessary resources to enable the demonstration of practice competence.

3. Work openly and co-operatively with learners, their line managers, workplace colleagues, other professionals, and service users and carers, in the planning of key activities at all stages of learning and assessment.

5. Monitor, critically evaluate and report on the continuing suitability of the work environment, learning opportunities, and resources. Take appropriate action to address any shortcomings and optimise learning and assessment.

Domain B: Enable learning and professional practice

1. Establish the basis of an effective working relationship by identifying learners' expectations, the outcomes which they have to meet in order to demonstrate competence, and their readiness for assessment. Agree the available learning opportunities, methods, resources, and timescales to enable them to succeed.

2. Discuss and take into account individuals' learning styles, learning needs, prior learning achievements, knowledge and skills. Devise an appropriate, cost-effective assessment programme which promotes their ability to learn and succeed.

4. Make professional educational judgments about meeting learners' needs within the available resources, ensuring the required learning outcomes can be demonstrated in accordance with adult learning models.

5. Identify which aspects of the management of the learning and assessment programme learners are responsible for in order to achieve their objectives.

Domain C: Manage the assessment of learners in practice

1. Engage learners in the design, planning and implementation of the assessment tasks.

2. Agree and review a plan and methods for assessing learners' performance against agreed criteria.

3. Ensure that assessment decisions are the outcomes of informed, evidence-based judgments and clearly explain them to learners.

4. Evaluate evidence for its relevance, validity, reliability, sufficiency and authenticity according to the agreed standard.

5. Use direct observation of learners in practice to assess performance.

6. Base assessment decisions on all relevant evidence and from a range of sources, resolving any inconsistencies in the evidence available.

7. Encourage learners to self-evaluate and seek service users, carers and peer group feedback on their performance.

8. Provide timely, honest and constructive feedback on learners' performance in an appropriate format. Review their progress through the assessment process, distinguishing between formative and summative assessment.

9. Make clear to learners how they may improve their performance. Identify any specific learning outcomes not yet demonstrated and the next steps. If necessary, arrange appropriate additional assessment activity to enable them to meet the standard.

10. Ensure that all assessment decisions, and the supporting evidence, are documented and recorded according to the required standard. Produce assessment reports which provide clear evidence for decisions.

Introduction

This chapter examines the process involved in the assessment of the student in practice.

It perhaps seems a somewhat needless question to ask *what is assessment?* when most social workers undertake some form of assessment on a daily basis, whether formally as part of the role or required by legislation, or as part of the informal, though often 'contractual' negotiations that determine a direction of travel with the people with whom you are working. However, assessment in practice education has a range of particular meanings which, although associated with modes and methods of assessment in working together with people using social care services, are different. Assessment in practice education is also related to the skills involved in conducting research, especially those of a qualitative nature, but it can also include a more quantitative approach.

Not only does assessment in practice education interlink with social work assessments in general and the conduct of social research, it is also a set of practices that are conducted on students, with students and by students, and, importantly for the reflective learning practitioner, by practice educators in respect of themselves.

In this chapter we will explore assessment in practice education in relation to its fit with social work practice and research, its particular meaning in practice education – drawing parallels, where appropriate, with higher education as a whole – and the functions and requirements demanded by it. This will be followed by an examination of ways in which practice educators might assess practice learning opportunities, encourage and use self-assessment, and continue to appraise their own skills as practice educators.

Meanings of assessment

Assessment means many things according to the context in which it is undertaken and the direction of assessment. The latter can be very complex indeed in respect of practice education (see Figure 4.1). The main thrust of most definitions concerns 'weighing up' the quality and value of something, the latter of which may be related to the amount in which this thing occurs. For instance, a student social worker will 'assess' the practice learning experience, learning opportunities and practice teacher/educator or daily supervisor, as well as undertaking professionally orientated assessments with people who use services and their carers. Practice educators and practice teachers are required to assess the competence of students to fulfil the roles specified for the level of placement undertaken. Such assessment is focused on students and their developing professional competence and expertise, on the university that set the goals for achievement according to the standards required, and, most importantly, it concerns the safety of the service users and carers with whom the student will work, and the potential benefits the student offer in their work. The practice teacher with overall responsibility for the experience may well assess the capacity and assistance of others – daily supervisors or other team members offering a learning

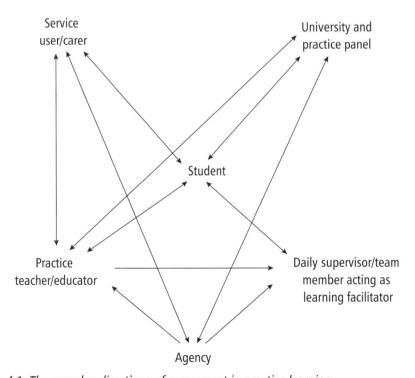

Figure 4.1 The complex directions of assessment in practice learning

experience – in facilitating the student learning process. Universities will assess the quality of the learning experiences offered, and often practice panels will provide feedback on the practice educator/practice teacher role, a report which is itself a form of assessment. Importantly, service users and carers 'weigh up' the value of the services offered and work done, including the qualities of those giving the service. When assessing in practice it is crucial that these views or assessments are taken into account and capitalised upon. Understanding that assessment is multifarious and undertaken in multiple directions is important, but it does not tell us what to do when working in practice education. What we will focus on in this chapter is the assessment of the student as a beginning practitioner.

REFLECTION POINT

Practice teachers and educators new to the role will probably have two distinct impressions of assessment. First, it is likely that you will relate it to your own work with people using your services and the assessments undertaken in this context. But, second, you will probably remember something of your own time as a student and the assessment made by your practice teacher about your practice. Both these experiences are useful. The core elements of assessment in practice situations are transferable to working as a practice educator, and your own experiences, perhaps of nervousness, apprehension and worry regarding the outcome – asking the question 'Am I good enough?' – may help foster an open and collaborative approach to practice education and judging progress, safety and learning.

Core characteristics and models of assessment

An examination of the core characteristics of assessments indicates that they can be construed in two discrete ways: as an outcome, such as a product or report, or as a process, and continuous iteration of progress. In practice, of course, these two elements are intertwined, but both can be seen in practice education which demands both a continuous process of assessment and a mutual and negotiated approach to learning and evaluation of that learning alongside a final report or summative assessment that makes a clear recommendation, based on evidence, as to whether the student is fit for practice as a social worker.

It is widely recognised that there is no clearly articulated theory of assessment in social work practice (Parker, 2007). However, there are common technical areas covered in each assessment, and shared ethical issues and potential dilemmas that can be exemplified , drawing on Smale et al. (1993), and shown in Table 4.1.

It is the case that a questioning approach will sometimes be useful and necessary in order to structure and gain required information. The process will also be aided by the use of set and previously developed pro formas, which have been designed with a particular purpose in mind. However, the assessment does not stop there and these forms of assessment should be triangulated with evidence gained from developing an exchange relationship with the student to negotiate and agree on the experiences, opportunities and modes of the assessment of learning.

Table 4.1: Areas of assessment and models

Assessment stages	Assessment model (after Smale et al. 1993)		
	Questioning	Procedural	Exchange
Planning for the assessment	Asking the student for a list of prior experience, qualifications, needs and so on. Asking colleagues and other professionals to take part in the student induction	Using university paperwork to formulate a learning and assessment plan	Negotiating experiences with student and others involved over time to develop an individualised assessment plan
Collecting the evidence	Collecting evidence by structured request for information from others	Using university and agency pro forma to collect and identify evidence that will contribute to the assessment	Considering the views and perceptions of all involved
Weighing the evidence	Questioning data against possible outcomes	Evaluating evidence and knowledge according to given criteria; using check-lists and so on	Critical evaluation of evidence
Producing a report	Focus on the summative outcome, less so on the process	Completing the required report using the given pro forma	Analysis of learning, negotiated and agreed process, identifying outcomes and future learning needs

ACTIVITY

Identify and write down some of the power imbalances that may arise or need to be taken into account in making an assessment of a student undertaking practice learning.

You may at first have thought that you held all the power as a practice educator – an anxiety-provoking situation in itself! – especially given your assessment function. However, you may also have recognised power imbalances in favour of the student and others, or certainly negotiable situations such as the student's feedback on your abilities, the practice panel assessment of your capacity to act as practice educator and its view of the learning opportunities offered and the assessment report submitted. Our conceptions of power have shifted significantly since the work of Foucault (1980). Power is not just something invested in those holding dominant and legitimised positions – in this case, you as practice educator, the university, the agency and the care councils – but is something that is negotiated between all involved in the process of practice learning. It is important to be aware of power issues and potential imbalances, and to plan open and honest assessments and engagement to maximise learning. (See also Chapter 5, for a discussion about power in the supervisory relationship.)

In practice education in social work, assessment takes place from the beginning of the learning activity through continual collection of data or information relating to the student, their prior experiences and capabilities, measured against achievements/goals identified in the learning agreement, informally rehearsed at each supervision session and formally reported upon at the midpoint or interim point of the practice opportunity and in the final report compiled at the end. Being clear and transparent about the process from the start of placement is central to minimising the negative impact of power imbalances, whilst acknowledging that 'equality of power', however defined, may not be possible. Using supervision to present non-negotiable requirements and to debate, plan and negotiate together with students how to meet these is likely to help promote trust in you and your assessment, and to facilitate the involvement of students in the assessment process.

CASE STUDY

At a university call-back day, Elaine and Nushra, student social workers, discussed their experiences of being assessed at the midpoint of placement. Both had passed so far. Elaine complained of not knowing what her practice educator was thinking, having had little discussion about how she was being assessed, only being told it was her job to provide the evidence and 'my [the practice educator's] job to assess the evidence'. Her experience was, Elaine said, preventing her from identifying clear experiences and opportunities for learning.

Nushra's experience was different. At a learning agreement meeting at the beginning of her placement, her practice educator set out what had to be achieved and then explored, in consultation with her, how this might be achieved given the opportunities the agency was offering. A plan was agreed which was discussed subsequently at each supervision session, identifying progress and issues or problems arising. This allowed Nushra and her practice educator to negotiate ways of overcoming any barriers to learning. She felt confident of meeting what was required of her.

What does the research say?

In 1990, Gleeson introduced a critical interview checklist as a means of encouraging self-assessment in practice, and recognised the long struggle social work has engaged in to implement a more scientific approach to the evaluation of practice. Edmond et al. (2006) echoed this earlier concern, stating that evidence-based approaches to the assessment of field education/practice learning remain patchy despite being desirable. Bogo et al. (2002)

identified the problem of a lack of consistent evaluation by practice educators or field instructors. This is a problem in searching for a viable assessment measure. Cowburn et al. (2000) identify further reasons why it has been difficult to develop and employ a scientific and evidence-based approach to assessment. They understand the assessment of practice as:

> . . . the process of making a judgement of a student's knowledge, skills and values. The structure through which these judgements are made is the practice curriculum. The student provides evidence from a variety of situations for the practice teacher to assess.
>
> (Cowburn et al., 2000: 630)

Making these judgements is complex, and using a competence-based model suggests the practice teacher can be neutral and objective whilst not recognising the socially and culturally specific context in which these judgements are made. For instance, the type of agency and its purpose impact on how evidence of competence is viewed, and individual characteristics and personality traits also have an influence. Using an example of a placement 'going wrong' – the student being in danger of failure – Cowburn et al. emphasise the need for negotiation and dialogue with the student, as opposed to the imposition of a standardised, rigid application of a competence framework. They suggest the application of 'standpoint theory'. This incorporates aspects of identity and social location, and acknowledges their impact on a situation in order to develop a pathway through. This model has important anti-oppressive features, allowing difference and diversity factors to be taken into account. However, it does not provide a framework for assessment that can be generalised across settings; rather, it offers a way of conducting the process. It does not get away from the need for clear assessment criteria.

A range of methods have been employed to assist in the assessment of practice. Many of these can be used in negotiation with students. Critical incident analyses have been popular (Crisp and Green-Lister, 2002; Davies and Kinloch, 2000; Noble 2001), or the use of reflective journals, portfolios and self-assessment (which we will deal with more fully later). Whilst clear empirical evidence in favour of learning styles remains equivocal (Cartney, 2000), these remain popular (see Honey and Mumford, 2000). Moore et al. (2004) employ a Myers-Briggs type indicator to assess learning needs and styles, and to attempt to improve practice educator/student relationships.

The assessment of students is central to the role of practice education. The relationship between practice educator and student and how it is perceived is important for learning (Knight, 2001; Kolevzon, 1979). Lefevre (2005) reports on a small-scale study into student perceptions of relationships with practice educators, and the significance of these for learning experiences and the accuracy of assessment. Her study found a rise in perception of the significance of practice teacher/student relationship from 82 per cent to 92 per cent between first and second placement. The central aspects of the relationship highlighted were support and availability, as well as more technical abilities to conduct high-quality work. Most students also believed that the relationship itself impacted on the effectiveness and accuracy of the practice teacher assessment of them. This research confirmed earlier research indicating that an open, collaborative partnership, which allows the sharing of power where possible, is important, and that a supportive and nurturing approach enables the development of trust and safety. These features are thought to facilitate accurate assessment. It is clear that the practice teacher educator has a pivotal role in assessment. Furness and Gilligan (2004) recognise this and the challenges that increased demands have put on those acting in this capacity.

ACTIVITY

Thinking of the importance of the working relationship for effective practice learning, and the power issues we discussed earlier, how do you think you might establish a profitable relationship with your students?

On the surface you may have thought this was a fairly straightforward activity – of course, you are a social worker and relationships are a social work strength! However, whilst an open, honest approach with clarity of expectations and responsibilities, clearly articulated and clearly delineated support mechanisms will all help, each student will have individual needs and each will perceive the power balance in the relationship differently. It is also possible that the level of input provided to a student may require negotiation across your team as a whole. Wherever possible, it is important to collect feedback from students and to seek their views on what helps. This will aid your development in the future.

The role of service users and carers in the assessment is growing in importance (Advocacy in Action et al., 2006; Thomas, 2002). This presents a management issue for practice educators, to ensure the accuracy of assessment and the safety of those service users and carers involved. Elliott et al. (2005) begin by asking people who use services to contribute to an assessment of safety to practise, by involving students in conversations with service users and carers, and asking students to complete a process recording which is then scrutinised for accuracy and the interpersonal skills of the student commented upon by service users. Baldwin and Sadd (2006) extend the reach of service user and carer involvement to all levels of the programme, which includes placements and their assessment. Edwards (2003) notes that practice teachers/educators must fully engage with the process in order to capitalise on the benefits, and move this emphasis on service user assessment from a perfunctory to a meaningful endeavour. One of the difficulties encountered within higher education social work has been the question of assigning marks, and the potential 'popularity factor' may play a part when asking for service user feedback. Therefore, argue Crisp et al. (2006) clear parameters are necessary for the assessment and lines of responsibility must be transparent:

> *Unless the parameters are carefully delineated, service users and practice teachers may develop quite different understandings as to the involvement of service users.*
>
> (Crisp et al., 2006: 730)

One key role of practice educators is to negotiate this process for student, university and especially for those people who use services.

ACTIVITY

How might you gain service user and carer views of your student's competence in working with people?

It is worth reiterating the need for meaningful involvement, and the need to ensure that those taking part do so in a voluntary and unimpeded way. Most agencies collect information from the people using their services. This can provide useful data, but you may need to collect specific information about individual students. Satisfaction questionnaires can help, but may need to be mediated, and you will need to think about whether you, the student or someone independent should collect this information. These questions remain if you decide that a personal interview is better for gaining such data. You will also need to bear in mind the cost implications of collecting service user and carer feedback in terms of time, finance and other costs. The daily practice learning funding only covers so much!

As a facilitator, your role as a practice educator may include the development and encouragement of student self-assessment strategies, which are seen as increasingly important (Burgess et al., 1999). Students may be quite hard on themselves (Parker, 2005), and part of the management process is to ensure a realistic and balanced approach. Garcia and Floyd (1999) suggest using a single system design to help students to evaluate their practice and interventions. In their study using this approach, however, they found that practice educators, whilst enthusiastic, needed support in providing useful feedback. Ellis (2001) sees possibilities for extending self-assessment to peer-assessment, which may be possible if your team or agency takes more than one student. Ellis suggests using a practice journal to encourage student reflection and self-knowledge, and to expose this deep learning to others by working in groups to develop a video presentation. This, of course, requires access to technology, time and other students. But it may be something you would wish to explore with other practice educators. Taylor et al. (1999) reported an analysis of an exploratory study into the use of portfolios. Whilst portfolios were found to encourage reflection and self-learning, the direct involvement of the practice educator was central. Interestingly, in this research Taylor et al. identify two distinct uses of the term 'portfolio', recognising that there is no agreed definition. They state that it could be used as a personal record of learning from which evidence can be taken for the assessment, or a continuous supervised piece of work that is integral to the assessment. The key element crucial to student learning was the development of a critically reflective dialogue about the portfolio. Taylor et al. suggest that clear guidance and ongoing support are important to the creation of a portfolio that will be assessed as containing adequate evidence; thus, more a negotiated and dialogic process than pure self-assessment.

Self- and peer-assessment seem to have potential, but more so as part of a wider assessment complex coordinated by the practice educator. Regehr et al. (2002) present a model for goal-setting in practice learning that draws on self-assessment skills to identify areas of disagreement and to address power differentials between practice educator and student. The structured negotiation of learning goals on the basis of agreed need forms the initial learning agreement, which is reviewed at the midpoint. A shared approach to assessment is also found within a use of self-efficacy assessment (Parker, 2005, 2006).

So, research would indicate that assessment is complex, often intuitive rather than scientific, and contested as to how it should be conducted. Assessments are interrelated with the student/practice educator relationship, and increasingly draw upon service user and carer evaluations and the self-report of those being assessed. It is important to consider these messages when formulating your own approach to student assessment.

Assessment in practice learning/ practice education

Assessment is a central part of being a student studying for any degree, including those with a vocational and professional element as well as those described as 'pure' academic degrees. Assessment provides the basis for determining whether or not a student is worthy of the academic qualification, and how their attainment should be measured, that is, the classification awarded. It is perhaps this purpose that marks out assessment in practice education from that which is purely academically focused. However, as we have seen, the core characteristics remain the same and it is dangerous to separate out academic from practice learning so starkly. To do so, suggests assigning different evaluations to each and fails to recognise the complex interaction of theoretical and practice- or skills-based learning (Parker, 2004).

What do the requirements state?

The Department of Health requirements for practice learning and all associated aspects are short and leave much to the individual programme to develop (DoH, 2002), which is one reason why you may find different criteria set if you are working as a practice educator with more than one university. The requirements for social work qualifying education simply state that students must spend at least 200 days in practice with at least two distinct user groups, and have experience of statutory social work tasks and legal interventions. Assessment is not explicitly referred to, except in mentioning satisfactory assessment prior to practice learning and to make reference to the 'full range of occupational standards and benchmark statements' (see Chapter 1 for further details).

Who you are, what your qualifications are and how much experience you have will have a bearing on what you are able to do in respect of assessment. As you will be aware, all candidates for post-qualifying awards must undertake study that will assist them in enabling others to learn. This allows a wide spectrum of involvement, from providing single opportunities for learning or tasks that you might supervise, to the full supervision and assessment of a placement. If, however, you are responsible for the final assessment of the student in practice towards their degree, you must be a qualified and experienced social worker.

It is uncertain at present whether there will be any standard education and training award equivalent to the Practice Teaching Award, although the higher specialist practice education pathway in the new post-qualifying framework may be considered a 'gold standard'. It is unclear how many practitioners will take this practice education pathway, whether there is, indeed, a market for it and how many universities will provide it or insist on its achievement in the future for those staff undertaking the final assessment of students. All social workers undertaking a Specialist level award, however, must take the unit concerned with enabling the learning of others, which involves learning about and undertaking assessment of learners' work and provides an imperative for contributing to the development of potential new entrants into the workforce. Kearney (2003) developed a framework for practice education that specified the skills levels and qualifications needed for assessing students at different levels that sees those with practice teaching awards supporting the education function of others and undertaking the final practice assessment. The enabling learning unit does not replace the Practice Teaching Award and its status is not yet fully defined. However, it is imperative that anyone undertaking assessment of final practice must engage in continuing development.

Continuing development and self-assessment as a practice educator

One important way of continuing your development is to engage, as a practice educator, in self-assessment. Elsewhere one of us has developed a model for the self-assessment of students in practice learning which is transferable to assessing your progress as a practice educator (Parker, 2004; see also section on self-efficacy, p. 93). This model describes three levels of assessment:

- Reflective – personal and self-critical learning;

- Formative – interpersonal learning with your post-qualifying (PQ) mentor or PQ peer group;

- Summative – completion of the prescribed assignments drawing on your reflections and development as a practice educator.

Developing a critically reflective approach through these levels, all of which intersect one another, and asking *'What situations have I experienced? What have I learned? What do I now need to do or learn? How can I achieve this and what resources or help do I need?'* will assist your continual learning and development, recognising that all practice education experiences are unique in some way and your learning is an ongoing process. This can be particularly important when making a recommendation to fail a student, which can have a profound impact on confidence and emotions. Reflecting on what you did, how you addressed your role and tasks and your future learning will be helpful in dealing with this situation.

The assessment of students

Social work students are measured against successful achievement of the *National Occupational Standards* and the subject benchmarks for social work degrees. Some universities separate achievement by placement and level of study, where others may expect a student to achieve all aspects at each practice learning level. Whichever is the preferred option for the university which your student attends, clear guidance should be provided and your role in the assessment should be made transparent. Explaining the basis for the assessment will help in establishing an open process which aids completion.

Social work academics and the profession as a whole have a history of commitment to partnership and valuing the input of practitioners in educating future social workers. However, universities have their own regulations and requirements that can make the assessment process complex. As a practice educator the outcome of your assessment is to make a recommendation rather than a final decision about a student; the final decision will be made according to the university's internal quality processes. Whilst it is unlikely that a practice educator's assessment recommendation made in good faith and based on practice evidence would not be listened to, it is important to be aware of the processes, especially given the increasing customer-focus in higher education and the growth of litigation by students in respect of decisions made. Many universities include practice partners or stakeholders in their assessment boards, which addresses some of these issues. If the regulations are not clear, ask.

The documentation provided by universities for practice assessment may seem bureaucratic, sometimes cumbersome and procedural, but should allow space for enabling the learning of others by the setting and assessing of individualised tasks designed to meet particular elements of the standards. It is important to negotiate and agree these tasks as part of the working relationship established between the students and yourself.

What and who are you assessing?

As a practice educator you are responsible for assessing: making a judgement of the practice of the student but also the student themselves. This is a subtle but important distinction that encompasses 'fitness for and to practise' as a social worker and so considers value and belief issues and how these inform practice behaviours.

ACTIVITY

Consider the following vignettes concerning students:

1. *George has shown highly developed empathic skills, forms effective relationships with service users and carers in the mental health team in which he is placed. In supervision he has demonstrated detailed knowledge of mental health issues, policies and legislation. Team members are impressed with George. Also, in supervision, he has expressed his belief that 'if only the service users and carers would turn to God and pray to accept Jesus into their hearts their problems would be resolved'.*

2. *Olga, an Estonian Jew now living in Britain, has described her pathway into social work, having experienced discrimination and violence since coming to Britain and wanting to create a more just and humane society. She is, according to her tutor, progressing satisfactorily in her studies. On an observed visit you note that she is quite authoritarian in her approach to service users, 'correcting' them when they say something she doe not agree with. When you discuss this with her she accuses you of being 'another anti-Semite who I can't work with!'*

3. *Zephaniah has shown skills in assessment, engagement with service users and in forming relationships with users, team members and other professionals. His qualities have been commented on as being 'as good as a qualified worker if not better'. In supervision discussions concerning the use of theoretical knowledge and the application of models for practice he shows little understanding or interest. He*

ACTIVITY CONTINUED

acknowledges that he has a limited knowledge base but argues this is not necessary as he is very practical.

Think about how these situations may influence your assessment of the students and how you might deal with them.

Of course, all students have different strengths just as qualified practitioners do, and we all have varying belief systems. The questions that you will need to ask as a practice educator include:

- How is this going to impact on service users and carers?

- How do these beliefs/issues affect meeting the requirements for the placement?

- How consonant are the student's personal beliefs with the required value base of social work or is there a 'good enough' fit?

The centrality of an open and honest approach cannot be underestimated, and the importance of seeing assessment as an activity that is wider than yourself can help alleviate some of the anxieties about making recommendations. However, the variety and complexity of students, their views and behaviours and, indeed, of our own, demand a flexible and individualised response.

The process of assessment as a practice educator

Let us return to the outline of assessment in Table 4.1. There are four key stages to the assessment of students in practice that you will be involved in as a practice educator. These comprise:

- Planning for the assessment

- Collecting the evidence

- Weighing the evidence

- Producing a report.

These elements rely on assessment being seen as both a process and an outcome, as something that occurs throughout the placement not just at the end, and as a tangible outcome in the form of a report and recommendation. We will look at each stage in turn.

Planning for the assessment

Planning is central to the overall process of educating others (see Chapter 6) and no less when it comes to assessment. There are, however, a number of key areas in which planning for the assessment of the student is crucial to a smooth and effective outcome. First, you need to understand what it is that is required from your assessment. You will no doubt have your own ideas of what makes a good social worker, of what qualities a practitioner needs to act in the capacity and role for which you are acting as practice educator. These are often important and drawn from your experiences and knowledge of the work. It is important sometimes, however, to put these to one side and to focus on exactly what is required and expected for the task you have taken on. So, before beginning work as a practice educator for any student you will need to immerse yourself in the requirements and standards that the student will have to meet, and understand the ways in which they will need to demonstrate them. Only with this knowledge are you fully able to judge whether your agency can provide the learning opportunities and activities that will contribute to the student's required learning, and whether you are able to plan a placement for them that will assess these areas.

As part of planning for the assessment you will need to undertake an assessment of the learning opportunities available within your agency. Ask yourself the following questions:

- What does the agency do?

- What roles and tasks are involved?

- What limits are there preventing non-qualified or employed workers from undertaking some of the work?

- What risks are there in setting learning opportunities and tasks?

- What risks are there that there will be too few opportunities or too few at the right level for the student?

These questions will help you decide whether or not you are able to take a student and to then develop a set of opportunities that can be discussed with the student and, where appropriate, the university tutor, to develop an individualised learning agreement for the placement (even where pro forma agreements are used, there is usually ample scope to write activities, tasks and other opportunities that meet particular student needs). The learning agreement is a central document for the assessment of practice learning. Where it is developed in a way that matches student needs with opportunities it can permeate supervision and form the basis for continued discussion between yourself and the student as to progress, barriers and solutions or revisions.

Gaining a picture and profile of the student is also a key part of prior planning for the assessment. If your learning agreement is to work effectively and to match student needs with what you and your agency can offer, understanding their starting point, experience and abilities is important.

Matching the individual student to learning opportunities and developing activities that will test the requirements the student needs to meet can be usefully condensed into a 'practice curriculum', a document that sets out the learning process for the placement. This curriculum can act as the plan or 'blueprint' for the assessment of student learning during the placement. The tasks, activities and work undertaken as set out in the practice curriculum should provide evidence to meet the requirements and individual needs of the student, and so form the basis for the continuous assessment and the final report.

Collecting the evidence

Developing a practice curriculum depends on adequate prior planning for the assessment process that meets the needs of both individual students and the wider programme of study. A good curriculum will detail the types of evidence to be collected and the means by which it will be developed. Types of evidence may include:

- Direct observation of practice

- Recordings of practice

- Feedback from other professionals internal or external to the team

- Feedback – written, verbal or other from service users and carers

- Case notes, assessment reports, letters, presentations to the team

- Discussion within supervision of cases, policy and theory understanding

- Self-assessment reports

- Role-play

- Critical incident reviews and reflective narrative accounts

- Learning journals

It is important for you as the practice educator to gather evidence from as many sources as possible with a view to judging the worth of that evidence in meeting the required outcomes. Part of your planning process prior to the collection of the evidence should be to develop a strategy for ensuring you have adequate evidence for the assessment. The responsibility of your role and the recommendation you will make is significant and you have a professional duty, to service users, other stakeholders involved in the student's education and to the students themselves, to make a sound assessment based on the best possible evidence available.

Weighing the evidence

First principles dictate that any evidence used should be 'fit for purpose' and measure what it sets out to measure, be clear and understandable to all parties and be appropriate for the task (see Parker, 2005; Pawson et al., 2003). Having collected a range of evidence, you can subject it to a number of key questions in order to assay its worth for your assessment of the student's competence as a practitioner. These questions work for judging your own assessment evidence and can be used by students undertaking their own self-assessment. The questions are included in Box 4.1.

The assessment you make has a profound impact on students and, potentially, their future. Therefore, reflecting deeply on the evidence and its meaning as regards student competence is important. However, it is worth remembering that you are not making the assessment alone, especially if you have garnered evidence from a range of sources, and your recommendation will be scrutinised by those making the final decision. Nonetheless, making recommendations about someone's competence in particular areas of practice can be anxiety-provoking. However, preparing for an assessment, gathering information and

---

Box 4.1: Judging the evidence (adapted from Parker, 2004, 2005)

- *Is it valid?* Does the evidence relate specifically to a requirement included in the practice learning agreement and practice curriculum, and does it demonstrate use of agency policy, procedure and practice?

- *Is it sufficient?* Has the evidence been seen frequently enough to justify your assessment and is it of sufficient depth?

- *Is it relevant?* Does the evidence relate specifically to the standard being considered or does it cover it in part or not at all?

- *Is it based in social work values?* Does it reflect anti-oppressive values and promote a value-based approach to social work?

- *Is it reliable?* Does the evidence build a consistent picture when taken together with other evidence from a range of sources?

- *Is it clear?* Can the description of the evidence and the evidence itself be understood by others to relate to an assessed objective?

- *Is it agreed?* Has the relevance and interpretation of the evidence been agreed by all involved, yourself as practice educator, student, colleagues, service users and carers?

---

evidence, deciding the value of that evidence and reaching a decision is something that most social workers do on a daily basis. It is likely that you have the skills and capacity for undertaking this task, although sharing responsibility and gaining experience in undertaking the assessment of students will confirm this to you.

Producing a report

As mentioned earlier in this chapter, student assessment is a process undertaken through dialogue throughout the placement. It is something that provides feedback on progress and helps students fine-tune their learning and practice to meet the outcomes set out for them in the learning agreement and practice curriculum, which should be grounded in the requirements and standards set out by the professional body and universities. However, placements and practice learning are finite activities and provide a judgement of competence at a particular moment in time, and therefore require an output or product. The practice educator's assessment product is the final report in which the opportunities provided are detailed, the process of the placement explained and critiqued, and the student learning analysed. All the skills involved in preparing assessment reports for people worked with in the agency are relevant to preparing an assessment report concerning a student. It is the focus and purpose that is different.

Each university is likely to have different, albeit broadly similar assessment documentation and requirements. Prior planning for the assessment is the key to competing this effectively and efficiently. If you have a clear understanding of what is required, what is being tested and how, and your learning agreement, curriculum and data collection have flowed from this, you will be in a position to address the requirements of the report. Most reports will require, from you as practice educator, the following components:

- An introduction to the agency, including what is on offer, who it serves and what its policies are that affect users of the service (e.g. confidentiality, data protection, complaints);

- An outline of learning opportunities offered to the student – this is likely to include the learning agreement and may include a practice curriculum detailing the process of the placement learning experience;

- Evidence from observations of practice, evidence from other professionals (internal/external to the team), evidence from service users and carers (these may be required as appendices and should be anonymised in respect of people who use services);

- A detailed analysis, drawing on the evidence, concerning how the student did or did not meet the requirements of the placement (this might require writing evidence against specific criteria such as the *National Occupational Standards*)

- A summary and recommendation – this may include a breakdown of future learning needs to assist the student in the future.

Often these reports will be combined in a portfolio of evidence in which the student's own self-evaluation and presentation of evidence will also be contained. Again, this may differ from university to university, but the purpose is the same. The report represents a final recommendation on a student's competence in practice that will help determine whether or not that student is appropriate for work in the particular role for which they are being assessed.

A self-efficacy model for assessing practice learning

Self-efficacy represents an important way for developing competence and effectiveness in a range of settings. It will be useful, briefly to introduce a self-efficacy model that may help in undertaking the assessment of practice learning which you might use with your students.

Theories underpinning self-efficacy

The concept of self-efficacy derives from the work of Bandura (1977, 1986) concerning social cognitive theory. Bandura proposes a model of learning – *triadic reciprocal causation* – which suggests that personal factors, behaviours and environmental events all interact and influence each other to produce future responses to situations. This provides a model for understanding differential performance by social work students dealing with similar events and situations, and offers practice teachers and assessors an opportunity to identify ways of assisting the learning process by building on constructive experiences.

Self-efficacy theory suggests that whilst a person may know what actions need to be undertaken in order successfully to execute a particular task (outcome expectations), there needs to be an element of belief or confidence in one's ability to perform those actions in order to achieve effective completion (efficacy expectations). Bandura (1986: 391) suggests that '[p]erceived self efficacy is a judgment of one's capability to accomplish a certain level of performance, whereas an outcome expectation is a judgment of the likely consequence such behaviour will produce'. It is, therefore, subtly different from self-esteem, which is global, whereas self-efficacy relates to the beliefs people have about their ability to produce certain behaviours or levels of performance in particular situations (Bandura, 1997).

A strong self-efficacy belief is associated with an approach that sees challenges as things to be mastered rather than threats to be avoided and this, in turn, increases a commitment to goal achievement and persistence when things initially may go wrong (Bandura, 1994). A strong belief in success in undertaking social work tasks will lead to persistence and commitment, and an active focus on the achievement of desired goals. Of course, students who have low perceptions of confidence in completing specific tasks may not perform well during practice learning and will need a greater level of support to succeed, or may counsel themselves away from a career in social work choosing a different option more suited to their needs. Thus being aware of your student's level of self-efficacy in key areas related to the requirements underpinning the assessment will help you in planning learning opportunities and tasks. The Practice Learning Self-Efficacy Scale included as Figure 4.2 looks at a student's confidence in areas of working with service users, written work, working with others, professional development and managing stress. You could, however, focus on one aspect of confidence in particular, and measure change throughout the placement.

Using self-efficacy scales with your students can provide a baseline of their confidence in undertaking core tasks. This can assist the development of a curriculum that accounts for the individual needs of students, providing tasks and activities that build up, in a task-centred way, to achieve required goals and targets. Figure 4.3 provides a task-centred model of practice learning self-efficacy, providing a pathway of smaller, manageable tasks for the less confident student and more complex challenges for the more confident student. With regular consideration of progress these tasks can be re-negotiated and altered as appropriate, and by repeating the self-efficacy questionnaire at key points and using it as a basis for discussion, you can assess learning and how the student is meeting the requirements.

ACTIVITY

Think of ways you have used an assessment in practice as a tool for learning for the people you are working with and as a tool for self-learning. Using this example, write down some of the pros and cons that might be associated with using a self-efficacy scale to assist student self-assessment.

How confident are you that you can work successfully with:

	Not at all Confident										Very Confident
• the particular service user group you are working with	0	1	2	3	4	5	6	7	8	9	10
• care-givers (family/informal)	0	1	2	3	4	5	6	7	8	9	10
• people from a different culture who speak English	0	1	2	3	4	5	6	7	8	9	10
• people from different cultures who do not speak English	0	1	2	3	4	5	6	7	8	9	10
• people with different values to yourself	0	1	2	3	4	5	6	7	8	9	10
• people who are loud, threatening, abusive or violent	0	1	2	3	4	5	6	7	8	9	10
• Please specify your area of practice (e.g. child care, children with disabilities, mental health etc)											

How confident are you that you can successfully:

	Not at all Confident										Very Confident
• establish contact with clients	0	1	2	3	4	5	6	7	8	9	10
• form working relationships with clients	0	1	2	3	4	5	6	7	8	9	10
• provide relevant information and advice	0	1	2	3	4	5	6	7	8	9	10
• collect relevant information	0	1	2	3	4	5	6	7	8	9	10

How confident are you that you can successfully:

	Not at all Confident										Very Confident
• write clear, explanatory and informative letters to clients	0	1	2	3	4	5	6	7	8	9	10
• write comprehensive, informative and relevant case notes	0	1	2	3	4	5	6	7	8	9	10
• write comprehensive, informative and relevant assessment reports	0	1	2	3	4	5	6	7	8	9	10

Figure 4.2 (continued overleaf): Practice Learning Self-Efficacy Scale (© Professor Jonathan Parker, Bournemouth University UK with acknowledgement to Professor Gary Holden, New York University USA)

How confident are you that you can work successfully with:

	0	1	2	3	4	5	6	7	8	9	10
• other social work students	0	1	2	3	4	5	6	7	8	9	10
• other social work staff	0	1	2	3	4	5	6	7	8	9	10
• your supervisor/practice teacher	0	1	2	3	4	5	6	7	8	9	10
• administrative staff	0	1	2	3	4	5	6	7	8	9	10
• other agency staff	0	1	2	3	4	5	6	7	8	9	10
• social workers external to the agency	0	1	2	3	4	5	6	7	8	9	10
• non-social work professionals from other agencies (e.g. teachers; health practitioners; housing officers; police officers – those relevant to your agency)	0	1	2	3	4	5	6	7	8	9	10

How confident are you that you can successfully:

	0	1	2	3	4	5	6	7	8	9	10
• apply theoretical models appropriately	0	1	2	3	4	5	6	7	8	9	10
• identify learning needs	0	1	2	3	4	5	6	7	8	9	10
• evaluate your practice	0	1	2	3	4	5	6	7	8	9	10
• make plans to increase learning opportunities	0	1	2	3	4	5	6	7	8	9	10
• recognise the ethical tensions inherent in the work	0	1	2	3	4	5	6	7	8	9	10

How confident are you that you can successfully:

	0	1	2	3	4	5	6	7	8	9	10
• manage the stress that you will feel in a fast-paced working and learning environment	0	1	2	3	4	5	6	7	8	9	10
• manage the frustration you will feel working with agency bureaucracy	0	1	2	3	4	5	6	7	8	9	10
• manage the feelings that you will have working with clients experiencing emotional and psychological distress	0	1	2	3	4	5	6	7	8	9	10
• manage the feelings you will have when clients or their families blame you for things going wrong	0	1	2	3	4	5	6	7	8	9	10
• manage the feelings you will have when team members from other disciplines blame you for things going wrong	0	1	2	3	4	5	6	7	8	9	10

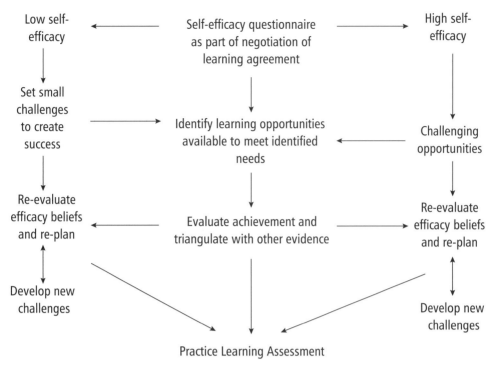

Figure 4.3: A task-centred model for facilitating assessment in practice learning (after Parker, 2005)

It may be argued that structured instruments deny the possibility of individual approaches, flexibility and creativity. However, if used alongside other methods they can make an important contribution to your assessment and can be used as further evidence to justify your recommendations. Using more structured and evidence-based approaches to assessment at a range of levels is an important and transparent way of working together and can be empowering to students with whom you are working. They can feel actively involved in the process.

Conclusion

This chapter has introduced you to the process of assessment as a practice educator, concentrating mainly on the management of that process, although also looking at planning and organisation, and enabling learning through the completion of planned tasks. We have considered what assessment means within the context of practice learning and education, and made links where appropriate with the assessment task undertaken by social workers in many aspects of their daily roles. We have looked at some of the research concerning assessment in social work practice education, and seen how feedback from others and team approaches, establishing a positive working relationship with the student, assessment by service users and self-assessment can combine to form a rigorous assessment of competence. A model for assessment that emphasises the centrality of planning was introduced and, finally, an example of using a structured scale to measure confidence development and task achievement was discussed.

FURTHER READING

Parker, J. (2004) *Effective Practice Learning in Social Work*. Exeter: Learning Matters.

This book provides a guide for student social workers undertaking practice learning. It gives details of the processes involved, some of the theories for learning in practice settings and ways in which learning can be managed and enhanced.

Williams, S. and Rutter, L. (2007) *Enabling and Assessing Work-Based Learning for Social Work: Supporting the development of professional practice*, Birmingham: Learn to Care.

This excellent book covers core elements essential to learning how to enable the development of others as part of a specialist award.

Chapter 5
What is supervision?

TThe material in this chapter links to the following Domain standards:

Domain B: Evaluate critically the methodologies and techniques that enable learning and professional development in practice

1. Establish the basis of an effective working relationship by identifying learners' expectations, the outcomes which they have to meet in order to demonstrate competence, and their readiness for assessment. Agree the available learning opportunities, methods, resources, and timescales to enable them to succeed.

2. Discuss, identify, plan to address and review the particular needs and capabilities of learners, and the support available to them. Identify any matters which may impact on their ability to manage their own learning.

3. Discuss and take into account individuals' learning styles, learning needs, prior learning achievements, knowledge and skills. Devise an appropriate, cost-effective assessment programme which promotes their ability to learn and succeed.

5. Identify which aspects of the management of the learning and assessment programme learners are responsible for in order to achieve their objectives. Describe and agree the roles of the work-based assessor in mentoring, coaching, modelling, teaching and supervision.

6. Establish how the learning and assessment programme is to be reviewed. Encourage learners to express their views, identify and agree any changes and how disagreements on any aspects of it are resolved.

7. Advise learners how to develop their ability to manage their learning. Deal with any difficulties encountered by them.

Domain C: Manage the assessment of learners in practice

1. Engage learners in the design, planning and implementation of the assessment tasks.

2. Agree and review a plan and methods for assessing learners' performance against agreed criteria.

3. Ensure that assessment decisions are the outcomes of informed, evidence-based judgments and clearly explain them to learners.

7. Encourage learners to self-evaluate and seek service users, carers and peer group feedback on their performance.

8. Provide timely, honest and constructive feedback on learners' performance in an appropriate format. Review their progress through the assessment process, distinguishing between formative and summative assessment

9. Make clear to learners how they may improve their performance. Identify any specific learning outcomes not yet demonstrated and the next steps. If necessary, arrange appropriate additional assessment activity to enable them to meet the standard.

Introduction

In this chapter we examine the concept of 'supervision' as a critical element of the practice placement for the student and the practice educator, especially in supporting learning and development, and in determining the outcome of the practice education experience of the student. Ultimately, high-quality supervision will influence the quality of the service, and experience of the service user with whom the student will be working.

Defining supervision

ACTIVITY

Think about your experience of supervision.

What do you see as the positive aspects of supervision?

What are the challenges of supervision for you?

Recall a time that you were a student. What was your experience of supervision in this context?

Supervision has a long history as an important process in the enabling professions. We bring our own experiences of supervision to the 'relationship' we develop with the student on placement. Supervision is a core process and a belief in the importance of supervision is at the heart of the practice placement experience of the student.

A number of authors have sought to define 'supervision': what they appear to demonstrate is the complexity of identifying the concept of supervision and encompassing the different processes and elements that form 'supervision'. All these definitions offer a useful starting point to reflect on the concept of supervision, to begin to reflect on the intricacies and specifics of a supervisory relationship, and the values and principles that underpin this relationship.

Each of these definitions offers different perspectives; there are those that describe the relationship; there are those that describe the functions of the supervisory role and others that focus on the development of the relationship. Supervision can be seen to be a contested term; it is value laden and can be seen by different practitioners to be different things.

Two final definitions specifically relate to the supervision of student in a practice learning situation.

> *By supervision we mean planned, regular periods of time that the student and supervisor spend together discussing the student's work in the placement and reviewing the learning progress.*
>
> (Ford and Jones, 1987: 63)

> *Supervision serves to benefit supervisee and service user by developing the practitioner's skills, understanding and ability.*
>
> (Parker, 2004: 65)

These definitions place an emphasis the learning that takes place within the supervision process, and role of the supervisor in the development of the individual. Supervision is about a relationship between one person, a supervisor, and another, a supervisee.

Box 5.1: Definitions of supervision

[Supervision is] an intensive, interpersonally focused one-to-one relationship in which one person is designated to facilitate the development of therapeutic competence in another person.

(Loganbill et al., 1982: 4)

Supervision is the process of reflecting on what you are doing with the help of another in order to help you do it better.

(Atherton, 1987: 12)

. . . [supervision] is an administrative and educational process used extensively in social agencies to help social workers further develop and refine their skills and provided quality assurance for the clients.

(Barker, 1995: 371)

Supervision is the primary means by which an agency-designated supervisor enables staff, individually and collectively; and ensures standards of practice. The aim is to enable supervisees to carry out their work as stated in their job specification as effectively as possible. Regular arranged meetings between supervisors and supervisees form the core of the process by which the supervisory task is carried out. The supervisee is an active participant in this interactional process.

(Brown and Bourne, 1996: 9)

Supervision can be defined as the overseeing of another's work with sanctioned authority to monitor and direct performance, to ensure satisfactory performance (which includes client safety).

(Caspi and Reid, 2002: 2)

Supervision is an interactional process, in which the student is an active participant. The student will need support from the supervisor to be helped to develop the skills and confidence to take a proactive approach to supervision. The supervisor (now referred to as the practice educator within the text) has authority (for example, from their organisation, from the academic institution) to ensure that the student is accountable for their work, and to support them in this. Ultimately, the accountability is to the service users and carers receiving the service; the overall aim of supervision is to ensure the best possible service to the user. The practice educator and student must take account of the individual and collective responsibility that they have – for example, to the team and organisation in which the practice takes place – and support the development of an appropriate ethos to support the development of practice in a wider context.

Within a practice learning experience, the process of supervision entails the practice educator creating the conditions for the student to acquire, be informed by and use knowledge, apply theories, develop skills and demonstrate the application of professional values in practice. Supervision therefore:

- Enables the student's learning and development through supporting their learning and development as a professional practitioner;

- Develops their knowledge of good practice and a knowledge and theory base of what works in a practice context;

- Facilitates the development and application of skills in practice;

- Supports the student in identifying their value base and in the development, application and promotion of their professional value within their practice. This will include an examination of the ethical and moral base of social work;

- Supports the student in understanding the impact of oppression and discrimination on the lives of service users and carers, including the wider impact of poverty and social exclusion. This will include support for the student in anti-oppressive practice;

- Draws on the practice educator's own professional knowledge, skills and practice, including their own commitment to their profession and the values and ethical base of practice, with a commitment to anti-oppressive practice;

- Provides an opportunity to support the learning and development needs of the student;

- Provides a forum for the practice educator to inform, evaluate, assess and encourage the student.

Functions of supervision

Different authors (such as Brown and Bourne, 1996; Ford and Jones, 1987; Hawkins and Shohet, 1989; Kadushin, 1992; Shardlow and Doel, 1996) have highlighted the three specific functions of supervision within the supervisory role: administrative, supportive and educational.

Box 5.2: Anti-oppressive practice

Dalrymple and Burke (2006; 20) define anti-oppressive practice as:

> A radical social work approach which is informed by humanistic and social justice values and takes account of the experiences and views of oppressed people. It is based on an understanding of how the concepts of power, oppression and inequality determine personal and structural relations.

They state that anti-oppressive practice requires:

- An empowering approach which aims to overcome barriers for service users in taking more control of their lives.

- Working in partnership so that, as far as possible, service users are included in decision-making processes about their lives. This is described as a 'vexed issues' (Healy, 2005: 186) for anti-oppressive practitioners because of the constraints that derive from the unequal power relations between themselves and service users.

- Minimal intervention to reduce the oppressive and disempowerment potential of social work intervention.

- Critical reflection and reflexivity. This involves a continual consideration of self in practice in order to understand how out values and our biographies impact on our practice relationships.

(See also Beckett, 2005; Clifford, 1998; Healey, 2005; Payne 2005a.)

ACTIVITY

Consider each of the three different functions of supervision in turn: administrative, supportive, educational. What do you consider to be the key elements of each these functions within supervision? What are the specific issues that you will need to consider as a supervisor of a student on placement?

Administrative

This is concerned with the promotion and maintenance of good standards of work, adherence to agency policy and procedures and external standards. This could also be described as the quality control function of supervision. This function could also be referred to as the 'managerial' function of supervision, which may include such requirements as target-setting, performance management, quality control and monitoring (Peach and Horner, 2007: 231).

As a practice educator you have a responsibility to make sure that standards are identified and maintained to ensure the protection of service users and carers. Your responsibility also includes ensuring the development of the student and their ability to understand and conform to the agency standards and procedures necessary to comply with these standards. This includes national, organisational and team standards highlighted in legislation, policy documents and the policy and procedures of the agency. Supporting the student in understanding and using relevant systems and processes, and completing the relevant paperwork, such as case records, will be a key part of ensuring that the student is accountable for their practice. In addition, you will need to work with the student to make certain that relevant competency standards for the assessment of their own practice are being identified and met within the work with service users and within the placement. Supporting the student to identify and maintain a professional standard of work will be critical; this will need to be discussed alongside issues of management of workload, both within the practice placement and in relation to academic work, and the management of the student's time.

Supportive

This is concerned with the support for the individual in the practical and psychological elements of their role. This includes ascertaining that the student has adequate support within the placement to ensure that they are demonstrating and maintaining high standards of professional and personal practice. Much of the work of those in enabling professions involves the 'personal' involvement of the supervisee themselves. Students will need the opportunity to discuss or off-load any problems or difficulties, sometimes feelings of distress or sometimes of happiness. Issues of 'self-care' will need to be examined; for example, support for the student in dealing with anxiety and stress, which may be linked to issues on placement such as:

- Dealing with the pressures of day-to-day complexities of working with service users and carers;

- Coping with particular challenges on placement; for example, working with service users at particular points of crisis, such as with children and their families when abuse is suspected; or with a service user with acute mental health needs; or dealing with the death of a service user;

- Dealing with value conflicts; and

- Dealing with personal memories

Students will need to know that they are being recognised for the contribution they are making and valued for their contribution.

Educational

This is concerned with the educational development of the individual and supporting the fulfilment of their potential. The primary focus is learning and development of professional competence; developing the student's knowledge, skills and abilities to undertake their work; their understanding; and demonstrating values within their practice. Working in an anti-oppressive and anti-discriminatory way is critical.

As a supervisor you will need to support the student in a process of 'discovery'. This will include the discovery of learning and knowledge within the workplace:

• Discovery of how learning from academic teaching transfers to practice. Students will need to be supported in making the links and applying the knowledge, skills and values they learn in the academic context to practice settings, particularly in direct work with service users. The issues of transfer of learning were discussed in Chapter 3.

• Discovery of 'what works'. This is the conscious integration of the student's theoretical knowledge and understanding with professional practice, including an understanding of the wider socio-political context of practice and of the application of values in practice. This should include recording and collating evidence, and research to build upon professional knowledge, to inform others and generate research that supports evidence-based practice.

• Discovery of 'self-knowledge' or self-awareness. Students will need to be given support to recognise the differences between their self-perception and others' perception of them to increase their self-awareness of the effect they have on others. You will able to support the student in this activity through such things as direct observation of their practice; obtaining feedback from service users, colleagues and other professionals; and in supporting the student to reflect on 'self' and their own performance as practitioner in training.

• Support with critically reflecting on their practice. For Harrison and Ruch (2007) this means moving from the 'What?' questions ('What do I do and how?') to the 'Why?' questions ('Why do I do that? Why did that happen?').

> *By engaging with knowledges derived from professional training and personal experience, practitioners can begin to answer the 'why' questions and model professional responses that are informed by their holistic and 'professional self' and are specific, dynamic and responsive to the unpredictable and complex nature of human behaviour.*
>
> (Harrison and Ruch, 2007: 44)

Models of supervision

A number of writers have noted that there are numerous models of supervision in the helping professions, which have borrowed from a range of disciplines (such as psychotherapy and interaction theory) to describe, explain and predict the behaviour of the supervisee (Kadushin and Harkness, 2002; Tsui, 2005). In the previous section we reviewed the three constituent parts of supervision: the administrative function, the supportive function and the educational function. All have important and interrelated functions within supervision. There is no one way of approaching or undertaking supervision (Thompson et al., 1994). What is apparent is that supervision is a complex and intricate process, with a number of levels, including the need to balance student needs with those of service users, others who are also involved, such as the agency in which the student is placed, and the requirements of the profession.

Models of supervision in social work and the helping professions tend to stress the developmental approach. Authors such as Hawkins and Shohet (2000), Gardiner (1989) and Brown and Bourne (1996) have all recognised of the importance of taking a developmental approach within supervision.

Underlying developmental models of supervision is the idea that each of us is continuously learning and developing within our practice. The object is to identify development and growth needed for the future. Developmental conceptions of supervision are based on two basic assumptions:

1. In the process of moving toward competence, supervisees move through a series of stages that are qualitatively different from one another.

2. Each stage requires a qualitatively different supervision environment if optimal supervisee satisfaction and growth are to occur (Chagnon and Russell, 1995).

Hawkins and Shohet (2000), adapting the work of Stoltenberg and Delworth (1987), outline an approach which focuses on the professional developmental stages in learning as individuals develop their professional competency.

Level 1: Dependence

This stage is characterised by the student's dependence on the supervisor. Students may not have the grounded experience or competence to make their own judgements. The student will need significant factual information and advice, guidance and support to build up their knowledge, skills and abilities, and develop their confidence. For the supervisor this stage is characterised by relationship-building and goal-setting. An important aspect of supervision is to negotiate a clear contract for supervision at the onset of the practice learning opportunity, which needs to be clear, explicit and focused (see Chapter 6; see also Parker, 2004: 78). This will ensure that the expectations, boundaries and objectives of supervision are explicit and made clear between the supervisor and supervisee. Brown and Bourne (1996) maintain that a supervisory contract should take into account nine elements:

- The nature of the relationship within supervision (see functions of supervision above)
- The format of the supervision
- Accountability
- Focus
- Scheduling
- Confidentiality
- Agenda-setting
- Record-keeping
- Values (the person-centred anti-oppressive value base for supervision)
- Evaluation.

Parker (2004: 78–82) provides a very useful example of a supervision contract.

Level 2: Dependence and autonomy

This stage is characterised by the student's fluctuation between dependence and autonomy. Hawkins and Shohet (1989) liken this stage to the adolescent phase of human development; whilst the student may be growing in confidence they may still feel overwhelmed by the range of issues and tasks facing them. As a supervisor you may find that you will move between the role of a 'therapist' and that of a teacher as the student is faced with issues in relation to the emotional impact of working in a practice setting and the need to develop their skills.

Level 3: Increased self-confidence

> . . . [the student] shows increased self-confidence, with only conditional dependency on the supervisor. He or she has greater insight and shows more stable motivation, supervision becomes more collegial, with sharing and exemplification augmented by professional and personal confrontation.
>
> (Stoltenberg and Delworth, 1987: 20)

This stage is characterised by increased professional self-confidence. The student will demonstrate greater confidence in their interactions and greater insight into their professional practice; the processes that impact on the service users guide their practice. The student's learning is being integrated within their practice. As a supervisor, the focus of your practice will be on adopting a more consultative/enabling approach as the student gains more confidence and expertise.

In working with students in a practice learning placement, this stage may be the level at which the student will be finally assessed within their placement, particularly as the final level suggests someone as performing at a 'master craftsman' (Hawkins and Shohet, 1989: 52) level of practice: for example, in drawing on 'practice wisdom' (practice knowledge that is deepened and integrated into practice) within their practice. However, we would outline final stage in the level of development and use of supervision.

Level 4: Personal autonomy

The supervisee will be demonstrating greater autonomy in their practice, and greater awareness and insight into the context of their practice. The supervisee should be able to integrate a wide variety of processes, views and experiences into their practice and offer professional, objective views on their practice, their practice with service users and in working with others. At this stage, the supervisee takes responsibility for his or her learning and development as a practitioner. The role of the supervisor will be to support, advise and facilitate the supervisee in analysis of, and reflection on, their practice.

This model is a useful tool in viewing supervision as a developmental process and in helping you to more accurately assess the needs of the student and to consider the tasks involved in developing the student at and between different stages of their development. However, there are limits to this model that need to be considered. First, this model was developed in America, so there are different 'cultural' differences in the concept of supervision; in addition, the model was developed for, and aimed at, those supervising counsellors and therapists. Second, the model does not take into account the individual needs of the student and their own strengths and abilities, particularly in taking responsibility for their own development and learning. As a supervisor you will also be developing your own skills in working with the student; the interaction and impact of both student and supervisor development at these different stages needs to be considered. Finally, this model seems to imply that the supervisor's roles and functions diminish as the supervisee gains greater insight and autonomy in their professional practice; this is certainly not the case in the supervision of a student. The practice assessor must maintain a clear focus on helping the student to think rigorously and systematically about their practice, and their learning and development, in a framework which examines values, beliefs and attitudes, and develops awareness of anti-oppressive practice.

The process of supervision through the 'life' of the placement

Taking a developmental approach to the supervisory relationship across the placement requires you to consider the processes that you will need to think about in developing, maintaining, assessing and supporting the student throughout the 'life' of the placement.

ACTIVITY

Consider the different processes that you will need to think about in your planning and preparation for supervision with a student.

'Beginnings'

In undertaking this task you will have been able to recognise the complexities and challenges of supervision, particularly of a student on placement in a practice setting. Managing the relationship that you have with the student within supervision requires you to balance a number of conceptual and practical elements. Sawdon and Sawdon (1995) refer to this as being able to 'wrestle creatively' with all of these different elements, seeing them as part of the whole. The supervisory process is a 'managerial' process to ensure that work is carried out and that standards are maintained that protect the rights of others, especially service users. You will be assessing and making a professional judgement on the practice of the student. At the same time, you will need to ensure that the student receives the appropriate support to learn about and develop their practice, to encourage new ideas, to create a comfortable atmosphere in which critical discussion can take place. As a supervisor you will need to be not purely reactive but also pro-active in your approach to supervision.

Prior to meeting for the first time you need to consider carefully the needs of the student. There is evidence that the student's initial positive experience of supervision is related to their feeling of satisfaction at the end of the placement. In addition, positive perceptions of supervision are important conditions for learning (Kissman and Tran, 1990). Some of the issues you will need to consider are:

Physical setting
Such basic arrangements as the physical setting should not be taken for granted. This section is intended to remind you of the importance of creating an appropriate 'space' for supervision to take place. Attention should be given to seating arrangements. The physical setting of the supervision session affects the atmosphere of the discussion; the basic principle underlying the choice of the physical setting for supervision is whatever makes the student feel secure, comfortable and respected.

Process
You will need to consider the learning opportunities that will be available to the student. Another important issue is your own time; you will need to do some advance planning to ensure you have adequate time and space for supervision. Demonstrating consistency shows a commitment to the supervisory relationship; it should be scheduled on a regular basis and take place without interruptions.

Structure
You will need to consider the way in which the time for supervision will be used. Clearly this will need to be negotiated with the student so that they have an opportunity to agree the structure and identify any regular issues they wish to be included and/or specific issues they may wish to discuss within an individual supervision session. The use of time within the supervision session will need to include opportunities not only to discuss specific casework issues but also opportunities for teaching and learning sessions; discussion about the student's academic work; the specific requirements for the placement (for example, observation of the student's practice and service user feedback on the student's performance); and progress with gathering evidence to demonstrate and assess the student's competence in practice. As we have indicated above, in examining the different levels of development of the student within supervision, the structure of supervision will vary over time.

Content
It is helpful for you to think about the formal process by which you will be assessing the student; reviewing this will help you to select appropriate learning opportunities to support the student in meeting the criteria. You need to consider how you will judge their performance; making this explicit to the student will ensure that the process is open and transparent. Providing ongoing, immediate and specific feedback about their performance will allow the student to identify their own strengths and areas that require development. Identifying poor implementation of skills early in the relationship will also allow the student to work with you in identifying their own learning and development needs. Being explicit in this way will demonstrate the principles of high-quality educational supervision.

Establishing a supportive, working relationship
Several objectives must be fulfilled in order to establish a successful teaching relationship. These include:

- establishing trust and respect;

- assessing the student's practice knowledge and skills;

- identifying learning and training needs;

- agreeing to a behavioural contract establishing the ground rules for the supervisory sessions; and

- setting learning and development goals.

In addition the supervisor must be familiar with the knowledge base, learning style, conceptual skills, suitability for work setting and motivation of the supervisee (Tsui, 2005: 127). The practice educator should encourage the student to share what they are thinking, feeling, to express feelings, fears and expectations, to share values and opinions. As a practice educator you need to model approaches within your supervisions that model reflective and anti-oppressive practice.

'Middles'

By the mid-phase of the placement you should have achieved a working alliance with the student, the core phase of the supervisory phase. Some of the issues you will need to consider are listed below.

'Tuning-in skills'

Shulman (1993) describes the essence of tuning in as facing problems, not avoiding them. For the student this should mean the opportunity to provide an honest reflection on their performance and consideration of the learning required in the next stage of the placement. For the practice educator this may mean an honest appraisal and sharing of the student's performance so far, and how any problems may be overcome. This will also mean reflecting on your own performance; in addition this will mean being aware of your own feelings about the student's performance. Being aware of your emotions and feelings will mean you are more open to the student's own feelings. Reflecting on the potential concerns of the student will also enable you to anticipate the student's needs and provide support and information that meets them.

Any specific problems that cause particular concern or may indicate that there are issues in relation to the student's performance (and therefore the possibility that they may not pass the placement) must be raised with the university tutor. Working as a partnership may result in a plan being put in place to resolve these difficulties or produce alternative strategies.

Reviewing

This involves a 'formal' review of the student's progress and learning so far and the opportunity to plan for the next stage of the placement. Looking back on and reviewing the Learning Contract constructed at the beginning of the placement will support this; you could also draw on the Practice Curriculum (see Chapter 6). You will need to review the evidence that you and the student have gathered so far that will inform the assessment of the student's competence. This could be informed by feedback from others, especially from service users and carers with whom the student has been in contact.

Maintenance

This relates to maintaining the momentum of the placement – ensuring that learning is developing and progressing, that the work being undertaken meets that student's learning needs, that progress is being made. This also means ensuring there is sufficient depth and breadth in the work being carried out within the placement by the student; is the student doing sufficient work? Sufficient variety of work? Sufficient complexity of work? Are there areas of their practice that could be developed?

Planning for 'endings'

Work being undertaken with service users and carers needs to be reviewed in order to make a judgement of the progress so far and anticipated 'end-point' in terms of the student's involvement.

'Ends'

As the placement comes to an end, there needs to be careful preparation for the end of work with service users and carers, with the team, with others, and with each other as student and practice educator.

Ending the supervisory relationship

This entails careful and systematic preparation; it involves reviewing what work needs to be completed and making practical decisions about such things as completion of paperwork and handing over of a case to another worker. It also involves thinking about the emotional reactions to the placement ending. In the supervisory relationship, you need to remind the student of the time that remains. Focusing on the end keeps attention on completing what needs to be done in a timely and organised way. The experience of stopping a relationship represents a loss, particularly if the relation has been positive and productive; confronting this reality may be difficult. Reviewing the work that has been done so far, and how the student has progressed in their knowledge and skills throughout the placement, will support the student in seeing how far they have come. The final evaluation of the student's performance is an important step in the relationship, reflecting with the student on their journey throughout the placement. This will allow the student and you to judge and reflect on how far the student has advanced during the course of the placement; reviewing important developmental moments and overall growth provides a complete picture of their progress. The end of the placement does not mean the end of the learning, and it is important for the practice educator and student to consider learning objectives for the future; planning for endings should include preparation for new beginnings.

Ending the relationship with the agency

You will need to schedule a clear process and time to ensure that all relevant paperwork is completed; this includes paperwork relating to the agency's work, for example case recording.

Ending rituals

Closing rituals, such as going out to lunch, a small gift and/or a card signed by yourself and other staff, provide acknowledgement of and thanks for the student's contribution. However, these informal rituals should not replace honest discussion about endings.

Ending relationships with service users

CASE STUDY

Mark feels sad and guilty about the ending of his relationship with Bill. He feels that he has been the only person advocating on behalf of this service user; now his placement has ended he feels that Bill will feel abandoned.

Jenny has been supporting Sarah settle into a new foster placement. She has promised to remain in contact.

Mark and Jenny's reaction to ending their working relationship with service users is not unusual. Both will need support to end their working relationship with the service user. As the student prepares to leave the agency, a review of each of the cases that they have worked with should take place to determine if the service user will need continuing support or if the service user's involvement with the agency may now end. Time needs to be given to considering the service user's own readiness to end the relationship with the student, and to allow the service user to prepare emotionally for this. Focusing on the needs of the service user in ending this relationship and engaging the student in an active discussion about the service user's experience of endings will maintain a focus on professional practice. A supportive supervisor enables students to express their reactions to the ending of the relationship with the service user and to learn how to handle endings, encouraging the self-awareness of the student. The supervisor should ensure that there is preparation for ending the relationship in an appropriate way and seek to anticipate any negative reactions, such as feelings of abandonment, anger, avoidance.

CASE STUDY

Dealing with issues in supervision

Nigel always comes to supervision unprepared, having not completed the work agreed in the previous supervision session. His case recording is poor and not up to date. When you challenge him he says: 'It's all this paperwork! It takes such a long time – it really gets in the way of what social work is about. We should be out there helping people not stuck behind a desk doing paperwork!'

Sara is always full of praise for your practice; in supervision she regularly praises you: 'You are a brilliant practitioner; you are so good with service users. I really hope that I can be as good as you some day!', 'You are just so helpful', 'I do not know how I would cope without you', 'You are the best practice educator I have ever had.'

In supervision Adrian constantly questions the practice educators' about their knowledge in relation to theories and contemporary approaches and debates about practice. He is clearly wide read and talks at length about contemporary theories and discussion from a number of sources. The questions he asks are often outside the practice educator's field of expertise.

Maria is always late for supervision and a number of sessions have had to be re-arranged. She is often late for work and leaves early claiming she is 'going on a visit'. You have asked to see Maria's portfolio of evidence, which she has to complete as part of the assessment of her competence in practice; she keeps 'forgetting it'.

It is now the half-way point of Wendy's placement. It has been going well; she has been energetic, keen and good at her work. However, in the last few days she has been distracted. In supervision she bursts into tears. She says that after months of disharmony her husband has left her. Her children are distressed and she needs some space to sort out her finances.

You may well have a great deal of empathy for Nigel's position! There a number of professionals who feel that their autonomy has been eroded by increased guidance, regulation and 'managerialism'. A number of processes have been introduced to alter poor practice in order to protect vulnerable children and adults and as 'tools' to support practice. This should not be used as an excuse not to carry out the necessary procedures. Increasing Nigel's understanding of the importance of processes in supporting the work with service users and carers, and potentially support with his workload and time management, could help him.

To be complimented is always very flattering – and of course it may well be true! However, continually putting her practice educator on a pedestal, as Sara has done, may well be distracting her from thinking about her own practice with the support of the practice educator. She will need support in thinking about what she brings to practice, increasing her skills and confidence, and developing her own sense of 'self' as a professional practitioner.

Whilst Adrian's attention to his learning about a subject is to be commended, the assumption that practice educator knows everything about everything has to be challenged! Learning needs to be seen as a joint sharing of knowledge; the practice educator needs to keep a focus on relevant knowledge for practice, and support the student to critically analyse information and reflect on its application in their professional practice.

In Maria's case, it appears that the practice educator needs to exert their authority. Whilst the aim of the supervisory relationship is to work cooperatively, there will be occasions where the practice educator will need to take control and bring the student 'back on track'.

Wendy may need the 'space' of a few days to sort out her current situation; and you could agree to this. You need to monitor the situation carefully, involving the university tutor, after consultation with Wendy. If she is unable to cope with the placement, it may be appropriate to agree between you the suspension of the placement until issues are more resolved and Wendy feels more able to cope and meet the demands of a practice placement.

Issues of power in the supervisory relationship

Issues to do with power, and how it is managed, lie at the heart of supervision and the supervisory relationship.

(Brown and Bourne, 1996: 32)

Authority and power are two major components of the supervisory relationship (Kaiser, 1997). Whilst they are used interchangeably they do have different meanings. It is important to differentiate between these two concepts, and to reflect on what they mean within a supervisory relationship and the implications for your practice in supporting a student.

ACTIVITY

Consider your role as a practice educator.

What do you understand by the term 'authority'? In what ways might you use 'authority' in a supervisory relationship?

What do you understand by the term 'power'? In what ways may 'power' be experienced in a supervisory relationship?

The *Oxford English Dictionary* defines authority as 'the power or right to give orders and enforce obedience'; power is defined as 'the capacity to influence the behaviour of others, the emotions, or the course of events'. Kadushin and Harkness (2002) suggest that authority is the right to control others; power is the ability to do so. Whilst these definitions may seem imposing, it is important that you understand what the use of authority and the experience of power may mean for your role in supervising a student. Many supervisors are not comfortable with the authority and power vested in the supervisor's role and may avoid it in various conscious and unconscious ways; this can confuse the student, who knows full well the supervisor is in a position of considerable authority and power (Brown and Bourne, 1996: 33).

Legitimate authority comes through legislation, policy and procedures. Within organisations, authority is designated through the purpose, functions and objectives of that organisation. Authority can be designated to another, for example, in the role of the supervisor. The use of supervisory authority is expected to demonstrate a commitment to, and ensure achievement of, the organisation's objectives. There is an expectation that the supervisor will demonstrate a subjective acceptance of the legitimacy of the agency, a sense of commitment to the agency. As a practice educator, you will need to support the student in understanding where the organisation's objectives have come from, and work with and support the student to ensure that you are committed to the same objectives. This is not to suggest that these objectives should not be challenged or questioned; indeed, this can be an important element of reflective practice within supervision. Nevertheless, supporting the student to understand the 'legitimate' authority of the agency is an important element of learning for the student; it is critical that you support the student in considering what this means for service users and within their practice – and what this means for their own professional practice and development. The contribution of the agency's objectives needs to be recognised and acknowledged as making a positive contribution to working with service users and to the work of the agency. The student will more freely grant the right to be 'controlled' by the legitimate authority of the organisation if they recognise their responsibilities towards the goals of the organisation and to the profession of social work. As a practice educator, further authority will also be designated and delegated to you from the academic institution in which the student is studying, to provide professional learning opportunities, and in supporting and assessing the student. This authority will prescribe responsibilities to you; for example, to undertake supervision with the student on a regular basis. Being prescribed authority does assume you will uphold and demonstrate your commitment to the profession of social work, and to the education and support of a social worker in training.

'Power' is derived from the supervisor's designated authority and also from the power that derives from their personal attributes. Power can be classified according to various criteria; the most frequently used classification was developed by French and Raven (1960).

As can be seen, the perception of 'power' is an important issue in supervision and is an even more significant aspect of the practice educator/learning relationship as the student has not yet qualified; if the student fails they will not gain a qualification. Shardlow and Doel (1996) highlight the 'inescapable' role of power in practice learning. When one person is in a position of authority over another, a dynamic is created that derives from the inequality of power. The use of authority and the power imbalance evident in a relationship between a practice educator and student has the potential to combine into a potentially complex abuse of power embedded in a typically hierarchical structure of supervision.

Brown and Bourne (1996) summarise the many types of power in practice learning as being derived from the formal and informal power associated with the role of the practice educator. Formal power derives from the role and position of the supervisor in relation to the person being supervised. Informal power can be manifest in both the supervisor and supervisee, and derives from the personal and professional attributes of each of them; for example because of personal attributes such as size, force of personality, interpersonal skills, energy, or their structural position in society (Kadushin, 1992). It can also derive from '*the structurally determined identities and roles based on key characteristics like race, gender, age, sexual orientation and (dis)ability*' (Brown and Bourne, 1996: 39, original emphasis). Power is not only manifested interpersonally but also culturally, structurally and institutionally. This may occur in a number of different ways: for example, reflect on the potential power imbalance between a black student with a white practice educator; a white woman student with a male practice educator.

Strategies that may help to address these issues include:

- Being aware and recognising the significance of acknowledging and addressing the issues of power, and discussing its ramifications in supervision sessions (Taylor and Baldwin, 1991). Discussion needs to work towards a shared understanding of the

> ## *Box 5.3: Types of power*
>
> French and Raven (1960) divided power into five categories. The first three kinds of power are perceived as 'administrative', and derive primarily from the authority of their role.
>
> 1. *Positional/legitimate power* – this relates to the formal power that relates more directly to the title of the supervisor and the authority with which the title is invested.
>
>   For students on placement this will be the power invested in the role that you have as their practice educator, delegated to you by the academic institution. Ultimately this could be related to the assessment function of the role – the ability to recommend a pass as well as a fail.
>
> 2. *Coercive power* – this relates to the kind of behaviours that are either encouraged or discouraged. This will include disapproval and the imposition of restrictions.
>
>   For a student on placement this will be linked to the
>
> 3. *Reward power* – this relates primarily to the capacity of the supervisor to control tangible rewards.
>
>   For a student on placement this could be linked to such things as desirable work assignments; the allocation of resources that the student has to carry out their role; opportunities to attend development events.
>
>   The final two kinds of power are perceived as 'functional', residing in the person of the supervisor.
>
> 4. *Referent power* – this relates to the person of the supervisor, the personal characteristics that make up the presence of the supervisor. This is the power that results from another person liking you or wanting to be like you.
>
>   For a student on placement this could be linked to having a good relationship between themselves and their supervisor.
>
> 5. *Expert power* – this relates to the profession knowledge and skills in practice of the practice educator.
>
>   For a student on placement this could be linked, for example, to being able to draw on the practice educator's expertise to support them in linking theories to practice; in day-to-day interactions with service users and carers; in developing their own professional skills and knowledge.

meaning of authority and power, and to recognise what could be shared between the student and practice educator; and how this could happen.

- Developing an open honest relationship in which the differences in power, both in formal position and in terms of identity, are acknowledged and considering how these power differences are likely to affect the supervisory relationship. There is a parallel process of power in the inequality of position in the worker–service user relationship.

- Recognising and trying to understand the obstacles to development that have arisen from past experiences and working actively to increase the student's personal confidence and professional competence. This includes a recognition of difference and disadvantage that may have been experienced because of class, gender, culture, race, age, disability and sexual orientation;

- Placing an emphasis on the human aspects of the relationship through a focus on mutual interests, and reinforcing the idea of the equal value of human beings.

> *An anti-oppressive approach would be one in which the whole style and perspective of a supervisor communicates a fundamental belief in the potential and ability of each supervisee.*

(Brown and Bourne, 1996: 37)

- Redressing unhelpful power differentials in the relationship by encouraging a wider collective approach on behalf of the less powerful person – for example, support networks or extra support for students who are structurally disadvantaged.

Conclusion

As we have outlined within this chapter, supervision plays an essential part in within the student placement. Supervision is a complex process with a number of functions. Supervision is about professional development. It is about accountability; supervision is also about the supportive, learning and educative elements within supervision. Supervision is also about discovery – the discovery of knowledge and values that underpin practice; discovery of innovative and best practice; discovery of 'self' and 'self' as a professional. Central to these processes is critical reflection. An opportunity for the student to evaluate your own performance as a supervisor can be helpful in critically reflecting your own performance. This could be in the form of an 'honest discussion'; this can not only support your own learning but also that of the student in evaluating the relationship and considering both strengths and areas for development. It is important that you maintain an open stance and do not retreat to a defensive position of authority. Timing the evaluation of your performance will need to be carefully judged; asking the student to evaluate your performance before all the relevant paperwork has been completed and a judgement has been made as to their success (or failure) in the placement, may put pressure on the student to present a 'positive' view of your performance rather than an honest one! Your own reflections on supervision will also support you in judging your own learning. Just as we have suggested with regard to reviewing the journey that the student has made, this is a process that should enable you to identify your own strengths and areas for development in your performance as a practice educator.

FURTHER READING

Hawkins, P. and Shohet, R. (2007) *Supervision in the Helping Professions*, 3rd edn. Buckingham: Open University Press.

This book provides a clear overview of the processes and techniques of supervision in the helping professions, including the CLEAR model for structuring the process of a supervision session.

Tsui, M. (2005) *Social Work Supervision: Contexts and Concepts*. Thousand Oaks, CA: SAGE.

This book examines supervision in social work generally and provides a sound review of theories and models of supervision.

Chapter 6

Managing and developing practice learning experiences

Domain C: Manage the assessment of learners in practice

1. Engage learners in the design, planning and implementation of the assessment tasks.

2. Agree and review a plan and methods for assessing learners' performance against agreed criteria.

6. Base assessment decisions on all relevant evidence and from a range of sources, resolving any inconsistencies in the evidence available.

7. Encourage learners to self-evaluate and seek service users, carers and peer group feedback on their performance.

Introduction

This chapter introduces you to the central importance of preparation, planning and management for the success of the learning opportunity that you are offering. Just as you are unlikely to undertake an assessment visit to a service user or to write a funding proposal for your agency or a report to court without meticulous planning, knowing that it is preparation that helps in overcoming – or at least recognising – potential problems and barriers, as well as presenting the best case for success, so too in offering a practice learning experience, you will need to prepare carefully the experience in terms of content and process. The clearer the initial plans the more organised the experience will seem to others in the team and to the student. Rigorous preparation also fits with the concept of evidence-based practice in providing targets and goals against which you can monitor student achievement, your own performance and the process of the placement, using the information to revise, refocus and re-plan any future placement experiences. The initial preparatory stages of a placement can be conceptualised as part of an action–research cycle, in which the lessons from prior experiences are integrated with planning for the next one in a continued search for improvement and enhancement of the effectiveness of the experience from a range of perspectives (Hart and Bond, 1995; Kemmis and McTaggart, 2000).

Planning for practice education is a multi-levelled activity. Not only does it concern making detailed plans for the placement of an individual student and, indeed, with the student, but it also concerns planning alongside your team and agency the levels and types of involvement suitable for enabling the learning of others. Furthermore, planning takes place across agencies and will involve your team and agency in negotiation with the university, determining the types of experience and placements that can be developed and offered.

ACTIVITY

Consider the different levels of planning involved in organising a placement for a student. Which have you been involved with? Are there elements in which you believe you could make a contribution? If so, how might you achieve this?

Domains A and B of the skills-sets identified for work-based assessors form the backdrop to this chapter. Preparation and prior planning are fundamental to creating learning experiences that are valuable and effective, and a structured approach to learning is acknowledged by students as important indicator of satisfaction and learning (Bogo et al., 2002). Key elements involved in preparing and planning for a student include:

- Creating a conducive learning environment within your team;

- Developing a set of potential opportunities for learning within the team, across teams and external to your agency, in which all involved are prepared and supported;

- Developing constructive working relationships with students which result in personalised learning plans.

The chapter will draw on your existing skills and knowledge as a professional practitioner and focus these on the practice learning experience. The chapter will examine:

- Planning before the placement

- The induction

- The development of learning agreements

- The practice curriculum

- Compiling the report.

It will be important throughout the chapter is to remember the SMART planning axiom; bearing in mind that whatever you decide, negotiate and plan should be:

Specific	*The outline of the experience and the expectations of all those involved in the experience at whatever level should be clearly understood. Use language, in any written plan, that is unambiguous and simple to understand; the placement will be complex enough once started!*
Measurable	*Make sure you can measure any outcomes that you specify and state clearly what will indicate that a goal or outcome has been achieved. This will help resolve any misunderstandings arising and assist in formulating your assessment at a later date.*
Achievable	*There is no point in deciding on and setting goals that are unlikely to be achieved successfully. Not only will this frustrate and reduce the confidence of students, but it will also create an unreasonable and unjustifiable expense to your agency and to those placing the student. Overall success is often increased by smaller achievements.*
Realistic	*This concerns the relevance of your plan to achieve what is required by the student's programme in line with your agency's remit. There is no point in developing a learning plan that does not cover what the student needs to cover,*

however interesting this might be; nor is it a profitable use of your time to develop learning experiences that are not covered within your agency brief. Plan experiences from within your role and remit.

Timely and time-limited | Focusing on the time-constraints involved in any learning experience provides clarity regarding what you need to complete and when. It is always worth starting at the end point and working backwards. For instance, you are likely to be required to complete a report at the end of a student learning experience. Therefore, starting at this point and asking what needs to be done when, in order for you to complete the report, will allow you to set timescales against elements of the plan which can then be discussed and evaluated within set supervision sessions (see Chapter 5).

Planning before the placement

Knowledge and understanding of adult learning, student programme characteristics, and expectations and demands of the work in acting as a practice educator are crucial prior to starting to plan and prepare for a student learning experience. Your practice educator's programme – at whatever level of study – should prepare you for understanding the different ways in which adults approach learning and refreshing yourself about these will help you to match a student to your agency and to prepare experiences that will maximise learning. If you wish, it might be helpful to read Chapter 2 of this volume again.

If you have been asked to enable the learning of a student it is worth spending a little time mapping what might be involved. This will help you to identify what you already know, which will be useful to this experience, and also to pinpoint the gaps you may need to work upon. Table 6. 1 shows some of the elements you may wish to focus on. It is not meant as an exhaustive list:

ACTIVITY

Using the categories and question outlined in Table 6.1 identify and write down how a social work student may be accommodated on a practice experience within your agency.

There are many possibilities when completing these preliminary preparations. It is always important to ask for clarification and details, however, from those requesting the practice opportunity. So, in respect of a social work student you would want to know from the university and your training department, assuming they act as intermediaries in negotiating placements, what are the standards and requirements; where can they be found; what would the student be expected to achieve; what would you (as a practice educator) be expected to do, and so on. Agency capacity and personal capacity may raise

Table 6. 1: Mapping the needs and requirements when providing learning experiences

Professional and legislative requirements	University and academic requirements	Agency function, capacity, requirements	Personal capacity, needs and requirements	Student need and requirements	Service user and carer needs
What do the professional body require in terms of standards, outputs and evidence?	What academic requirements and outputs does the university need from the student? (If you are being assessed as a practice educator, what requirements are there for you to fulfil?)	Can the agency provide experiences that meet the requirements of the professional body, legislation and university or educational body?	Do you have the space (in physical and work-capacity terms) at work to provide a learning opportunity?	What learning styles, experience, qualities and characteristics does the student possess?	What particular role will service users and carers have in the practice education experience?
Are there any legislative requirements attached to the learning opportunity?			Do you have the support of the team, your manager and others in providing this experience?	What does the student need to complete during the course of this learning opportunity?	Are there any training, support or practical needs that service users and carers may need to fulfil their role in the experience?
			Do you have the right knowledge and skills for this work?		
			Are there any special needs you require or must negotiate?		

other issues of course, and these may fluctuate depending on the personal and work pressures experienced.

Let's now turn to consider agency capacity, personal capacity, and service user and carer needs in terms of planning before a placement starts.

Agency capacity depends on a range of factors. The first question must be whether your agency undertakes work that can offer a valid, measurable and realistic experience to a student in their particular course of study. If the answer is no then you will not be in a position to accept a student for that course. However, if, as the world of social and health care changes over time, you can offer some learning opportunities but not the whole placement experience, you may be able to negotiate and plan a set of opportunities that will allow the student to achieve some or part of their requirements and outcomes. This may be increasingly important and should be recognised as contributing to the learning of others.

If your agency can offer a full practice learning opportunity you will then need to consider the philosophical and practice orientation of the team, and whether a particular student would gain from being placed there and whether or not you need to stipulate specific student qualities, characteristics, interests and experiences. For instance, a student interested in developing psychodynamic practice may well be usefully challenged by working in a Youth Offending Team using a cognitive-behavioural approach but it may not present the best use of the agency, yourself or the opportunity. Carefully checking the request for a placement made by students will allow you to match their needs with the placement offered. It is also important at this point to check what students are required to bring to the learning opportunity in order to complete their placement. For instance, a social work student must complete self-declarations of health status and good character, the latter being supplemented by a current Criminal Records Bureau (CRB) check. It is the student's responsibility to highlight any special needs resulting from health conditions and important that, with prior knowledge, you are able to take advice and plan for the placement accordingly.

If you meet the criteria for the placement and can offer appropriate opportunities to enhance the student's learning, you will need to evaluate whether you have management support and the backing of your team before going ahead. The former is important in terms of your workload and appraisal, and the latter crucial to ensuring the student has a positive and constructive learning experience. Research indicates that where the responsibility for enabling the learning of others is shared across teams and not seen as the sole responsibility of the primary assessor or educator, that experience is valued (Doel, 2006; Parker et al., 2006a). It is also helpful to ensure that the team are aware of what the student can and cannot do whilst undertaking practice learning. This will prevent an inappropriate use of the student's time and learning, and also may help in developing learning opportunities supervised by others, which adds to the veracity and validity of the report at the end.

A final agency issue to be considered concerns physical capacity or space. Team norms as regards desks, mobility of work stations and so on can form an important part of the learning, but there is no excuse for treating a student as less important than other members of the team and providing them with fewer resources. If team workers have a desk, a telephone and a computer – or access to them – then so too should the student. If there is not the physical space available the student may feel ostracised and disadvantaged, and may not be able to avail themselves of the learning opportunities in the placement. It is important that these factors be taken into account prior to committing to a student placement.

When you have determined that the team has the capacity and is supportive of providing learning experiences to students, you will need to consider your *personal capacity* for the role. It is assumed, if you are reading this book that you have an interest in and commitment to enabling other people's learning and developing the future workforce; and that you are probably undertaking post-qualifying education of which this forms part. However, enthusiasm and commitment alone are not enough. Social work is multi-faceted and highly pressured, and you need to be realistic as to whether you have the time and space to commit to this role; it is a heavy responsibility and will have an impact on the work your team expects from you, the student's future career path and, most important of all, on the outcomes for those people with whom you are working. If you have the space to undertake the practice educator role, it is important to consider what support needs you might have, in terms of supervision and management backing, and what training you may need in order to fulfil the role successfully.

The centrality of including service users and carers in the education of the future workforce represents a significant shift in the mind-set, culture and philosophy of social and health care agencies (Beresford et al., 2007). The participation of service users and carers is still at an embryonic stage, however, with complications and barriers being identified, and fears of tokenistic involvement preventing the development of constructive partnerships. Before you embark on a placement with a student it is worth determining how, and in what ways, you can legitimately and appropriately employ the skills and knowledge of people who use your services. This may be in providing feedback in some way to you about the student (see Chapter 4). It may be in talking with students about the experience of receiving and working with social care services. In whatever ways you may develop service user and carer involvement, it will benefit from being clearly delineated so that all involved know what is expected from them and what they are likely to be called upon to do. You can be innovative in developing the involvement of users of the service and their carers, but it is important to keep to the fore the need to act ethically and alongside those with whom you work.

Once you have decided – in consultation with your manager, team and learning advisors – that you are able to take a student, you can begin to plan and develop the placement learning experience.

It is worth considering the use of tools developed for project planning. Placements are, to a large extent, projects of learning, and can be broken down into tasks and activities, and set against timescales, in a similar way to other projects. Many tools for project planning are available free on the Internet (see www.mindtools.com or www.businesballs.com). The two most commonly used are GANTT charts and critical path analyses. An example of a simple GANTT chart is provided in Figure 6.1. The steps involved include listing the various activities and tasks that must be achieved in the placement, considering when they have to be achieved by and whether they can be undertaken in parallel or sequentially, with

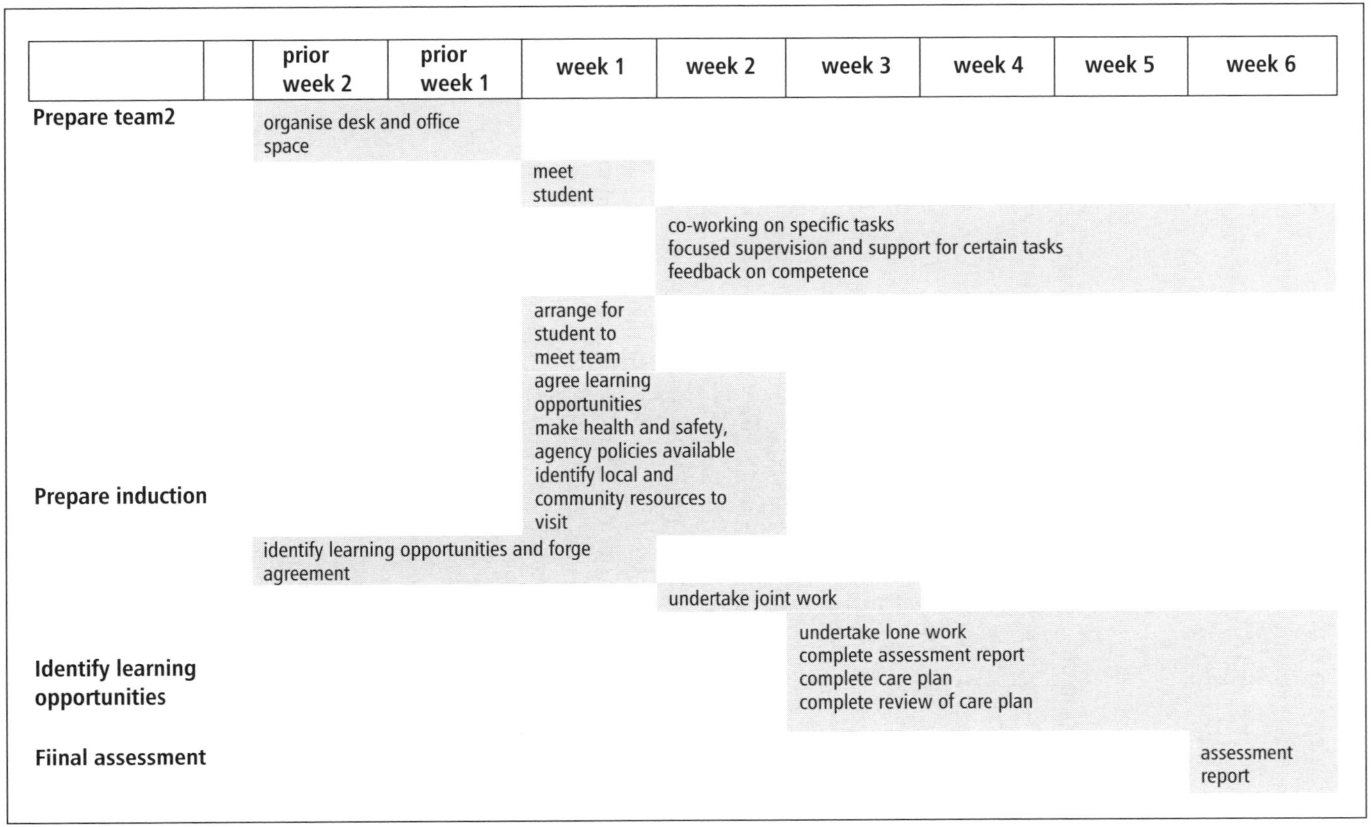

	prior week 2	prior week 1	week 1	week 2	week 3	week 4	week 5	week 6
Prepare team2	organise desk and office space	organise desk and office space						
			meet student					
				co-working on specific tasks focused supervision and support for certain tasks feedback on competence				
Prepare induction	identify learning opportunities and forge agreement	identify learning opportunities and forge agreement						
			arrange for student to meet team agree learning opportunities make health and safety, agency policies available identify local and community resources to visit					
Identify learning opportunities				undertake joint work				
					undertake lone work complete assessment report complete care plan complete review of care plan			
Fiinal assessment							assessment report	assessment report

Figure 6.1: A simple GANTT chart to develop a project plan for a placement

some tasks being prerequisites for others. Once you have answered these questions for your placement you can fit the information on a chart according to the weeks (or whatever time it is) you have to complete the placement. A critical pathway analysis displays and organises information in a similar way but is more diagrammatic as shown in Figure 6.2. If you are using any of these tools for planning the placement it is worthwhile starting from the end-point and working backwards. In this way you will be able to grasp better how to fit in your learning objectives and how much time you have for each stage, creating a focus for accomplishment and achievement.

Induction

Consultation and participation are important concepts in planning an effective practice learning experience and, wherever possible, you should strive to include the student in the design of the placement. However, you will also need to do some work to develop a structured experience and, indeed, students welcome this planning and knowledgeable approach from the person managing their learning (Bogo et al., 2002; Parker et al., 2006a, 2006b). Planning an induction may be one of those tasks that, apart from the negotiation and individualising that occur when you first meet your student – hopefully prior to the placement! – you might develop yourself.

Induction should be a part of every new worker's experience on starting with a social care agency, and Skills for Care (2005) and the Children's Workforce Development Council (CWDC) (2006) have developed and agreed common induction standards for people new to or moving across social care organisations. These standards set out what people should know and understand within six months of employment. Whilst students undertaking practice learning will have a far shorter period in which to be inducted into the agency, there are common elements which they need to be aware of and you may, as part of a developing practice curriculum, develop an induction around these. The six standards identified by Skills for Care (2005) are:

- Understanding the principles of care
- Understanding the organisation and the role of the worker
- Maintaining safety in the workplace
- Communicating effectively
- Recognising abuse and neglect
- Developing as a worker.

The CWDC adds a standard relating to values. It is clear that students need an orientation to the agency and its ways of working, communication strategy, complaints policy and confidentiality, and access to records policies. They need to be aware of health and safety issues, and responsibilities such as when to sign in and out, how to record when you are visiting a service user external to the agency, when to inform others and so on. It is likely that students will also require informal meetings of staff members, going out with staff members and perhaps visiting key personnel in other agencies with whom you work closely. In planning an induction for your student it is worth asking some of the questions set out in Table 6.2.

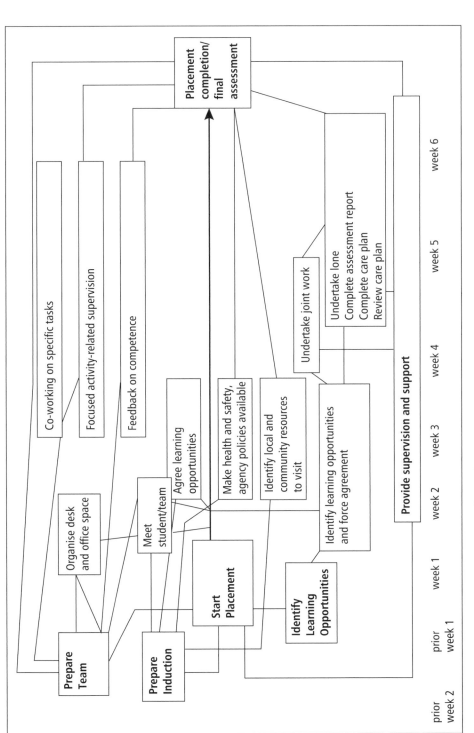

Figure 6.2: A simple critical path analysis for a placement

Table 6.2: Induction planner

	Who to meet	Where to visit	What to know
Within the agency/team			
Within the organisation			
Within the community			

Core knowledge and understanding can be developed within a structured induction as shown in the following case study.

CASE STUDY

Jeremy was an experienced social worker in a team working with older people with a range of long-term conditions. He was taking a student for a short placement as part of a split experience between the local adult mental health team and his own team. Thus he wanted to ensure that Geraldine, who was new to the area, gained an understanding of the team, got to know people and was accepted as part of it. He was also concerned that Geraldine had a constructive experience and was equipped with necessary information for the people who used the team. Information-giving and knowledge of local resources had surfaced many times in service evaluations as the most common need and request.

Geraldine was pleasantly surprised, having heard stories about poor and last-minute planning from her peers, when Jeremy emailed her to arrange a meeting before the placement to plan her induction. This act in itself helped to establish trust and a positive relationship between them that lasted through the placement.

At the meeting, Jeremy used the questions 'who, where and what?' to identify people and agencies to visit and information to find out from them. This helped Geraldine to think about what she needed from the placement and provided them both with a structure to identify 'how and when' the induction would take place.

The development of learning agreements

It is a debatable point, and will depend on your agency and the university you are working with, whether the induction takes place before or following the negotiation of a learning agreement. A learning agreement is part of the overall practice curriculum, which we will deal with next, but is considered here separately because this agreement represents a planning process crucial to the rest of the placement.

The learning agreement is a quasi-contractual arrangement setting out what the placement will offer in terms of learning opportunities, supervision and support, and what expectations the student may have of you and the agency alongside the responsibilities of the student, what he or she will commit to and what you can expect from them. It is important to get this right for the smooth running and assessment of the placement. A simple, understandable and clear agreement at this stage can prevent untold misunderstandings and complications later. You can use project planning models such as GANTT charts or critical path analyses in developing the learning agreement. This can work even if the format of the learning agreement is set by the university you are working with and may individualise it in a constructive way (see Figure 6.3 for an example of a learning agreement form).

CASE STUDY

The induction plan negotiated prior to the short placement formed the initial part of Geraldine's learning agreement. Geraldine was encouraged to meet with workers from other agencies, to develop an understanding of the ways in which they worked, and to compare and contrast this with her role in the practice agency in supervision with her practice educator. This helped her to identify how this learning met some of the requirements of the placement, and to develop new learning opportunities and experiences in an iterative but guided way.

Practice curriculum

What is a practice curriculum?

The use and development of a practice curriculum in practice education has been introduced in Chapter 4 as an aid to the process and completion of assessment. However, it is much more than this. As noted elsewhere, a practice curriculum is a systematic collection of learning opportunities and experiences designed to meet the demands and needs of a range of stakeholders involved in practice education (Parker, 2004). These may include:

- professional, registration and training bodies;

- the university; and

- each individual student (see Shardlow and Doel, 1996).

Much of what follows builds on the use of a practice curriculum for student social workers (see Parker, 2004). Systematic approaches to practice learning and education are based around a curriculum setting out the key learning opportunities and issues that will be covered by students undertaking practice learning within that agency. In respect of social work, these relate to the prescribed areas of knowledge, skills and values set by the Department of Health (2002), the GSCC (2002a), the *National Occupational Standards* (Topss/SfC, 2002a; see also 'Introduction' in this volume), and the subject benchmarking criteria (QAA, 2000). However, each agency or practice educator may develop individually tailored activities and learning opportunities to meet prescribed and negotiated needs. A good practice curriculum aims to do this in a flexible way that accounts for individual and particular needs, and will build on the learning agreement for practice learning. An

Student Details
Name: ....
Contact Details:.............................
....
....
email: ....

Practice Supervisor Details
Name: ....
Contact Details:.............................
....
....
email: ....

Practice Educator Details
Name: ....
Contact Details:.............................
....
....
email: ....

University Tutor/liaison Details
Name: ....
Contact Details:.............................
....
....
email: ....

Signature: ....
Signature: ....
Signature: ....
Signature: ....

Role and expectations of student:
 – time keeping/work time
 – dress code
 – sickness policy
 – lone working
 – health and safety
 – supervision

1.
2.
3.
How will these be adressed?
How will these be monitored and reviewed?
How will these be assessed?

Role and expectations of practice educator/supervisor/agency:
 – supervision, support and availability
 – contact and support
 – policy and procedure information

Review details

Learning opportunities:
Opportunity:
How will this be achieved?
How will this be assessed?

Resolution of difficulties, disagreements and conflicts:

Particular student learning needs:

Figure 6.3: An exemplar learning agreement form

130

important task for negotiation with your student concerns the identification of learning goals and needs that will assist in the preparation of a unique learning and development plan, which covers both the required areas included in the standards and requirements, and individually negotiated needs, which may be included in the learning agreement.

The practice curriculum specifies and structures the learning opportunities your agency can offer and sets them in the context of the overall student's learning needs. This may be flexible and fluid according to a process of negotiated learning or it may be that a sequential or 'building-block' approach to the practice curriculum is adopted (Shardlow and Doel, 1996). Parker (2004) suggests that important steps in designing a practice curriculum include:

- defining the aims of the curriculum;
- identifying the content;
- considering the merits of sequence;
- devising the methods and strategies of learning;
- considering issues of measurement of learning;
- presenting the material in accessible form;
- reviewing and evaluating the curriculum;
- writing the final version.

To reiterate, however, the key elements of an effective practice curriculum are negotiation with the student, clarity, simplicity and measurability.

Some students find it useful to include a systematic learning plan as part of their practice learning opportunity. To help develop this way of recording and keeping track of learning, a plan is included in the Box 6.1. This can be adapted to suit individual styles of learning. It can be useful to attempt this for yourself. This will help identify potential blocks to learning and ways you may encourage students to deal with them.

A continuing curriculum may consider more agency-specific aspects of learning or the development of advanced skills in practice, and should be guided by the requirements the student has to fulfil, their prior learning and experience, and your negotiations. Content may include:

- agency-specific models of practice;
- integrating theory and practice;
- service user and carer knowledge and/or feedback;
- legislative, policy and practice knowledge;
- critical reflection.

Whatever elements form the core of your agency- and student-specific practice curriculum, the outcomes from it will assist your assessment of the student and the subsequent report-writing.

Box 6.1: *Action and learning plans (after Parker, 2004)*

My list of strengths
(Consider here anything that you consider yourself to be good at, including personal qualities, practical tasks and more abstract qualities. List as many as you can and don't be shy!)

My list of needs
(Here you should include experiences, practice skills, knowledge, learning and core qualities that you feel you need to increase, develop or introduce into your repertoire of skills and behaviour. Again, as with the list of strengths, it is important to be honest in order for you to judge your progress throughout the practice learning opportunity.)

ACTION PLAN
Need identified:

Resources required to meet need:
(It may be useful to list the practical resources, the learning and knowledge resources, the skills base and the personal resources in such an order or to take a thematic approach listing resources of a particular type.)

List methods by which resources can be gained:
(At this point you should begin to work out an action plan within the plan to gain access to resources, i.e. if you need to acquaint yourself more fully with a particular aspect of the case you may need time to spend researching this in the library, or you may need to speak with a relevant authority, or attend a workshop or lecture.)

What do you need from your practice teacher?

What do you need from colleagues?

Methods by which you will evaluate your learning:
(List some of the ways in which you will check out that you are meeting your learning needs. This may include discussion and feedback from colleagues, clients and practice teacher. It may include self-report in relation to confidence. It may involve presenting your learning to colleagues for critical review.)

The Action Plan:
(Write down a series of steps and stages that are involved in your meeting your identified learning needs.)

Writing the report

The onus is on students to collect, demonstrate and write about the evidence that shows they have met the outcomes required for their learning experience. However, that does not mean that you do not need to complete a report. Each university that you work with will have its own requirements for and expectations of the completion of the assessment report they wish you to undertake for students. However, these tend to follow similar formats and will concern the particular outcomes, standards and requirements for the course studied. It is important to consider the completion of the report as part of this chapter on managing the learning experience because, as noted in Chapter 4, students are aware of the assessment of their competence and the power you have can have a significant impact on the placement. Therefore, it can help to include the student in the process of writing the report, as well as their collecting and presenting evidence on which you can comment. This helps to re-balance some of the power issues and also allows you both to negotiate what it is that needs to be presented as evidence, how much is needed, from whom and by when.

A time-managed approach to writing your report is just as important as it is for the student. Planning time to address the criteria that have been set and using your observations, supervision notes and the comments of colleagues can feed into the development of an overall assessment throughout the placement. Indeed, the process of report writing is, to a degree, iterative, and your perceptions will go through stages and develop as the student demonstrates, hopefully, a greater aptitude for the work throughout. When you prepare to take a student at the outset, it is crucial to factor in sufficient time to make a valid assessment and produce a high-quality report: it has potentially a huge impact on the professional career of the student involved and we owe it to those people who use social services. Consider the two following vignettes.

CASE STUDY

Tomas

Tomas had gained much from taking a student. The experience had given him an enthusiasm for learning and sharing that learning with others. The student had also commented on the commitment, high level of knowledge and much valued support that had been offered. When it came to the end of the placement, Tomas prepared to write his report but was unfortunately called away to deal with two of his families who were experiencing crises and needed immediate assistance. This took three days, after which was the weekend. Tomas caught 'flu and was off work for a further week, missing the deadline for submission of the report. This was managed by the university, which agreed to look at the report outside of the meetings if necessary. However, Tomas was again busy at work and had put the report to one side. As a result, when he did finally write it, he omitted much of relevance that his student could have used to develop further or could have been commended on. Indeed, when he did submit the report it was quite rushed and done in response to a plea from the university, which by now had received an official complaint from the student who said the delay was having an impact on their ability to qualify and work.

Nushra

Nushra was aware that she needed to be methodical in her work otherwise it got 'out of control' for her. In the placement she offered Michael, she collected weekly summary sheets of work done and reflection on learning, alternated with him the completion of supervision notes, used part of each session to look at the standards and requirements to be met on the placement and identified where the evidence being presented and discussed at that session could fit. She completed the report on time, included all relevant evidence and found the process fairly stress free.

Evaluating your plans and the managed process

After offering a placement, and as part of the process of managing it effectively, it is important to spend some time reflecting on the experience. Asking questions about your role, involvement, style, knowledge and practice are all useful and will help you evaluate the placement. In turn, your reflections will help in revising the way you manage placements in the future. It is a constantly evolving and iterative process: an action–research cycle. As with planning and managing the placement, project management tasks can be helpful in evaluating how it has gone and what you might do differently in the future. Undertaking a SWOT analysis – looking at strengths, weaknesses, opportunities and threats – can be extremely useful in evaluating the placement from your perspective (see Figure 6.4).

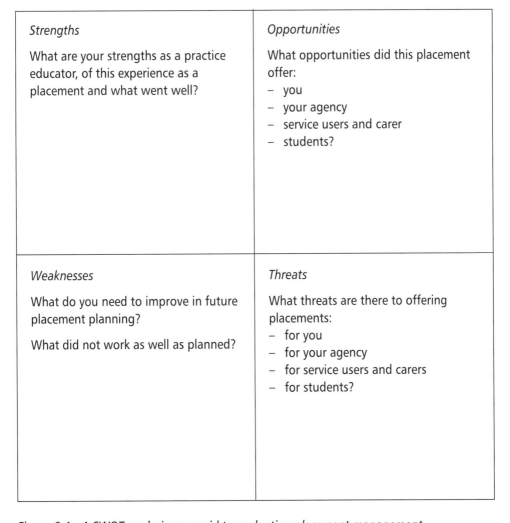

Strengths	*Opportunities*
What are your strengths as a practice educator, of this experience as a placement and what went well?	What opportunities did this placement offer: – you – your agency – service users and carer – students?
Weaknesses	*Threats*
What do you need to improve in future placement planning? What did not work as well as planned?	What threats are there to offering placements: – for you – for your agency – for service users and carers – for students?

Figure 6.4: A SWOT analysis as an aid to evaluating placement management

You will be able to identify areas that can be enhanced and those that can be improved, as well as keeping a careful eye on whether the agency is best placed to offer further placement opportunities.

Conclusion

Preparation and planning are central to the effective management of practice learning and this chapter has introduced and explored a number of ways in which you might plan the placement, conceptualising this as an iterative or action–research process. Pre-placement planning was considered prior to the development of an induction, a learning agreement and practice curriculum. A key element in the process is negotiation with and participation of the student undertaking the placement.

FURTHER READING

Williams, S. and Rutter, L. (2007) *Enabling and Assessing Work-based Learning for Social Work: Supporting the Development of Professional Practice*. Birmingham: Learn to Care.

The processes covered in this excellent volume will contribute to planning and managing, as well as pointing you in the direction of other materials.

Chapter 7
What about 'me'?

MEETING THE POST-QUALIFYING SOCIAL WORK STANDARDS

This chapter will meet the following standards:

As a social care worker, you must be accountable for the quality of your work and take responsibility for maintaining and improving your knowledge and skills.

(GSCC, 2002a: point 6)

Think critically about their own practice in the context of the GSCC codes of practice, national and international codes of professional ethics and the principles of diversity, equality and social inclusion in a wide range of situations, including those associated with inter-agency and inter-professional work.

(GSCC, 2005a: 16)

Thus, according to the General Social Care Council:

... professional development is a holistic process ... whereby individuals acquire knowledge and skills in different areas, which then combine with one another to promote a deeper sense of overall professional identity.

(GSCC, 2005a: 8).

Introduction

This chapter will examine the development of self, considering the personal strategies that could support you, as a practice educator, in managing your role and responsibilities. Within the chapter you will look at the concepts of reflection, reflexivity and knowledge-informed practice, as examples of the ways in which you might continue your own development as a practitioner and practice educator. The chapter also considers support processes that may be available to you individually, as well as exploring the potential for support and learning generated through a wider network of colleagues and practice educators working together in 'communities of practice' (Wenger, 1998).

'Social work and social care is a rapidly developing field in which innovation and change are becoming commonplace' (GSCC, 2005a: 7) and it is therefore necessary for practitioners, learners and their educators to 'use reflection and critical analysis to continuously develop and improve their specialist practice, including their practice in interprofessional and inter-agency contexts, drawing systematically, accurately and appropriately on theories, models and relevant up-to-date research' (2005: 17).

The notions of accountability, continuous development and critical reflection are further embedded in the GSCC *Codes of Practice for Social Care Workers* and the generic-level criteria for post-qualifying awards in social work.

Why do I need to think about my support and development needs?

This book has enabled you, as a practice educator, to examine contemporary theories and knowledge in relation to practice learning, teaching and education, with a focus on ways of working that develop the skills and practice of the individual with whom you are working. This chapter, however, shifts that focus somewhat, as it encourages you to examine how you continue to develop your own skills and practices, as someone based in practice who undertakes learning, teaching and assessment of others. Therefore, the emphasis on this chapter will be exploring strategies and support mechanisms that may enable you to reflect on your role and continuing professional development as a practice educator.

As you have seen in the epigraph to the chapter, the idea that as professionals we are ethically required to continually improve our professional knowledge and skills through learning and professional development at all stages in our careers, is embedded in the professional value base. This requirement is demonstrated through, for example; the codes of practice; national policy standards such as the national occupational standards; post-registration training and learning requirements and the post-qualifying framework.

The GSCC *Codes of Practice* for social care workers describe the standards of conduct and practice within which all practitioners, including learners and qualified social workers, should work. The codes suggest that you use the codes to examine your own practice and to look for areas in which you can improve. So, for example, the sixth code of practice, as cited in the epigraph to this chapter, requires workers 'to be accountable for the quality of your work and take responsibility for maintaining and improving your knowledge and skills' (GSCC, 2002a). The codes of practice develop this further by stating that this can be achieved through:

- Meeting relevant standards of practice;

- Working in a lawful, safe and effective way;

- Maintaining clear and accurate records;

- Informing your employer or appropriate authority about any personal difficulties that might affect your ability to do your job competently and safely;

- Seeking assistance if you do not feel able or adequately prepared to carry out any aspect of your work;

- Working openly and cooperatively with colleagues; treating them with respect;

- Recognising that you remain responsible for work that you have delegated to other workers;

- Recognising and respecting the roles and expertise of workers from other agencies and working in partnership with them; and

- Undertaking relevant training to maintain and improve your knowledge and skills and contributing to the learning and development of others.

(adapted from GSCC, 2002a)

It is self-evident that all of these points are relevant to your role as a practice educator, but perhaps the most pertinent, in terms of the objectives of this chapter of the book, is the last bullet point.

ACTIVITY

Read the GSCC Codes of Practice (2002a) point six again (this is cited in the epigraph to the chapter). Then consider the last bullet point on the list of 'activities' – reflect upon what this might mean for you and your practice. Is this statement satisfactory and comprehensive?

It is likely that, as you read through this chapter you will consider that whilst 'undertaking relevant training to maintain and improve your knowledge and skills and contributing to the learning and development of others' is a valid and important activity, it is by no means the only way in which you can develop and learn in professional practice. Indeed, in this chapter, you will look at a range of ways in which you can 'improve your knowledge and skills and contribute to the learning and development of others' that are not necessarily associated with 'undertaking training'; examples include reflection, reflexivity, awareness and development of tacit knowledge, practice wisdom, undertaking practitioner research and participating in collegiate learning in the workplace.

You will also be familiar, through your practice educator role, with the *National Occupational Standards for Social Work* (Topss/SfC, 2002) which describe the functions of social work and provide a standard of best practice in social work competence (see also Chapter 1). The *Codes of Practice* described above have been incorporated into the *National Occupational Standards* and thus within the six key roles, particularly in key roles 5 and 6, the requirement for social workers to take responsibility for their own practice and continuing development is evident. The standards are available from the Sector Skills Council (www.gscc.org.uk).

Additionally, as a practice educator, you are likely to be a registered social work practitioner, responsible for evidencing continuing training and learning in order to maintain your registration. The GSCC uses the term *Post Registration Training and Learning* (PRTL) and it is useful to see these requirements as integral and continuing elements of your professional development. Details of the requirements are available from the GSCC (www.gscc.org.uk) – Box 7.1 contains an extract from the web pages.

Box 7.1: Extract from GSCC requirements for post-registration training

The rules state that:

- every social worker registered with the GSCC shall, within the period of registration, complete either 90 hours or 15 days of study, training, courses, seminars, reading, teaching or other activities which could reasonably be expected to advance the social worker's professional development, or contribute to the development of the profession as a whole;

- every social worker registered with the GSCC shall keep a record of post-registration training and learning undertaken;

- failure to meet these conditions may be considered misconduct.

What sort of post-registration training and learning activities should I undertake?

We realise there are many ways to continue to learn and develop as a social worker so we have deliberately avoided being too specific about the type of activities which will meet our requirements.

We expect you to choose training and learning activities that:

- will benefit your current employment;

- will benefit your career progression;

- reflect your preferred learning style;

- make the most of the learning opportunities available to you form part of your wider professional development.

For example, you may wish to:

- arrange to shadow the work of a colleague in a related team or profession;

- negotiate protected time to research latest policy and good practice developments in your field of practice;

- undertake a piece of research related to your practice.

If you are studying for a certificated post-qualifying award, you can use those studies as evidence that you meet the post-registration training and learning requirements. www.gscc.org.uk

---

As you consider the GSCC's PRTL requirements stated on their web page and reproduced in Box 7.1, you might reflect upon our earlier critique of the GSCC codes of practice in respect of professional development. The descriptions of potential activities for PRTL are much more comprehensive, broad and inclusive. It is likely, therefore, that the strategies, ideas and concepts proposed in this chapter will all fall within these requirements. In fact, by using this whole book to enhance your knowledge and skills as a practice educator you are exploring *the latest policy and good practice developments in your field of practice*, which are likely to 'benefit your current employment', to 'benefit your career progression'; 'reflect your preferred learning style' and 'make the most of the learning opportunities available to you form part of your wider professional development'.

Furthermore, and closely linked to the requirements for maintenance of registration, the new GSCC post-qualifying framework for social work is underpinned by the principle that professionals must continuously develop and improve their practice. The framework has three levels: Specialist level; Higher Specialist level; and Advanced level, with additional generic-level criteria which are to be embedded into any programmes of learning at all levels. Within each of the generic-level criteria there are criteria that stress critical reflection upon practice and continuing learning; some of these are cited in the epigraph to the chapter.

This initial discussion has presented the discourse, rhetoric and policy-level requirements that provide the context and background for contemporary professional development in social work. Perhaps, then part of the answer to the question set out in the heading 'Why do I need to think about my support and development needs?' has not been made explicit. In other words, the details above lay out the standards and formal requirements, but what is missing from this are the less tangible, more informal reasons for participating in your own learning and progression. Thus, notions of self-fulfilment; genuine interest; motivation; commitment to maintaining best practice; personal satisfaction; achievement; and a desire to learn are all part of understanding what you can accomplish through learning and development and hence 'why you need to think about your support and development needs'. These concepts are, of course, also important when thinking about the learners that you work with and their support and learning needs.

As you now read further, you will be invited to consider and appraise, in more practical terms, exactly what some of this might mean in practice, to you, the learners you work with and your colleagues in practice. Thus, in the next section you will read about reflective and reflexive practice, both of which are arguably entrenched in all areas of practice- and work-based learning.

What is the place of reflective and reflexive practice for me as a practice educator?

Before discussing the efficacy of reflection and reflexivity it may be helpful to consider exactly what these terms mean. It is likely that you feel very familiar with the notion of *reflection* from your own qualifying studies, your practice experience and your work to facilitate effective reflection with learners. Thus, as you read through the extracts in Box 7.2, which summarise a way of interpreting how reflection and reflective learning might be understood, you could consider how they mirror the meanings you attribute to the term *reflection* when working with learners.

> ## Box 7.2: Literature summary – extracts from Moon (2004: 80–84)
>
> . . . a common sense view of reflection can be stated as follows:
>
> > Reflection is a form of mental processing – like a form of thinking – that we may use to fulfil a purpose or to achieve some anticipated outcome or we may simple 'be reflective' and then an outcome can be unexpected. Reflection is applied to relatively complicated, ill-structured ideas for which there is not an obvious solution and is largely based on the further processing of knowledge and understanding that we already possess.
> >
> > (Based on, but extending the definition in Moon, 1999)
>
> . . ..we can add to the common-sense definition of reflection as follows:
>
> > Reflection/reflective learning or reflective writing in the academic context, is also likely to involve a conscious and stated purpose for the reflection, with an outcome specified in terms of learning, action or clarification. It may be preceded by a description of the purpose and/or the subject matter of the reflection. The process and outcome of reflective work are most likely to be in the represented (e.g., written) form, to be seen by others and to be assessed. All of these factors can influence its nature and quality.

In these short excerpts from Moon's work, it is clear that whatever terminology is chosen, the processes of reflection are fundamentally associated with the acquisition of knowledge and understanding. Alongside this, 'the concept of "reflexivity" has become increasingly significant in social work literature in relation to social work education, theory and practice' (D'Cruz et al., 2007: 73). However, in their review of the literature on the concept of *reflexivity*, D'Cruz et al. concede that there is little agreement or precision about what the term means and how reflexivity is 'played out' in practice. In Box 7.3 there is an extract from D'Cruz et al.'s article which is a very brief summary of their typology of three different variations of meaning of *reflexivity* identified in their literature review. Note though, that this is only one paragraph from a 17-page article, so it cannot give a full representation of the complexity that the authors critique – it is recommended that you source and read the full article to fully appreciate their findings.

Following extensive research of the relevant literature, D'Cruz et al. (2007) also discuss the concepts of *reflection* and *critical reflection*, alongside the complexities of *reflexivity*. Gardner (2006: 144) tells us that 'critical reflection as a theory and a process unsettles dominant thinking and unquestioned beliefs, which can lead to greater clarity about underlying assumptions and values'. Potentially the most helpful definitional contribution, also cited by D'Cruz et al., is provided by Jan Fook who, referring to reflexivity in research, offers clarity in making distinctions between some of these terms.

> *Reflectivity seems in this sense to refer more to a process of reflecting upon practice, whereas reflexivity in the latter sense refers more to a stance of being able to locate oneself in the picture, to appreciate how one's own self influences the research act*
>
> (Fook, 1999, cited in Fook, 2002: 43 emphasis in original)

Box 7.3: Literature summary – extract from D'Cruz et al. (2007: 75)

In presenting different meanings of the concept of reflexivity in the following discussion, we have separated them into three categories that we have described as variations. Within the three variations, there are subtleties and nuances of meaning which we explore through the differences and the articulations between them.

The first variation regards reflexivity as an individual's considered response to an immediate context and making choices for further direction. This variation is concerned with the ability of individuals to process information and create knowledge to guide life choices, and has implications for both the role of social workers and the relationships between social workers and clients. The second variation defines reflexivity as an individual's self-critical approach that questions how knowledge is generated and, further, how relations of power operate in this process. The third variation is concerned with the part that emotion plays in social work practice.

Reflectivity and reflexivity, can be shown, therefore to have significant value for you as a practice educator and experienced practitioner, and for the learners you support. It is likely that the learners you are working with are required to keep a reflective diary or journal providing reflective commentaries on their practice. It may be some time since you last kept such reflective records, but it is acknowledged good practice for all practitioners to record reflections that inform their developing practice, not only those who are undertaking formal programmes of learning. Moon (2004) offers many helpful suggestions of ways in which reflective writing can be developed to ensure it is effective in supporting and enhancing the depth of your continued learning. Further to this Crawford (2006: 141) uses Kolb's (1984) model of experiential learning to illustrate some examples of reflective activities that can be associated with different stages in the learning cycle. This is reproduced in Figure 7.1.

So far in this section we have considered how reflective and reflexive practices are defined, and looked at some of the ways within practice education that you might develop these approaches. To start with, the activity below asks you to think about the different methods and processes that help you to evaluate your work in enabling the learning and development of others.

ACTIVITY

As a practice educator how do you appraise your own practice? Make some notes in response to the questions below:

How do you know you are doing a good job – that the way in which you approach things is effective?

What strategies do you have to evaluate your efforts?

Where do you gather information from to inform your self-appraisal? Is this formal or informal?

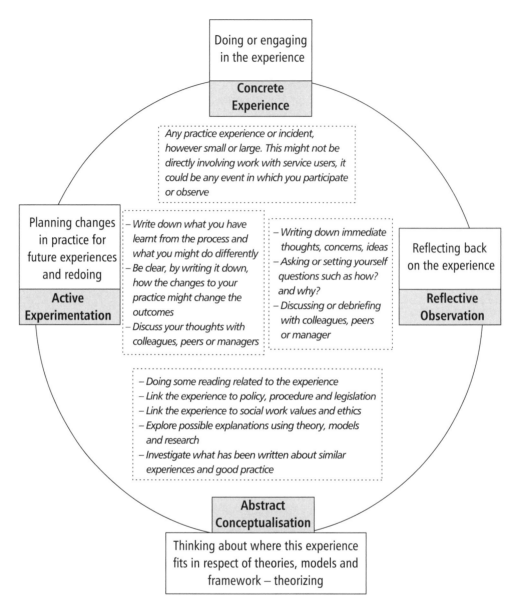

Figure 7.1: Examples of practical reflective practice activities associated with Kolb's experiential learning cycle

Source: Crawford (2006: 141)

There are many ways in which you might evaluate your work as a practice educator, perhaps including formal organisational processes of supervision and regular line-manager appraisal, as well as more informal approaches, for example, personal reflections on practice as a form of self-appraisal. A further source of feedback on practice is comments from the learner/s that you work with and, potentially, peer observations of your practice, perhaps undertaking a supervision session or learning activity with a learner in practice. As an extension of this exercise think about ways in which you could record your self-appraisal and reflections, as such records would provide a further mechanism for future evaluation of further development.

The next reflective activity is a suggested way of 'reflecting-*before-action*' that you would thus use as you prepare for a particular episode of practice with a learner. Try the reflective activity below and see whether it is a helpful approach for you.

ACTIVITY

This is an activity that may help you reflect on and prepare for working with a learner in practice, through reflective thinking dialogue.

Think about a particular situation in your practice as an educator, which is complex or requires certain potentially contentious decisions to be made. If you are not able to think of such a case, then build up an imaginary situation in your mind. Next, consider that you are planning to go into a practice supervision session with your own supervisor, whose knowledge you respect and whose views/reflections you always find very helpful and inspiring.

Develop the dialogue that may take place. This is almost like role-playing the scenario through, but in your imagination. Think through and 'listen' for the sorts of responses, ideas, knowledge and direction that might come from your supervisor. Frame your questions and concerns about the practice education situation and then frame the responses. This activity may be more effective for your reflection on practice if you verbalise – and perhaps record or write down the dialogue as you might perceive it.

(adapted from Moon, 2004: 212)

The activity is often particularly helpful if you find the concept of reflection difficult to perceive. This notion of 'role-playing' in the imagination enables some people to enter a form of reflective mode in their minds. Of course, the responses that you might think your supervisor would provide, are actually your own reflections and ideas, but somehow they are given credibility and credence through this activity.

Finally, for this section of your reading, there is one more reflective activity that you could try. This activity could be usefully adapted for the learners you work with to think through.

ACTIVITY

If you accept that 'critical reflection . . . unsettles dominant thinking and unquestioned beliefs, which can lead to greater clarity about underlying assumptions and values' (Gardner 2006: 144), what are the questions that, as a practitioner and educator, you need to be pondering on? Think about yourself as you work in practice with learners and make a list of some reflective questions that you could use to help you become more critical about your own practice. These might be questions that you muse on in your own head, that you use to frame a reflective diary or that are useful for discussions with colleagues, the learners you work with or your supervisor.

You may have developed some very specific questions in response to this activity, perhaps particular questions about a particular situation that you are working with. However, I think it is possible to have some key questions, like a reflective tool-kit that you can refer to, that will prompt or stimulate your 'reflective juices' in practice! Here are some examples that I thought of in response to this activity – I am sure there are many more that you may have thought of;

- Why do we (or am I) working with this learner in this way?

- Are there other ways of enabling and facilitating this learner's development?

- What is my experience (or that of other practice educators) of working with similar situations previously? What can we (I) learn from this?

- What knowledge, research or theory underpins this practice? Where is it? Who developed it? When was it developed and how?

- Is this practice informed by professional values and the principles of anti-oppressive practice – if so, can I articulate, describe and locate those values and principles?

- Is there a formal theory of learning or a body of knowledge that I should explicitly draw upon for this area of practice education?

- How have I incorporated the views, wishes, experiences of the learners I work with in determining my approach to this practice? Additionally, how have the views of service users and carers contributed to or influenced this practice?

- Are there any particular issues about the context of my work as a practice educator; the time, the environment, the individuals that I need to consider?

- If I try to take another perspective on this (for example, the learner's my manager's, a service user's or a colleague's) would I approach it differently?

- How do I feel about this practice? What emotions, concerns, anxieties does it give rise to for me?

- Is there other information, viewpoints, ideas, opinions, knowledge or details that I should consider?

The important issue here, is not the detail of the questions, but that you develop for yourself, a 'culture of inquiring about' or 'researching practice' (Gardner, 2006: 153) and are prepared to ask 'questions about what is happening at a deeper level and what this might mean for processes and outcomes' (2006: 153).

How do I continue to develop as a knowledge-informed practice educator?

Throughout this book you have been presented with a range of different knowledge, used to inform practice education in social work. You have been encouraged and assisted to link this knowledge, the models, theories and research to your practice as an educator, whilst also critically evaluating the different data by questioning, making comparisons, looking for links to other literature and overall taking a critical viewpoint. It is these approaches to knowledge, or evidence for practice, that you are encouraged to develop and maintain.

ACTIVITY

Reflect back upon your learning across this book and, perhaps taking one chapter at a time, draw out the knowledge, theories, research and literature that particularly resonates with your practice in enabling learners.

- *As a practice educator, which particular areas of knowledge inform your practice?*
- *Which areas are of less relevance to your practice as an educator?*
- *In what ways do they make a difference to your work with learners?*

It is likely that all of the knowledge evidence produced in this book is relevant to your particular work as a practice educator, to some extent. It is important, though, that you are able to articulate the actual ways in which this learning and the knowledge base influence what you do in practice.

There is a lively and ongoing debate in academic literature about knowledge- (or evidence-) based practice and whether it is a science or an art. So, for example, quantitative research is given more status and credibility as it is conceived of as being scientific – in the perceived 'hierarchy of knowledge' (McLaughlin 2007: 86). Qualitative studies, which reflect views, experiences and opinions, are seen as being less valued and less rigorous. Smith (2004: 15) confirms this when he states that 'science promises what managers long for: control, certainty, predictability and an end to ignorance and doubt'. He goes on, however, to caution that such certainty is not possible in the real world, and that 'the social world is inherently unpredictable and uncertain (2004: 15). Thus the knowledge base for social work practice and social work education can inform, influence and guide practice, but must always be set in the context of the individual situation (be it that of the service user or the learner), which is where the 'art' of social work, the skills, judgement and practice experience become significant in the integration of knowledge and practice. In an article in the *British Journal of Social Work*, Taylor and White (2006) argue that, for social work practice, the skill of questioning the knowledge base, working through decisions and reasoning are all an integral part of making judgements in conditions of uncertainty. They suggest that, for example, new assessment processes in social work (and similarly in assessing social work practice as part of assessing learning) are all part of a drive to make practice more 'scientific' and that such moves towards 'technical-rational applications of knowledge to practice' result in knowledge becoming 'increasingly synonymous with mere information' (2006: 950). Hence Taylor and White (2006: 950) conclude that we 'need to place much greater emphasis on the critical evaluation of how research and theory get invoked in practice' – which links to the activity (see Activity box: 'Reflect back on your learning across this book …') that you have undertaken earlier.

At the outset of this chapter, you read about some of the requirements for continuing professional development in social work practice, and the place of formal, tangible, measurable learning was contrasted with the value of more tacit forms of learning.

Tacit knowledge development, such as that which happens through reflection and reflexive practice, developing practice wisdom through the experience and skill of 'doing' social work have a valid place in professional development. However, such knowledge is not tangible, not easily quantified or articulated, and therefore becomes questioned and challenged. O'Sullivan (2005: 222) conceptualised practice wisdom as consistent with 'critical, accountable and knowledge-based practice' but noted that practice wisdom and knowledge acquired through informal, tacit processes can be perceived as 'unreliable, personal, idiosyncratic knowledge built up through practice experience'. Similarly, Brechin (2000: 41) connects knowledge of evidence-based practice with critical practice, seeing the two together as 'increasingly forming a basis' for professional development.

Corby (2006: 158) states that 'the prevailing view of social work practice held by key policy-makers is that it is a largely reactive activity and one that is not particularly well informed by research evidence'. Corby also cites research which demonstrates that 'social workers do not spend much time discussing research in supervision and that an appreciable minority do not read about research at all (because of lack of time)' (Sheldon and Chilvers, 2002 cited in Corby, 2006: 158). Such findings clearly add to the debate about whether knowledge-based practice is 'panacea or pretence'. However, conversely, in reviewing how research is applied to social care, Walter et al. (2004: 13) state that 'a theme that recurs throughout all the studies is of a commitment to and belief in the importance and value of research for improving social care practice' and that 'there are a lot of people actively involved in many, wide-ranging activities aimed at increasing research use in social care'.

What strategies and support processes are available to support me in managing my role and responsibilities as a practice educator?

Throughout this book you have examined strategies, practical ideas and approaches that may help you support the practice learning of others. It is also important, however, that you consider the strategies and processes that are available to support you in your role as a practice educator. Your concerns and needs for guidance or support in the practice learning situation may often be very similar to those of the learners you work with, being likely to centre on issues such as managing a number of roles in practice and a busy workload, and/or managing difficult, unpleasant or complex situations that involve the learners you are supporting.

It is widely acknowledged that 'an excessive workload is counterproductive, in so far as it can lead to less being achieved, rather than more' (Thompson, 2006: 110). This may be nothing new to you, but it is a significant statement that you should have in your mind as you consider your own responsibilities in the workplace and those of the learners you support.

> ## Box 7.4: Literature summary – Clutterbuck (2001) cited in Thompson (2006: 109)
>
> It's a true but sad reflection on the way that we organise work that very few people come to work to think. In seminar after seminar, around the developed and increasingly in the developing world too, I find that people do their real thinking out of office hours, in the car, on the train, or in the period between going to bed and going to sleep. Working time and, to a large extent, non-working time is primarily about doing. Top management often reinforces this view by expecting people to be seen to work. Putting one's feet on the desk and relaxing is not perceived as a constructive activity . . . Yet all the evidence we have is that reflective space – time to think deeply and in a focused way – is critical to effective working. Instead of back-to-back meetings, companies can encourage people to build buffer periods in which they can reflect on what they have just done and what they want to achieve from the next meeting. Practical experience shows that people who manage their time in this way accomplish far more, more quickly. Decisions taken in meetings where participants have thought about what they want to say, hear and achieve, are clearer and achieved in much shorter time.

Again, the 'picture painted' by the extract in Box 7.4 may be nothing new to you, it may have made you smile, and it is also very likely that much of this resonated for you in your own practice. So, what can be done about it? Thompson (2006) suggests four principles of time and workload management; he also offers four sets of skills that support those principles. These have been adapted and reproduced in Figure 7.2 to reflect some strategies that you might consider employing to manage your workload and time more effectively.

ACTIVITY

Consider the strategies in the Figure 7.2. Work through each one and reflect upon the extent to which you already use these strategies and skills in your work. Try to list some actual examples where you have effectively used these strategies, as well as some points how and you might further develop these skills. Are there other skills or strategies that you would add here?

In this activity, and so far in this section, we have been focusing on what you can do, individually, to improve how you manage the different roles you undertake in practice and your busy workload. As you considered the latter part of this activity, you may have thought about strategies or processes that involve support mechanisms or other individuals in your workplace, and it is to these that we now turn, considering, for example: supervision; using a mentor; using your manager; and working with others who support practice learning.

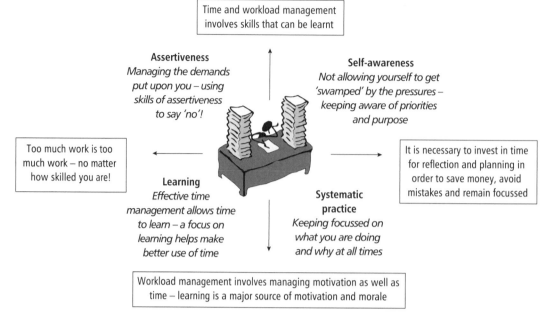

Figure 7.2 content:

Time and workload management involves skills that can be learnt

Assertiveness
Managing the demands put upon you – using skills of assertiveness to say 'no'!

Self-awareness
Not allowing yourself to get 'swamped' by the pressures – keeping aware of priorities and purpose

Too much work is too much work – no matter how skilled you are!

It is necessary to invest in time for reflection and planning in order to save money, avoid mistakes and remain focussed

Learning
Effective time management allows time to learn – a focus on learning helps make better use of time

Systematic practice
Keeping focussed on what you are doing and why at all times

Workload management involves managing motivation as well as time – learning is a major source of motivation and morale

Figure 7.2: Strategies and skills for managing time and workload

Source: Adapted and developed from Thompson (2006: 107–8)

In professional social work practice *supervision* exists to support you and learners working in practice. Supervision, with its regular meetings between practitioner and supervisor and agendas focused on the work of the individual, provides a process that has a range of functions: supportive, educative and managerial. The educative/formative function is about 'developing the skills, understanding and abilities' of staff (Statham, 2004: 90). Statham goes on to state that: 'this emphasises the need for reflection on practice to be very much part of the supervision encounter. . . . Supervision uses reflection on direct practice as a method for professional learning' (2004: 90). This is an example of supportive workplace interaction that also values reflective learning and practice. Additionally, in respect of formal processes that may exist in your workplace, you could reflect upon how procedures that are set up to appraise performance (sometimes called 'employee develop-ment reviews' or 'appraisal schemes'), for example, can be supportive not only of your continuing development needs, but also in prioritising the variety of roles and responsibilities that you hold.

Elsewhere in this book you have considered the role of supervision in supporting practice learning. However, you should also consider how the supervisory process, your manager and potentially a mentor too, can support you in your role as a practice educator. Furthermore, you may have a named link-person who represents the institution or agency that is supporting the learner with their academic programme; if this applies to your role, you should also plan for how you work with them and make use of the type of support that they may be able to offer you. In considering how you can be supported by others in your role as a practice educator, you should contemplate the strengths of collegiate working with practice educators and team colleagues.

How can my needs for support and learning be met within my networks of colleagues and other practice educators?

Being alive as human beings means that we are constantly engaged in the pursuit of enterprises of all kinds, from ensuring our physical survival to seeking the most lofty pleasures. As we define these enterprises and engage in their pursuit together, we interact with each other and with the world and we turn our relations with each other and with the world accordingly. In other words, we learn.

Over time, this collective learning results in practices that reflect both the pursuit of our enterprises and the attendant social relations. These practices are thus the property of a kind of community created over time by the sustained pursuit of a shared enterprise. It makes sense, therefore, to call these kinds of communities communities of practice.

(Wenger, 1998: 45)

Given the heading of this section, perhaps a good starting point is to achieve clarity about your professional working networks or *communities of practice* – who is within in them and what they are. Therefore, as a precursor to your reading on this section undertake this first activity.

ACTIVITY

It is highly likely that in a similar way to holding a number of roles in your professional life, you are also part of a number of networks. Think about your daily practice activities and make a list of the networks that you are part of.

It is not possible for us to know the details of your individual practice or the networks that your work in. However, these may include very small local networks through to some larger national networks, for example you may have listed some of the following (realistically this list could be endless, so these are just some possibilities!):

- Your immediate social work practice team;
- A multi-disciplinary or interprofessional team;
- A small group of practitioners that specialise in a particular area, either geographically or in terms of specialist practice, or sometimes both; for example a group of Approved Social Workers who form a local network and meet regularly to discuss dilemmas and good practice;
- A multi-agency team – one that comes together to consider a particular practice issue, for example local services for people with learning difficulties or child protection issues; or a team that comes together to consider particular complex decisions in working with an individual, their family and carers;
- A network of practice educators;

- Collectively, the individuals who work for your agency, or employer – who may, of course, not all be engaged in social work or social care activities;

- A group of practitioner students undertaking post-qualifying education;

- A national employees body or union such as the British Association of Social Workers.

Realistically, then, at any one time, you could be part of numerous *communities of practice*. Wenger (1998: 127) develops the notion of 'constellations of interconnected practices' which may be helpful in understanding the complexities and interrelations of such networks. As we have seen earlier, *communities of practice* are seen as places of *collective learning* and in this book you have read about social learning theory. Guile and Young address the concept of learning as a 'relational process that is generated socially' through the learner's participation in a range of interrelationships (2002: 153), and go on to explore existing practices and models to show ways in which they might be integrated and developed to address contemporary concerns about the 'separation of formal and informal learning' (2002: 158). The authors ground their ideas in Vygotsky's Zone of Proximal Development (ZPD) and more recent expansions of that work by Cole, by Lave and Wenger and by Engeström (cited in Guile and Young, 2002: 151–4). The ZPD is the potential for further learning which is realised through analytical work with others or under guidance. Hence, Guile and Young's proposition, that learning is a social process that can occur in different situations through a practical problem-solving approach, can be seen to be supported by a Vygotskian perspective on learning. In this way, an inclusive explanation of learning that takes account of cultural and social difference and a variety of learning contexts is provided. We see here, then, the overt connection between working in teams and networks, and the opportunity for learning and development for individuals.

Thus whilst, earlier in this chapter, you explored the potential for reflection and reflexivity to support your own development, with such reflections potentially challenging tacit understanding, we might question how this can be effective without interaction and the perspectives, guidance and advice of others. In addition, as you have read about learning within *communities of practice* you may have felt that some of the possible consequences for individuals' professional development of working within the complexities of many integrated and changing *communities of practice*, need further consideration; for example, where power differentials might compound discriminatory practices which may already exist, such as disablism, ageism, racism or sexism, or where poor practices may be embedded in the *community of practice*.

Despite the potential critique, however, as a practitioner and practice educator your support and continuing professional development needs will largely be met within the socially situated learning environment of the practice workplace.

ACTIVITY

If learning and support for learning can be achieved through a process of engagement in shared practice within communities of practice, how is this manifested in your own practice? In what ways do you gain support or develop your learning through the networks and communities of practice of which you are a member?

You have already identified that you belong to and interact with a number of *communities of practice*, and it is acknowledged that within these social learning structures you can disseminate, share and reflect upon your own learning. For example, as you have worked through the learning in this book, you could find ways of sharing your learning or discussing your thoughts with colleagues, this could be with the learners you are supporting, other post-qualifying learners, your own supervisor or colleagues.

You may be part of a community of practice educators within which you can share and develop knowledge about practice in supporting learners. If such a network does not operate in your area, you could consider setting one up. Such a network would have similar features to those of *Teaching Circles*, which are 'semi-formal meetings designed to promote scholarship about teaching, enhance teaching practice and provide a forum for professional development' (Pearson, 2002: 9). Whilst Pearson describes teaching circles for part-time lecturers, the process and possibilities are transferable to meet the needs of practice educators, as the teaching circles focus on 'teaching practice . . . and . . . relied heavily on learning through peer discussion' (2002: 9).

Where do I go from here?

We hope that you have found the content of this book stimulating and motivating – within it there have been many suggestions for how you can take your own learning forward in such a way that it will support you personally and professionally, but will also enhance your work with other learners. Here are just a few additional examples of ways in which you can continue your learning beyond the content and activities of this text.

Extending your reading and studying further

Throughout the book, we have recommended texts, models, theories, journal articles and research that you might explore to extend your understanding of particular areas of practice education. There is a 'Further reading' section at the end of each chapter too. It is recommended that you select and read around the areas that are of interest and particular relevance to your practice, but do so in a systematic way, keeping bibliographic records and personal notes on your learning and progress.

Undertaking or participating in research into practice education

Often practice educators have ideas or hypotheses about how some area of practice learning might work better, or might be experienced by those involved. As part of your professional development and to increase your understanding about your own practice as an educator, you could consider investigating a discrete area of practice that interests you. The potential for practitioner research in social care may be underdeveloped (Shaw and Lishman, 1999; Statham, 2004), but it remains a valued method of learning and continuing professional development. If you are studying within the post-qualifying framework for social work, it is likely that your programme of study will include some element of research or research methodology. You should note that practitioner research does not have to be large-scale, grand or involve large numbers of respondents. It is also

very possible to join together with other practice educators, in a *community of practice*, to carry out a small-scale research project. Your employing agency and the education provider that you work with are likely to be very interested in any research ideas or proposals that you put forward.

Developing clarity about your professional aspirations

Crawford (2006: 145) states 'that the process of thinking through and planning your short, medium and long-term professional goals can be very helpful in assisting you to decide upon the focus of your learning and development activities'. It is not necessary for all practitioners to be highly ambitious in terms of career progression, but all practitioners, in line with responsibilities for continuing professional development, will have aims and objectives related to their practice.

ACTIVITY

As a practice educator, what are your professional developmental aims? Make a list of the areas in which you want to learn more and develop professionally in respect of your practice with learners. Then consider how you might achieve these aims, and what you need in order to achieve them.

This activity helps you to begin to map out a future learning pathway, reflecting on the skills and knowledge you already have and looking forward to those you need to acquire and develop. Your work on this activity might mirror, or supplement, thinking that you have undertaken as part of a 'training needs analysis' exercise, or an 'appraisal' or 'staff development' process. As such, it might be a useful activity to share with your supervisor, manager or, if you are engaged in post-qualifying learning, with your tutor.

Conclusion

Throughout this book you have been developing your knowledge and skills about your role as a practice educator, facilitating learning, assessing, supporting and mentoring learners in practice. However, the focus in this chapter has been more inwardly reflective, encouraging you to think about what this means for you, your own developing practice and the support that you may need. Effectively, many of the concepts explored in this chapter are mirrored in earlier chapters; however, this chapter has changed the emphasis from your work with others, to your reflections about your own needs. Thus, for example, you have looked at reflection and reflexivity; knowledge-informed practice; and, finally, strategies and processes for support, including supervision and working in communities of practice, as different approaches to thinking about your own support and development needs. Any or all of these may be beneficial to you and your practice as an educator at different points in time.

FURTHER READING

Moon, J.A. (2004) *A Handbook of Reflective and Experiential Learning: Theory and Practice*. London: RoutledgeFalmer.

This book provides an accessible text that explores how knowledge is acquired and learning takes place through experience and reflection. The final section of the book may be of particular interest for you as a practice educator as the author provides a range of reflective activities and guidance in the process of writing reflectively, which you may want to use with the learners you support.

Thompson, N. (2006) *Promoting Workplace Learning*. Bristol: Policy Press.

Whilst this text is not promoted as being specifically about practice learning in the helping professions, it does develop an earlier work by the same author that focuses on practice learning in social work. The book is a useful resource for you as a practice educator as it considers the wider aspects of learning in the workplace and within its eight chapters covers a comprehensive range of issues related to the development of a learning culture.

Wenger, E. (1998) *Communities of Practice: Learning, Meaning, and Identity*. Cambridge: Cambridge University Press.

If the discussion in this chapter about learning and developing in *communities of practice* sparked your interest, then this text provides a good foundation for your reading on the topic. There are other, later books by this author and others related to this approach, however, in this text, the influential theory is thoroughly explored and, as the title suggests, given meaning within the context of learning in practice.

Summary

As we have sought to highlight throughout this book, practice educators have a critical role to play in developing students' practice, working alongside academic institutions and teaching professionals in supporting the transfer and development of learning in practice. Service users and carers should be at the heart of this learning: to ensure they receive high-quality, best practice based on sound knowledge and a sound theoretical base, using highly skilled activities, demonstrating a professional value base and demonstrating anti-oppressive practice in action. Service users and carers should inform and contribute to the learning and development of the student. For the student and the practice educator, demonstrating critical reflection in and on their practice is essential.

Practice is complex, 'messy' and unpredictable. The complexity of social work practice involves the combination of multiple roles and tasks. In day-to-day practice social workers are frequently dealing with situations where there is tension between people's interactions and the 'social' world. The distinctiveness of social work is in working 'holistically' with different people in different situations; professional practice is developed through the capacity to select and combine different approaches and multiple roles to meet each unique situation. Empowerment and emancipation of service users is essential; this must be balanced with appropriate support and protection of vulnerable people. As a practice educator you will be working with the student to transfer their learning from the academic institution, and further developing their knowledge, skills and understanding to make sense of their professional roles and responsibilities as a social worker. Identifying and clarifying individual and cultural values will help the student to identify their starting point in developing their professional values and beliefs in action within their own practice. This will also contribute to the wider aims of the profession. Competence is a central concept of contemporary social work requirements, which develop over time as part of the continuous cycle of learning.

The practice educator is central to creating the learning experience for the student. Through application of theories and processes that support learning you are applying frameworks and processes to support students in developing their practice. You are also empowering them to identify and take control of their own learning. Providing structured learning and teaching activities supports students' development; in addition, practice educators encourage students to identify learning opportunities and learn for themselves. An essential feature of the practice placement will be your role in assessing the student's competence as a learning social worker. Assessment is vital to any teaching and learning. It is not simple. Assessment is learning. The methods and process of assessment should be made clear to the student and their contribution identified. Essentially you should be identifying the strengths and areas for development in and with the student, identifying gaps in knowledge or skills and putting in place teaching strategies to develop these. Formative assessment will support and provide feedback to the student on their progress and performance. Any assessment should reflect the student's achievement and provide guidance for the future. Supervision provides a forum for enhancing and developing practice, and for development, assessment and reflection by the student. Supervision also provides a forum for the development of an effective working relationship with the student and for power-sharing within existing power structures. It is a crucial forum for promoting critical reflection on practice.

Taking on a student involves prior planning across the placement, for example, preparing the team and identifying learning opportunities; negotiating with the academic institution to take a suitable student; meeting and connecting with the student prior to the start of the placement. This involves preparing a practice curriculum, ensuring the student receives an induction, and constructing a learning agreement between the student, you and the academic institution. You need to maintain learning, development and support throughout the placement, as well as reviewing progress and development of the student and of your own practice as a practice educator. Planning and support is also necessary around the ending of the placement and the completion of the relevant tasks; for example, the student's work; the work that the student undertakes as part of the assessment of their practice; and your own assessment of the student's competence. This will include supporting the student to identify future learning needs. As the student leaves, you need to critically reflect on your own performance and learning in working with the student, and the implications for your own practice and your practice as a practice educator.

Your own preparation and reflection on your 'readiness' to support a student is essential. This may involve reviewing your own approach to practice with service users; the knowledge, theories and skills you use in practice; the professional values you draw on; and the demonstration of your commitment to anti-oppressive and anti-discriminatory practice. You will need to consider your readiness to work with another; this involves practical aspects, such as time and commitment, including the commitment of your team and your manager to taking a student. It also means thinking about your engagement with 'another' in developing and forming a relationship that supports their personal and professional development. This may involve reviewing and developing your knowledge and skills to support learning, teaching and the development of a learner 'in training'. A commitment to developing your knowledge and skills through undertaking a professional programme of learning in relation to practice education will significantly enhance your practice.

Partnership with others in developing and managing learning opportunities is essential. Working in partnership with the student involves such things as identifying their learning and development needs through the process of supervision. It also involves working with the university tutor and academic institution as partners in the three-way relationship between the student, practice educator and tutor; and partnership with service users and carers in the learning and development of the student, and in support of the assessment of the student, for example through direct feedback about the student's involvement with them. You will also be working with other colleagues, the team and other professionals as partners in enhancing teaching and learning opportunities and to support the development of the student.

Supporting a student's learning in practice requires an integrated approach that makes practice learning 'everybody's business' (Practice Learning Taskforce, 2003). This is more likely to be achieved, it is argued, within a culture of 'learning organisations' with a 'team approach' to students on placement. Learning organisations, according to Senge (1990) are those that excel at tapping people's commitment to and capacity for learning. Learning organisations have systems and processes in place to support learning and have a culture within which learning is embedded, a 'way of life'. Learning organisations cope with change and the need for continual improvement as they comprise 'a group of people continually enhancing their capacity to create what they want to create' (Senge, 1991: 42). Your contribution to the 'learning organisation' is demonstrated in your commitment to supporting the development of the student as a professional practitioner, as well as your contribution to the learning of the team and organisation. Essentially it is also reflected in your own critical reflection on your practice as a social worker and as a practice educator, especially as 'the continuous testing of experience, and the trans-formation of that experience into knowledge' (Senge, 1991: 49).

For the student undertaking their learning in practice as a significant proportion of their qualification programme, practice should be recognised as contributing to their learning as part of their commitment to continuous learning and development throughout their professional lives. As a practice educator you will be modelling this and acting as an exemplar, demonstrating your own commitment to continually developing and using the skills of critical reflection within your practice. Supporting and developing others takes time. Working as a practice educator you make a significant contribution to the develop-ment and maintenance of the profession of social work. You are also contributing to the learning of the team and organisation. You are part of the wider community of practice educators supporting students. Through your work as a practice educator you are demonstrating your own commitment to learning and professional development as a life-long process.

Appendix: Guidance on the Assessment of Practice in the Workplace

Foreword

This document was developed in the context of a number of strategic changes within the field of social work and social care education and training, which have considerable relevance for work based assessment.

These changes are one part of major legislative reforms intended to raise the standard and consistency of services. The essential links between effective work-based assessment, a competent workforce and quality of service provision have never been so clearly articulated in social care service provision and education and training policies.

We hope that this guidance will prove to be a useful tool for those responsible for developing work based assessment strategies within organisations and for individual practitioners' career development.

Mike Wardle
Director of Standards and Regulation
GSCC

Andrea Rowe
Chief Executive
Topss

Introduction

1   This guidance for work-based assessors is intended to put in place a framework of generic statements or benchmarks which define and describe the core activities involved in assessing the practice of others, irrespective of the purpose of the assessment. It is designed to be used by training and education providers to identify the competence of individuals to assess candidates' practice. It can also be used for workforce development purposes to identify the competence required by those involved in performance appraisal and confirmation of continuing role competence for registration and continuing professional development (CPD) purposes. It will therefore be of particular interest to those involved in work-based assessment in relation to education and training, but may also have relevance to managers in performance assessment and the analysis of training and development needs.

2   The statements are grouped in three domains:

- The organisation of opportunities for the demonstration of assessed competence in practice

- Enable learning and professional development in practice; and

- Manage the assessment of learners in practice.

Background

3   This guidance has been developed by a project group from the General Social Care Council (GSSC), the new social care workforce and training regulator in England, and Topss England, the former national training organisation for social care. The first stage of the project, undertaken in 2000, was a consultation exercise conducted by a questionnaire sent to all providers of approved social work training. There was a 50 per cent response rate. The general messages given in response to the questionnaire were:

- Many providers had concerns about the variability of practice assessment and the criteria for the role of practice assessor;

- Most providers recognised that work-based assessment should be a core function of social care workers and other professionals and an essential component of continuous professional development;

- Most providers agreed that there should be standard 'requirements' for assessors across the continuum of training from National Vocational Qualifications (NVQ) to the Advanced Award in Social Work (AASW);

- Many providers felt that it would be helpful to have National Occupational Standards for work-based assessment; and

- Many providers felt that the requirements for the Practice Teaching Award (PTA) should be reviewed, with specific mention of the current level of post–qualifying (PQSW) professional credits.

4   By the time that this consultation was completed the following developments were underway:

- The National Training Organisation for Employment was undertaking a review of the Training and Development National Occupational Standards and related qualifications;

- Topss England had finalised 'Modernising the Social Care Workforce', the first training strategy for the social care sector. It was clear from this report that in order to meet the aspiration of all social care agencies to become learning organisations, the function of work-based assessment was to be integrated into the role of social care workers, social workers and their managers; and

- The Department of Health had initiated projects associated with the reform of social work education and training. The future needs and requirements for practice and work-based learning were to be considered as part of the reform agenda.

5   In response to these developments, the GSCC/Topss England work-based assessment project group agreed to work specifically on the areas of competence which could be identified as key to the role of a work-based assessor in order to provide guidance to providers of education and training.

6   Draft guidance on the competence required for the task of assessing practice in the workplace was developed from a range of other professions' standards and qualifications for practice assessors and from the draft Learning and Development national occupational standards. A second consultation exercise was conducted on this draft guidance with GSCC-approved post-qualifying (PQ) training providers. Three well-attended workshops were held to discuss both the general approach and the detail of the draft guidance and written responses were received from individuals and organisations such as the National Organisation for Practice Teaching (NOPT). The consultation process revealed some key themes that have been reflected in the guidance:

- A recognition of the importance of adult learning theories in the assessment process;

- Multiple ownership of the assessment process and role differentiation;

- Engagement with learners as active participants and recognition of their rights, needs, entitlements and obligations; and

- Participation in assessment quality assurance systems which contribute to training and development strategies.

7   Work-based assessment of competence in practice is neither new nor specific to social care. Regulatory, awarding and professional bodies, educational institutions, employers and other organisations have long experience of developing this type of education and training provision. Typically, it makes explicit links between occupational standards, individuals' performance, learning programmes and evidence-based assessment of practice. It may be certificated, leading to vocational, academic and professional qualifications. NVQs in social care, qualifying social work training, probation officer training, nursing and midwifery pre-qualifying training, and post-qualifying or professional training in health and social work, to name but a few, all require assessment of the learner in practice in the workplace.

8   Participants in the consultation process, many of whom have developed inter-professional courses and other vocational training, were able to draw upon wider perspectives to help inform the debate. These included:

- the Employment National Training Organisation's review of 'The Learning and Development and Assessment and Verification' national occupational standards (2002);

- existing National Occupational Standards related to work based assessment, developing others and continuing professional development;

- the Nursing and Midwifery Council's 'Revised standards for the preparation of teachers of nursing and midwifery' (2001); and

- the Institute of Learning and Teaching's knowledge base and six professional requirements for membership.

9 The range of assessor activities described in this guidance has been developed with the benefit of the particular experience and practice wisdom of post-qualifying social work training providers. There is a clear consonance with models of assessment in other sectors, reinforcing the belief that there is a generic core activity amenable to description. To illustrate the point, the links between the statements set out in this guidance and a number of National Occupational Standards and professional requirements are shown in annex 1.

10 The guidance does not replace existing qualifications, schemes and awards which involve learning about assessment, or the requirements already in place that establish criteria for the suitability of assessors. It will enable stakeholders to identify the extent to which work-based assessors are able to provide evidence of suitability for the assessment task irrespective of the context and specific knowledge-base required to assess learners' practice. For some assessment purposes, assessors may also have to provide evidence of occupational and/or professional competence in the area of social care work being assessed.

11 Programme providers, educational institutions and employers may use the statements to develop systems for the accreditation of prior learning, training programmes, and modules of certificated learning in assessment to complement the wide range of existing programmes and awards. The links with National Occupational Standards and other professional requirements will enable managers, learners and assessors to identify appropriate units across the range of assessment levels, functions and roles, and may inform human resource planning to meet individual and organisational requirements. The guidance therefore offers a benchmark to employers to widen their pool of workers who could be considered for the task of work-based assessment.

Choice of language

12 One of the most confusing aspects this guidance acknowledges is terminology. For example, we have consciously chosen the term 'work-based assessor', rather than practice teacher, practice assessor, practice educator, practice tutor, on-site or off-site supervisor. It implies no specific status, level or range of assessment activities or linkages to particular types of education or training. It seeks to capture the essence of the generic assessment task.

13 The choice of the term 'learner' to describe the person being assessed is derived from the same debate. Rather than using definitions such as students, candidates, or trainees to describe people who may well be employees in practice, 'learner' is used to describe anyone undergoing work-based assessment in order to demonstrate learning outcomes that confirm and validate standards of practice competence. In that role they are participants in the learning and development cycle.

14 It is through work-based assessment that the learning achieved is demonstrated. The relationship between work-based assessment and teaching is complex. People undergoing assessment engage in a process and sometimes a programme of learning that inevitably informs the work-based assessor's own intervention. The core question is whether teaching the learner is integral to the assessment process, or a complementary but additional role carried out by an assessor.

15 The guidance does not attempt to define arbitrarily the relationship between assessment and learning: it is likely that it will always be situation-specific. The statements draw upon the application of adult learning theories. There is an explicit recognition that coaching, mentoring, supervision, teaching and also role modelling are activities linked to work-based assessment. It is for providers to clarify the expectations of participants as appropriate to the learning process or programme and in accordance with the work context.

Values, reflective practice and continuing professional development

16 The individual guidance statements do not set out in any detail either the necessary underpinning commitment to core social care values and anti-discriminatory practices, or the broader continuing professional development and critical self reflection required of all practitioners. There has been considerable debate on this issue in developing the guidance. The consensus is that people engaged as work-based assessors should bring those commitments with them and always operate accordingly, no matter what the context.

17 The suggested applied value base for the work-based assessor role is presented in this spirit. It has been linked to the GSCC Codes of Practice, the core values requirements of the post-qualifying framework, the National Organisation for Practice Teaching statement on anti-oppressive and anti-discriminatory practice teaching and the Institute of Learning and Teaching professional values base.

Guidance layout

18 The guidance identifies three domains of activity in which the applied value and professional development base for work-based assessors should be integrated but which may be thought to be sets of activities carried through in all work-based assessment. The choice of the word 'domain' to group assessment activity under the three headings, as opposed to, for example, performance criteria, elements, requirements or competences, avoids undue association with any particular scheme, award or standards.

19 They are:

- *Domain A*: Organise opportunities for the demonstration of assessed competence in practice
- *Domain B*: Enable learning and professional development in practice
- *Domain C*: Manage the assessment of learners in practice

20 The statements represent the minimum expectations embedded in the assessment process: programme providers, educational institutions, employers and organisations may wish to complement them to meet their own circumstances.

Values for work-based assessors

21 Values for social care work-based assessors have been developed in addition to the core values of social care and social work and the General Social Care Council's Code of Practice for Social Care Workers. Work-based assessors are key people in training and development strategies that enable staff to carry out their responsibilities as outlined in the Code of Practice for Social Care Employers.

22 This guidance focuses on the implications of these values in relation to the assessment process. In order to promote anti-oppressive and anti-discriminatory practices, work-based assessors will:

- identify and question their own values and prejudices, the use of authority and power in the assessment relationship, and recognise and act upon the implications for their assessment practice;

- update themselves on best practice in assessment and research on adult learning and apply this knowledge in promoting the rights and choices of learners and managing the assessment process;

- respect and value the uniqueness and diversity of learners and recognise and build on their strengths, and take into account individual learning styles and preferred assessment methods;

- accept and respect learners' circumstances and understand how these impact on the assessment process;

- assess in a manner that does not stigmatise or disadvantage individuals and ensures equality of opportunity. Show applied knowledge and understanding of the significance of

    - racism

    - ill health and disability

    - gender

    - social class

    - sexual orientation

    - in managing the assessment process;

- recognise and work to prevent unjustifiable discrimination and disadvantage in all aspects of the assessment process, and counter any unjustifiable discrimination in ways that are appropriate to their situation and role; and

- take responsibility for the quality of their work and ensure that it is monitored and appraised; critically reflect on their own practice and identify development needs in order to improve their own performance, raise standards, and contribute to the learning and development of others.

Guidance statements

Domain A: Organise opportunities for the demonstration of assessed competence in practice

Work-based assessors should:

1. Take responsibility for creating a physical and learning environment conducive to the demonstration of assessed competence.

2. Negotiate with all participants in the workplace, including service users and carers, the appropriate learning opportunities and the necessary resources to enable the demonstration of practice competence.

3. Work openly and co-operatively with learners, their line managers, workplace colleagues, other professionals, and service users and carers, in the planning of key activities at all stages of learning and assessment.

4. Co-ordinate the work of all contributors. Ensure they are fully briefed, understand their roles and provide them with feedback.

5. Monitor, critically evaluate and report on the continuing suitability of the work environment, learning opportunities, and resources. Take appropriate action to address any shortcomings and optimise learning and assessment.

6. Contribute to the learning and development of the agency as a training organisation. Help to review and improve its provision, policies and procedures and identify barriers for learners.

Domain B: Enable learning and professional development in practice

Work-based assessors should:

1. Establish the basis of an effective working relationship by identifying learners' expectations, the outcomes which they have to meet in order to demonstrate competence, and their readiness for assessment. Agree the available learning opportunities, methods, resources, and timescales to enable them to succeed.

2. Discuss, identify, plan to address and review the particular needs and capabilities of learners, and the support available to them. Identify any matters which may impact on their ability to manage their own learning.

3. Discuss and take into account individuals' learning styles, learning needs, prior learning achievements, knowledge and skills. Devise an appropriate, cost-effective assessment programme which promotes their ability to learn and succeed.

4. Make professional educational judgments about meeting learners' needs within the available resources, ensuring the required learning outcomes can be demonstrated in accordance with adult learning models.

5. Identify which aspects of the management of the learning and assessment programme learners are responsible for in order to achieve their objectives. Describe and agree the roles of the work-based assessor in mentoring, coaching, modelling, teaching and supervision.

6. Establish how the learning and assessment programme is to be reviewed. Encourage learners to express their views, identify and agree any changes and how disagreements on any aspects of it are resolved.

7. Advise learners how to develop their ability to manage their learning. Deal with any difficulties encountered by them.

Domain C: Manage the assessment of learners in practice

Work-based assessors should:

1. Engage learners in the design, planning and implementation of the assessment tasks.

2. Agree and review a plan and methods for assessing learners' performance against agreed criteria.

3. Ensure that assessment decisions are the outcomes of informed, evidence-based judgments and clearly explain them to learners.

4. Evaluate evidence for its relevance, validity, reliability, sufficiency and authenticity according to the agreed standard.

5. Use direct observation of learners in practice to assess performance.

6. Base assessment decisions on all relevant evidence and from a range of sources, resolving any inconsistencies in the evidence available.

7. Encourage learners to self-evaluate and seek service users, carers and peer group feedback on their performance.

8. Provide timely, honest and constructive feedback on learners' performance in an appropriate format. Review their progress through the assessment process, distinguishing between formative and summative assessment

9. Make clear to learners how they may improve their performance. Identify any specific learning outcomes not yet demonstrated and the next steps. If necessary, arrange appropriate additional assessment activity to enable them to meet the standard.

10. Ensure that all assessment decisions, and the supporting evidence, are documented and recorded according to the required standard. Produce assessment reports which provide clear evidence for decisions.

11. Ensure that disagreements about assessment judgments and complaints made about the assessment process are managed in accordance with agreed procedures.

12. Seek feedback from learners on their experience of being assessed, and the consequences of the assessment programme for them. Incorporate the feedback into future assessment activity.

13. Contribute to standardisation arrangements and the agreed quality-assurance processes which monitor the organisation's training strategy.

Annex 1: Mapping the statements with existing roles, credits, qualifications and standards

Participants in the consultation process drew attention to the generic nature of work-based assessment and how its core activities cut across specific provision. Suggested links between the guidance statements and some existing vocational and professional qualifications, awards and programmes of learning are identified below.

Relevant extracts from the rules and requirements of different types of provision relating to work-based assessment are quoted. **A tick (✓) indicates that one or more guidance statements are normally applicable. A circle (○) indicates that one or more of the statements are compatible, applicable or relevant, according to the work context.**

1. Roles for work-based assessors

Programme rules and requirements for the Diploma In Social Work
Assessment of students and observation of their practice

✓ Programme providers responsible for assessment, particularly practice teachers, will have to judge the quality, coherence and sufficiency of evidence provided by students to show that they have met the practice requirements.

✓ *A report by the practice teacher evaluating the student's practice in meeting the six competences.*

✓ It is recommended that all first time practice teachers should receive a minimum of five days training in student supervision.

✓ One piece of direct observation may be carried out by a link supervisor, or be in the form of a video recording, but on at least two occasions in each assessed practice experience, the practice teacher must directly observe the student working with service users.

Accreditation of universities to grant degrees in social work
Criteria for key personnel and involvement

✓ Appoint enough academic and practice assessors with appropriate values, academic and professional qualifications and experience.

✓ Make sure that those who are responsible for the final assessment that a student is qualified to practise include qualified and experienced social workers and professional educators. The views of people who use services must be taken into account in the assessment process.

✓ Provide for an assessment by an experienced and qualified social worker of the competence and safety of a student to become a social worker.

167

○ Develop, promote and monitor activities for shared learning with other professions.

○ Secure, approve, allocate and audit appropriate practice learning opportunities in line with the curriculum

○ Make sure resources are available for teaching and assessment.

○ Provide opportunities for practice assessment based on the student providing a service over an extended period of time to people with a range of needs.

Programme requirements for mental health social work and the training of Approved Social Workers (ASW)
Evidence of candidates' competence and key staff

✓ A report by a practice assessor or practice supervisor from the programme, based on observation of the candidate's application of learning.

✓ Staff with relevant qualifications and experience to meet candidates' learning and assessment needs, including practice assessors and practice supervisors who would normally be expected to be practising approved social workers (ASWs) or mental health officers (MHOs).

✓ Programmes must address the needs of practice supervisors or assessors for adequate preparation for their role and for the standardisation of assessment.

Programme requirements for the Child Care Award
Evidence of candidates' competence and key staff

✓ A report by a practice supervisor/assessor from the programme which includes a report on the direct observation of the candidate's practice in relation to the five practice requirements, verifying and evaluating the direct evidence contained in the candidate's portfolio.

✓ The practice supervisor/assessor referred to above should have relevant practice experience and understanding and should normally be a practising child care worker. Programmes must address the needs of practice supervisors/assessors for adequate preparation for their role and for the standardisation of assessment.

Programme requirements for the Regulation of Care Services Award
Evidence of candidates' competence and key staff

✓ Confirmation and supporting evidence from a practice assessor that the practice requirements integrated with the values requirements have been met. This should include a report on a minimum of two direct observations of the candidate's practice as well as other sources identified as necessary by the practice assessor in relation to the six practice requirements. The report will verify and evaluate evidence contained in the candidate's portfolio and confirm whether the candidate has failed or passed the practice element of the programme.

✓ The practice assessor referred to above should have relevant practice experience and knowledge and would normally be a senior inspector or have recently been an inspector. Programmes must recruit practice assessors according to specified criteria, demonstrating that they are competent to assess candidates. Practice assessors might have a qualification in assessing practice; although programmes may recruit assessors who do not hold formal qualifications but would need to verify they are competent to assess practice at PQ level.

Programme requirements for the Practice Teaching Award
Key staff and role of the practice assessor

✓ The practice assessor is the person designated by the programme to write a report about the candidate's competence as a practice teacher.

✓ The evidence for the practice assessor's report will be derived from observing the candidate acting as a practice teacher on a minimum of two occasions.

✓ The practice assessor's report will provide complementary evidence and an overall assessment of the candidate's competence as a practice teacher.

✓ The practice assessor will normally be a qualified social worker or allied professional with at least two years experience of practice teaching, staff supervision, PQ mentoring or teaching/assessment.

✓ The scope of the practice assessor's role with the candidate should be made clear, i.e. whether the practice assessor will provide support and mentoring in addition to assessing the candidate's performance or whether the support role will be undertaken by someone else such as the line manager.

2. Credits which work-based assessors may accumulate

Requirements for the Post-Qualifying Award in Social Work
Core requirements

✓ Evaluate the effectiveness of their practice using a relevant knowledge base, including an understanding of legal and policy contexts and appropriate research.

✓ Demonstrate an explicit adherence to the values of social work and to the provision of ethically sound practice.

General requirements part II

✓ PQ5: competence in identifying and maintaining purposeful networks and collaborative arrangements.

✓ PQ6: competence in enabling others through management, education, supervision, consultation, practice teaching or direct contributions to education and training.

Requirements for the Advanced Award in Social Work
Core requirements

○ Demonstrate analysis and critical reflection which informs and influences practice and service provision.

○ Provide evidence of a commitment to sustaining the values of social work in the light of continuing social and political change and be able to define and develop policies and practices accordingly.

General requirements

○ AA1: Provide evidence of significant contribution to the development, delivery and evaluation of the service provided in a chosen area by demonstrating the ability to research, plan, implement, monitor and evaluate strategies for improvement or change.

✓ AA4: demonstrate competence in enhancing the capabilities of others as a means of informing and improving practice or service delivery.

○ AA8: Provide evidence of leadership in their chosen field including the ability to work independently, and to be accountable, in fulfilling the responsibilities of their role.

The Institute for Learning and Teaching (ILT) in Higher Education
Members of the Institute will be expected to have knowledge and understanding of:

✓ The subject matter that they will be teaching;

✓ Appropriate methods of teaching and learning in the subject area and at the level of the academic programme;

✓ Models of how students learn, both generically and in their subject;

✓ The use of learning and technologies appropriate to the context in which they teach;

✓ Methods for monitoring and evaluating their own teaching;

✓ The implications of quality assurance for practice.

Members of the Institute will be expected to adhere to the following professional values:

○ A commitment to scholarship in teaching, both generally and within their own discipline;

✓ Respect for individual learners and their development and empowerment;

✓ A commitment to the development of learning communities, including students, teachers and all those engaged in learning support;

tick; A commitment to continued reflection and evaluation and consequent improvement in their own practice.

Application routes are focused on the following six areas of professional activity:

○ 1. Teaching and/or the support of learning in higher education;

✓ 2. Contribution to the design and planning of learning activities and/or programmes of study;

✓ 3. Assessment and giving feedback to learners;

✓ 4. Developing effective learning environments and learner support systems;

✓ 5. Evaluating your practice and personal development;

✓ 6. Using your research, scholarly activity or relevant professional work to inform and impact on your teaching.

3. Some qualifications and standards relevant to work-based assessment

Requirements for the GSCC Practice Teaching Award

Values: Demonstrate and integrate the values of social work in all aspects of practice teaching.

✓ A1. Acknowledge and respect the rights of service users and students and value difference.

✓ A2. Promote and value student self-determination within an adult learning process.

✓ A3. Identify, analyse and take action to counter discrimination, racism and disadvantage using appropriate strategies in the context of own role and practice with the student.

✓ A4. Demonstrate fair and equal assessment of competence.

✓ A5. In Wales, promote practice teaching though the medium of Welsh.

Management: Manage the placement and the student's practice and be accountable with others for the quality of service to and safety of users.

✓ B1. Plan the placement and facilitate available practical resources and effective working relationships to support the student in placement.

✓ B2. Manage the integration of the student's learning needs, DipSW programme requirements and the agency context.

✓ B3. Manage and monitor the student's practice and progress within the placement and safeguard the quality of service to and safety of users.

✓ B4. Communicate effectively about specific tasks in relation to the student placement, within and across settings, contexts and disciplines.

Teaching: Plan, deliver and evaluate practice learning opportunities and assist the student's personal and professional development.

✓ C1. Negotiate, agree and review the student's practice learning objectives within the context of the rules and requirements for the DipSW, current legislation and agency procedures.

✓ C2. Deliver and evaluate effective practice learning opportunities for the student.

✓ C3. Provide an effective learning process and environment to ensure the student's personal and professional development.

Assessment: Assess the student's performance in the workplace against agreed criteria.

✓ D1. Agree and review a plan and methods for assessing the student's performance.

✓ D2. Collect and judge performance evidence against agreed criteria.

✓ D3. Collect and judge knowledge evidence against agreed criteria.

✓ D4. Make assessment decisions and provide feedback against agreed criteria which are communicated verbally throughout the placement and in a written assessment report to the student and the programme.

✓ D5. Assess the student's performance using differing sources of evidence.

Reflective practice: Critically reflect on own practice teaching and analyse policies and developments with respect to practice teaching.

✓ E1. Pursue own continuing professional development.

✓ E2. Critically evaluate own performance as a practice teacher and the quality of the learning opportunities and assessment provided.

✓ E3. Analyse and evaluate research, policies and developments with respect to practice teaching.

Standards for the preparation of teachers of nursing and midwifery-practice educators and practice education

The content of the programme of education should enable the following outcomes to be achieved:

Communication and working relationships enabling:

✓ The development of effective working relationships based on mutual trust and respect.

✓ An understanding of how students/registered practitioners integrate into a new setting and assisting with this process.

✓ Provision of ongoing and constructive support for students and registered practitioners.

Facilitation of learning in order to:

✓ Demonstrate the ability to facilitate effective learning within an area of practice.

○ Demonstrate the ability to be the prime educator in practice.

○ Demonstrate the ability to facilitate learning for those intending to become specialist practitioners.

✓ Identify individual potential in students and practitioners through appropriate systems; as an expert in practice, advise on educational opportunities that will facilitate the development of and support of specialist knowledge and skills.

○ Demonstrate strategies that will assist with the integration of learning from practice and educational settings.

Assessment in order to:

✓ Demonstrate a good understanding of assessment and ability to assess.

✓ Implement approved assessment procedures.

Role modelling in order to:

○ Demonstrate effective relationships with patients and clients.

✓ Create an environment in which practice development is fostered, evaluated and disseminated.

Creating an environment for learning in order to:

○ Ensure effective learning experiences and opportunities to achieve learning outcomes for students through mentorship, and for registered practitioners through preceptorship, clinical supervision and provision of a learning environment.

✓ Explore and implement strategies for quality-assurance and quality audit.

Improving practice in order to:

✓ Contribute to the creation of an environment in which change can be initiated and supported.

○ Identify ways in which multi-professional working would benefit patients and clients and contribute to the development of strategies to deliver quality care within a multi-disciplinary/multi-agency context in partnership with patients and clients.

A knowledge base in order to:

✓ Identify, apply and disseminate research findings within their area of practice.

○ Identify areas of practice which require evaluation and establish strategies for effecting this.

Course development that:

○ Contributes to the development and/or review of courses.

The Employment National Training Organisation Learning and Development Standards catalogue
Identify learning needs:

✓ Develop a strategy for learning and development.

✓ Identify the learning and development needs of the organisation.

✓ Identify individual learning aims and programmes.

Plan and design learning:

✓ Design learning programmes.

✓ Agree learning programmes with learners.

○ Develop training sessions.

✓ Prepare and develop resources to support learning.

○ Plan how to provide basic skills in the workplace.

Deliver learning:

✓ Manage the contribution of other people to the learning process.

✓ Create a climate that promotes learning.

○ Enable learning through presentations.

○ Enable learning through demonstration and instruction.

○ Enable individual learning through coaching.

○ Enable group learning.

○ Support learning by mentoring in the workplace.

✓ Support and advise individual learners.

○ Provide learning and development in international settings.

○ Introduce training for basic skills in the workplace.

○ Support how basic skills are delivered in the workplace.

○ Support people learning basic skills in the workplace.

Evaluate learning outcomes:

✓ Assess candidates using a range of methods.

✓ Assess candidates' performance through observation.

✓ Conduct internal quality assurance of the assessment process.

○ Conduct external quality-assurance of the assessment process.

✓ Monitor and review progress with learners.

✓ Evaluate and improve learning and development programmes.

✓ Respond to changes in learning and development.

✓ Support competence achieved in the workplace.

References

Adams, R. (2007) 'Reflective, Critical and Transformational Practice', in W. Tovey, (ed.) *The Post-Qualifying Handbook for Social Workers*. London: Jessica Kingsley.

Adams, R., Dominelli, L. and Payne, M. (2005a) 'Engaging with Social Work Futures', in R. Adams, L. Dominelli and M. Payne (eds) *Social Work Futures: Crossing Boundaries, Transforming Practice*. Basingstoke: Palgrave Macmillan

Adams, R., Dominelli, L. and Payne, M. (2005b) *Social Work Futures: Crossing Boundaries, Transforming Practice*. Basingstoke: Palgrave Macmillan.

Advocacy in Action, Charles, M., Clarke, H. and Evans, H. (2006) 'Assessing Fitness to Practise and Managing Work-based Placement', *Social Work Education*, 25(4): 373–84.

Armstrong, T. (2003) *The Whole-brain Solution: Thinking Tools to Help Students Observe, Make Connections and Solve Problems*. Ontario, Canada: Pembroke Publishing.

Atherton J.S. (1987) *Professional Supervision in Group Care: A Contract Based Approach*. London: Tavistock.

Baldwin, M. and Sadd, J. (2006) 'Allies with Attitude! Service Users, Academics and Social Service Agency Staff Learning How to Share Power in Running Social Work Education Courses', *Social Work Education*, 25(4): 348–59.

Bandura, A. (1965) 'Influence of Model's Reinforcement Contingencies on the Acquisition of Imitative Responses' *Journal of Personality and Social Psychology*, 1: 589–95.

Bandura, A. (1977) 'Self-efficacy: Toward a Unifying Theory of Behaviour Change', *Psychological Review*, 84(2): 191–215.

Bandura, A. (1986) *Social Foundations of Thought and Action: A Social Cognitive Theory*. Englewood Cliffs, NJ: Prentice Hall.

Bandura, A. (1994) 'Self-efficacy', in V.S. Ramchandran (ed) *Encyclopaedia of Human Behavior*, vol. 4. New York: Academic Press.

Bandura, A. (1997) *Self-efficacy: The Exercise of Control*. New York: Freeman.

Barker, R.L. (1995) *Social Work Dictionary*, 3rd edn. Washington, DC: NASW Press.

Barnett, R. (2002) 'Learning to Work and Working to Learn', in F. Reeve, M. Cartwright and R. Edwards (eds), *Supporting Lifelong Learning, vol. 2: Organizing Learning*. London: Routledge.

Barnett, R. and Hallam, S. (1999) 'Teaching for Supercomplexity: A Pedagogy for Higher Education', in P. Mortimore(ed.) *Understanding Pedagogy and its Impact on Learning*. London: Paul Chapman.

Beresford, P. and Wilson, A. (1998) 'Social Exclusion and Social Work: Challenges and Contradictions of Exclusive Debate', in M. Barry and C. Hallett (eds) *Social Exclusion and Social Work*. Lyme Regis: Russell House.

Beresford, P., Adshead, L. and Croft, S. (2007) *Palliative Care, Social Work and Service Users: Making Life Possible*. London: Jessica Kingsley.

Biggs, J. (2003) *Teaching for Quality Learning at University*, 2nd edn. Maidenhead: Open University Press.

Blewitt, J. (2008) 'Social Work in New Policy Contexts: Threats and Opportunities', in S. Fraser and S. Matthews (eds) *The Critical Practitioner in Social Work and Health Care*. London: SAGE.

Blewitt, J., Lewis, J. and Tunstall, J. (2007) *The Changing Roles and Tasks of Social Work: A Literature Informed Discussion Paper*. London: GSCC.

Bogo, M., Regehr, C., Hughes, J., Power, R. and Globerman, J. (2002) 'Evaluating a Measure of Student Field Performance in Direct Service: Testing Reliability and Validity of Explicit Criteria', *Journal of Social Work Education*, 38(3): 385–401.

Bolton, G. (2005) *Reflective Practice: Writing and Professional Development*, 2nd edn. London: SAGE.

Brechin, A. (2000) 'Introducing Critical Practice', in A. Brechin, H. Brown and M.A. Eby (eds) *Critical Practice in Health and Social Care*. London: SAGE, pp. 25–47.

Brookfield, S.D. (1986) *Understanding and Facilitating Adult Learning*. San Francisco, CA: Jossey Bass.

Brown, A. and Bourne, I. (1996) *The Social Work Supervisor*. Buckingham: Open University Press.

Burgess, H., Baldwin, M., Dalrymple, J. and Thomas, J. (1999) 'Developing Self-assessment in Social Work Education', *Social Work Education*, 18(2): 133–46.

Burt, M. and Worsley, A. (2008) 'Social Work, Professionalism and the Regulatory Framework', in S. Fraser and S. Matthews (eds) *The Critical Practitioner in Social Work and Health Care*. London: SAGE.

Caffarella, R.S. (1993) 'Self-directed Learning', in S.B. Merriam (ed.) *An Update on Adult Learning Theory: New Directions for Adult and Continuing Education*. San Francisco, CA: Jossey Bass.

Cameron-Jones, M. and O'Hara, P. (1997) 'Support and Challenge in Teacher Education', *British Educational Research Journal*, 23(1): 15–25.

Cartney, P. (2000) 'Adult Learning Styles: Implications for Practice Teaching in Social Work', *Social Work Education*, 19(6): 609–26.

Caspi, J. and Reid, W.J. (2002) *Educational Supervision in Social Work: A Task-centered Model for Field Instruction and Staff Development*. New York: Columbia University Press.

Central Council for Education and Training in Social Work (CCETSW) (1991 [1989]) *Improving Standards in Practice Learning: Requirements and Guidance for the Approval of Agencies and the Accreditation and Training of Practice Teachers*. Paper 26.3. London: CCETSW.

Central Council for Education and Training in Social Work (CCETSW) (1995) *The Requirements for Post-Qualifying Education and Training in the Personal Social Services*. Paper 31. London: CCETSW.

Chagnon, J. and Russell, R.K. (1995) 'Assessment of Supervisee Developmental Level and Supervision Environment across Supervisor Experience', *Journal of Counseling and Development*, 73(5): 553–8.

Charles, M. and Butler, S. (2004) 'Social Workers' Management of Organisational Change', in M. Lymbery and S. Butler (eds), *Social Work Ideals and Practice Realities*. Basingstoke: Palgrave Macmillan.

Children's Workforce Development Council (2006) *CWDC Induction Standards*, URL (consulted October 2007): http://www.cwdcouncil.org.uk/projects/cwdcinductionstandards.htm

Clifford, D. (1998) *Social Assessment Theory and Practice*. Aldershot: Ashgate.

Cooper, A. and Lousada, J. (2005) *Borderline Welfare: Feeling and Fear of Feeling in Modern Welfare*. London: Karnac.

Corby, B. (2006) *Applying Research in Social Work Practice*. Maidenhead: Open University Press.

Cowan, J. (1998) *On Becoming an Innovative University Teacher: Reflection in Action*. Buckingham: SRHE and Open University Press.

Cowburn, M., Nelson, P. and Williams, J. (2000) 'Assessment of Social Work Students: Standpoint and Strong Objectivity', *Social Work Education*, 19(6): 627–37.

Cox, D. and Pawar, M. (2006) *International Social Work: Issues, Strategies and Programs*. London: SAGE.

Crawford, K. (2006) *Reflective Reader: Social Work and Human Development*. Exeter: Learning Matters.

Cree, V. and Davis, A. (2007) *Social Work: Voices from the Inside*. London: Routledge.

Cree, V.E. (2005) 'Students Learning to Learn', in H. Burgess and I. Taylor (eds) *Effective Learning and Teaching Social Policy and Social Work*. Abingdon: RoutledgeFalmer.

Cree, V.E. and Macaulay, C. (2000) *Transfer of Learning in Professional and Vocational Education*. London: Routledge.

Crisp, B.R. and Green-Lister, P. (2002) 'Assessment Methods in Social Work Education: A Review of the Literature', *Social Work Education*, 21(2): 259–69.

Crisp, B.R., Green-Lister, P. and Dutton, K. (2006) Not Just Social Work Academics: The Involvement of Others in the Assessment of Social Work Students, *Social Work Education*, 25(7): 723–34.

D'Cruz, H., Gillingham, P. and Melendez, S. (2007) 'Reflexivity, its Meanings and Relevance for Social Work: A Critical Review of the Literature', *British Journal of Social Work*, 37: 73–90.

Dalrymple, J. and Burke, B. (2006) *Anti-oppressive Practice: Social Care and the Law*, 2nd edn. Maidenhead: Open University Press.

Davies, H. and Kinloch, H. (2000) 'Critical Incident Analysis: Facilitating Reflection and Transfer of Learning', in V.E. Cree and C. Macaulay (eds) *Transfer of Learning in Professional and Vocational Education*. London: Routledge, pp. 137–47.

Davies, M. and Connolly, J. (1994) 'The Price of Taking Students', *Health and Social Care*, 2: 339–46.

Department for Education and Skills (DfES) (2004) *Every Child Matters: Change for Children*. Nottingham: DfES.

Department of Health (DoH) (1996) *Community Care (Direct Payments) Act*. London: Department of Health.

Department of Health (DoH) (2002a) *Quality in Social Care: The National Institutional Framework*. Norwich: The Stationery Office.

Department of Health (DoH) (2002b) *The Requirements for Social Work Training*. Norwich: The Stationery Office.

Department of Health (DoH) (2006) *Our Health, Our Care, Our Say*. London: Stationery Office.

Department of Health (DoH) and Department for Education and Skills (DfES) (2006) *Options for Excellence: Building the Social Care Workforce of the Future*. London: Stationary Office.

Doel, M. (2006) *Effective Practice Learning in Local Authorities (1): Strategies for Improvement*, Capturing the Learning Series. Leeds: DoH/Skills for Care.

Doel, M. and Shardlow, S.M. (2005) *Modern Social Work Practice: Teaching and Learning in Practice Settings*. Aldershot: Ashgate.

Edmond, T., Megivern, D., Williams, C., Rochman, E. and Howard, M. (2006) 'Integrating Evidence-based Practice and Social Work Field Education', *Journal of Social Work education*, 42(2): 377–96.

Edwards, C. (2003) The Involvement of Service Users in the Assessment of Diploma in Social Work Students on Practice Placements', *Social Work Education*, 22(4): 341–9.

Elliott, T., Frazer T., Garrard, D., Hickinbotham, J., Horton, V., Mann, J. et al. (2005) 'Practice Learning and Assessment on BSc (Hons) Social Work: "Service User Conversations"', *Social Work Education*, 24(4): 451–66.

Ellis, G. (2001) 'Looking at Ourselves – Self-assessment and Peer-assessment: Practice Examples from New Zealand', *Reflective Practice*, 2(3): 289–302.

Eraut, M. (1994) *Developing Professional Knowledge and Competence*. London: Falmer.

Eraut, M., Alderton, J., Cole, G. and Senker, P. (2002) 'Learning from Other People at Work', in R. Harrison, F. Reeve, A. Hanson and J. Clarke (eds), *Supporting Lifelong Learning, vol. 2: Perspectives on Learning*. London: Routledge.

Fish, D. (1995) *Quality Mentoring for Student Teachers: A Principled Approach to Practice*. London: David Fulton.

Fook, J. (1999) 'Critical Reflectivity in Education and Practice', in B. Pease and J. Fook (eds) *Transforming Social Work Practice: Postmodern Critical Perspectives*. St Leonard's: Allen and Unwin.

Fook, J. (2002) *Social Work: Critical Theory and Practice*. London: SAGE.

Fook, J. (2007) 'Uncertainty: The Defining Characteristic of Social Work?', in M. Lymbery and K. Postle (eds) *Social Work: A Companion to Learning*. London: SAGE.

Fook, J., White, S. and Gardner, F. (2006) 'Critical Reflection: A Review of Contemporary Literature and Understandings', in S. White, J. Fook and F. Gardner (eds) *Critical Reflection in Health and Social Care*. Maidenhead: Open University Press and McGraw-Hill Education.

Ford, K. and Jones, A. (1987) *Student Supervision*. London: Macmillan.

Foucault, M. (1980) *Power/Knowledge: Selected Interviews and Other Writings 1972–1977*. Brighton: Harvester Press.

Freire, P. (1972) *Pedagogy of the Oppressed*. Harmondsworth: Penguin.

French, J.R.P. and Raven, B. (1960) 'The Bases of Social Power', in D. Cartwright (ed.) *Studies in Social Power*. Ann Arbour, MI: Institute of Social Research.

Furness, S. and Gilligan, P. (2004) '"Fit for Purpose": Issues from Practice Placements, Practice Teaching and the Assessment of Students' Practice', *Social Work Education*, 23(4): 465–79.

Garcia, J.A. and Floyd, C.E. (1999) 'Using Single System Design for Student Self-assessment: A Method for Enhancing Practice and Integrating Curriculum', *Journal of Social Work Education*, 35(3): 451–61.

Gardiner, D. (1989) *The Anatomy of Supervision: Developing Learning and Professional Competence for Social Work Students*. London: Society for Research into Higher Education and Open University Press.

Gardner, F. (2006) 'Using Critical Reflection in Research and Evaluation', in S. White, J. Fook and E. Gardner (eds) *Critical Reflection in Health and Social Care*. Maidenhead: Open University Press.

General Social Care Council (GSCC) (2002a) *Codes of Practice for Social Care Workers and Employers*. London: GSCC.

General Social Care Council (GSCC) (2002b) *Guidance on the Assessment of Practice in the Work Place*. London: GSCC.

General Social Care Council (GSCC) (2005a) *Post-Qualifying Framework for Social Work Education and Training*. London: GSCC.

General Social Care Council (GSCC) (2005b) *Specialist Standards and Requirements for Post-qualifying Social Work Education and Training: Practice Education*. London: GSCC.

Gleeson, J.P. (1990) 'Engaging Students in Practice Evaluation: Defining and Monitoring Critical Initial Interview Components', *Journal of Social Work Education*, 26 (3): 295–309.

Gould, N. and Taylor, I. (1996) *Reflective Learning for Social Work*. Aldershot: Ashgate.

Gregory, J. (2006) 'Facilitation and Facilitators' Style', in P. Jarvis (ed.) *The Theory and Practice of Teaching*, 2nd edn. Abingdon: Routledge.

Griffin, C. (2006) 'Didactism: Lectures and Lecturing', in P. Jarvis (ed.) *The Theory and Practice of Teaching*, 2nd edn. Abingdon: Routledge.

Guile, D. and Young, M. (2002) 'Beyond the Institution of Apprenticeship: Towards a Social Theory of Learning as the Production of Knowledge', in R. Harrison, F. Reeve, A. Hanson and J. Clarke (eds) *Supporting Lifelong Learning, vol. 1, Perspectives on Learning*. London: Routledge.

Hafford-Letchfield, T. (2006) *Management and Organisations in Social Work*. Exeter: Learning Matters.

Harden, R.M. and Crosby, J.R. (2000) 'The Good Teacher is More than a Lecturer – The Twelve Roles of the Teacher. *AMEE Medical Education Guide*, 20.

Harris, J. (2003) *The Social Work Business*. London: SAGE.

Harrison, K. and Ruch, G. (2007) 'Social Work and the Use of Self', in M. Lymbery and K. Postle (eds) *Social Work: A Companion to Learning*. London: SAGE.

Hart, E. and Bond, M. (1995) *Action Research for Health and Social Care: A Guide for Practice*. Buckingham: Open University Press.

Hawkins, P. and Shohet, R. (1989) *Supervision in the Helping Professions: An Individual, Group and Organizational Approach*. Buckingham: Open University Press.

Healey, K. (2000) *Social Work Practice: Contemporary Perspectives on Change*. London: SAGE.

Honey, P. and Mumford, A. (2000) *The Learning Styles Questionnaire*. Maidenhead: Peter Honey.

Jarvis, P. (2006) 'The Socrates Method', in P. Jarvis (ed.) *The Theory and Practice of Teaching*, 2nd edn. Abingdon: Routledge.

Jordan, B. and Jordan, C. (2006) *Social Work and the Third Way – Tough Love as Social Policy*, 3rd edn. London: SAGE.

Kadushin, A. (1992) *Supervision in Social Work*, 3rd edn.) New York: Columbia University Press.

Kadushin, A. and Harkness, D. (2002) *Supervision in Social Work*, 4th edn. New York: Columbia University Press.

Kaiser, T.L. (1997) *Supervisory Relationships: Exploring the Human Elements*. Pacific Grove, CA: Brooks/Cole.

Kearney, P. (2003) *A Framework for Supporting and Assessing Practice Learning*. SCIE Position Paper No. 2. London: SCIE.

Kemmis, S. and McTaggart, R. (2000) 'Participatory Action Research', in N.K. Denzin and Y.S. Lincoln (eds) *Handbook of Qualitative Research* , 2nd edn. Thousand Oaks, CA: SAGE, pp. 567–605.

Kissman, K. and Tran, T.V. (1990) 'Perceived Quality of Field Placement Education among Graduate Social Work Students', *Journal of Continuing Social Work Education*, 5(2): 27–30.

Knight, C. (2001) 'The Process of Field Instruction: BSW and MSW Students' Views of Effective Field Supervision', *Journal of Social Work Education*, 37(3): 357–9.

Knowles, M.S. (1980) *The Modern Practice of Adult Education: From Andragogy to Pedagogy*. Englewood Cliffs, NJ: Cambridge Adult Education.

Kolb, D. (1984) *Experiential Learning*. Englewood Cliffs. NJ: Prentice Hall.

Kolevzon, M.S. (1979) 'Evaluating the Supervisory Relationship in Field Placements', *Social Work*, 24(3): 241–4.

Ladyman, S. (2004) 'Foreword', in Practice Learning Taskforce, *Practice Learning Taskforce First Annual Report*. London: Department of Health.

Lave, J. and Wenger, E. (1991) *Situated Learning: Legitimate Peripheral Participation*. Cambridge: Cambridge University Press.

Lave, J. and Wenger, E. (1998) *Communities of Practice: Learning, Meaning, and Identity*. Cambridge: Cambridge University Press.

Lefevre, M. (2005) 'Facilitating Practice Learning and Assessment: The Influence of Relationship', *Social Work Education, 24(5): 565–83.*

Lehmann, J. (2006) 'Telling Stories . . . and the Pursuit of Critical Reflection', in S. White, J. Fook and F. Gardner (eds) Critical Reflection in Health and Social Care*. Maidenhead: Open University Press and McGraw-Hill Education.

Light, G. and Cox, R. (2001) *Learning and Teaching in Higher Education: The Reflective Professional*. London: SAGE.

Loganbill, C., Hardy, E. and Delworth, U. (1982) 'Supervision: A Conceptual Model', *Counselling Psychologists*, 10: 3–42.

Lymbery, M. and Butler, S. (eds) (2004) *Social Work Ideals and Practical Realities*. Basingstoke: Macmillan.

Lymbery, M. and Postle, K. (2007) 'Social Work in Challenging Times', in M. Lymbery and K. Postle (eds) *Social Work: A Companion to Learning*. London: SAGE.

Macaulay, C. (2000) 'Transfer of Learning', in V.E. Cree and C. Macaulay (eds) *Transfer of Learning in Professional and Vocational Education*. London: Routledge.

Martin, G.P., Phelps, K. and Katbamna, S. (2004) 'Human Motivation and Professional Practice: Of Knights, Knaves and Social Workers', *Social Policy and Administration*, 38(5): 470–87.

Marton, F. and Saljo, R. (1997) 'Approaches to Learning', in F. Marton, D. Housell and N. Entwistle (eds) *The Experience of Learning*, 2nd edn. Edinburgh: Scottish Academic Press.

McLaughlin, H. (2007) *Understanding Social Work Research*. London: SAGE.

Merriam, S. and Caffarella, R.S. (1998) *Learning in Adulthood: A Comprehensive Guide*. San Francisco: Jossey Bass.

Moon, J.A. (1999) *Reflection in Learning and Professional Development*. London: Kegan Paul.

Moon, J.A. (2004) *A Handbook of Reflective and Experiential Learning: Theory and Practice*. London: RoutledgeFalmer.

Moore, L.S., Dettlaff, A.J. and Dietz, T.J. (2004) 'Using the Myers-Briggs Type Indicator in Field Education Supervision', *Journal of Social Work Education*, 40(2): 337–49.

Noble, C. (2001) 'Researching Field Practice in Social Work Education: Integration of Theory and Practice through the Use of Narratives', *Journal of Social Work*, 1(3): 347–60.

O'Connor, I., Hughes, M., Turney, D., Wilson, J. and Setterlund, J. (2006) *Social Work and Social Care Practice*. London: SAGE.

O'Sullivan, T. (2005) 'Some Theoretical Propositions on the Nature of Practice Wisdom', *Journal of Social Work*, 5(2): 221–42.

Parker, J. (2004) *Effective Practice Learning in Social Work*. Exeter: Learning Matters.

Parker, J. (2005) 'Should You Encourage Students to Assess Themselves in Practice Learning? A Guided Self-efficacy Approach to Practice Learning Assessment', *Journal of Practice Teaching in Health and Social Work*, 6(3): 8–30.

Parker, J. (2006) 'Developing Perceptions of Competence during Practice Learning', *British Journal of Social Work*, 36(6): 1017–36.

Parker, J. (2007) 'The Process of Social Work: Assessment, Planning, Intervention and Review', in M. Lymbery and K. Postle (eds) *Social Work: A Companion to Learning*. London: SAGE, pp. 111–22.

Parker, J. and Bradley, G. (2003) *Social Work Practice: Assessment, Planning, Intervention and Review*. Exeter: Learning Matters.

Parker, J., Whitfield, J. and Doel, M. (2006a) *Improving Practice Learning in Local Authorities (2): Workforce Development, Recruitment and Retention*. Capturing the Learning Series. Leeds: DoH/Skills for Care.

Parker, J., Doel, M. and Whitfield, J. (2006b) 'Does Practice Learning Assist the Recruitment and Retention of Staff?', *Research Policy and Planning*, 24(3): 179–96.

Parton, N. (ed.) (1996) *Social Theory, Social Change and Social Work*. London: Routledge.

Parton, N. and O'Byrne, P. (2000) *Constructive Social Work: Towards a New Practice*. London: Palgrave Macmillan.

Pawson, R., Boaz, A., Grayson, L., Long, A. and Barnes, C. (2003) *Types and Quality of Knowledge in Social Care*. Knowledge Review 3, London: SCIE.

Payne, M. (2002) 'Social Work Theory and Reflective Practice', in R. Adams, L. Dominelli and M. Payne (eds) *Social Work: Themes, Issues and Critical Debates*, 2nd edn. Basingstoke: Palgrave.

Payne, M. (2005) *Modern Social Work Theory*, 3rd edn. London: Palgrave Macmillan.

Peach, J. and Horner, N. (2007) 'Using Supervision? Support or Surveillance?', in M. Lymbery and K. Postle, *Social Work: A Companion to Learning*. London: SAGE.

Pearson, C. (2002) *Teaching Circles as a Response to the Staff Development Needs of Part-time Teachers in Higher Education*. LTSN Generic Centre, URL (consulted): www.heacademy.ac.uk

Practice Learning Task Force (2003) *Practice Learning in Focus*. Edinburgh:

Prochaska, J.O. and DiClemente, C.C. (1983) 'Stages and Processes of Self-change of Smoking: Toward an Integrative Model of Change', *Journal of Consulting and Clinical Psychology*, 51: 390–5.

Quality Assurance Agency (QAA) (2000) *Subject Benchmark Statements: Social Policy and Administration and Social Work*. Gloucester: Quality Assurance Agency for Higher Education.

Quality Assurance Agency for Higher Education (QAA) (2000) *Social Policy and Administration and Social Work: Subject Benchmark Statements*. Gloucester: QAA.

Ramsden, P. (1992) *Learning to Teach in Higher Education*, 2nd edn. London: RoutledgeFalmer.

Regehr, C., Regehr, G., Leeson, J. and Fusco, L. (2002) 'Setting Priorities for Learning in the Field Practicum: A Comparative Study of Students and Field Instructors', *Journal of Social Work Education*, 38(1): 55–65.

Sawdon, C. and Sawdon, D. (1995) 'The Supervision Partnership: A Whole Greater than the Sum of its Parts', in J. Pritchard (ed.) *Good Practice in Supervision*. London: Jessica Kingsley.

Schön, D.A. (1983) *The Reflective Practitioner: How Professionals Think in Action*. London: Temple Smith.

Senge, P. (1990) *The Fifth Discipline*. London: Random House.

Senior, B. with Lodes, E. (2008) 'Best Practice as Skilled Organisational Work', in K. Jones, B. Cooper and H. Ferguson (eds) *Best Practice in Social Work: Critical Perspectives*. Basingstoke: Palgrave Macmillan.

Shardlow, S. and Doel, M. (1996) *Practice Learning and Teaching*. Basingstoke: Macmillan.

Shaw, I. and Lishman, J. (1999) *Evaluation and Social Work Practice*. London: SAGE.

Sheppard, M. (2006) *Social Work and Social Exclusion*. Aldershot: Ashgate.

Shulman, L. (1993) Interactional Supervision. Washington, DC: NASW Press.

Skills for Care (2005) *The State of the Social Care Workforce 2004*. London: Skills for Business.

Smale, G., Tuson, G. with Biehal, N. and March P. (1993) *Empowerment, Assessment, Care Management and the Skilled Worker*. London: National Institute of Social Work.

Smith, D. (ed.) (2004) *Social Work and Evidence-based Practice*. London: Jessica Kingsley.

Statham, D. (ed.) (2004) *Managing Front Line Practice in Social Care*. London: Jessica Kingsley.

Stoltenberg, C. and Delworth, U. (1987) *Supervising Counsellors and Therapists*. San Francisco: Jossey Bass.

Taylor, C. and White, S. (2006) 'Knowledge and Reasoning in Social Work: Educating for Humane Judgement', *British Journal of Social Work*, 36: 937–54.

Taylor, I., Thomas, J. and Sage, H. (1999) 'Portfolios for Learning and Assessment: Laying the Foundations for Continuing Professional Development', *Social Work Education*, 18(2): 147–60.

Taylor, J. and Baldwin, M. (1991) 'Travelling Hopefully: An Anti-racist Practice and Practice Learning Opportunities', *Social Work Education*, 10(3): 5–32.

Thomas, R. (2002) 'Creative Assessment: Involving Service Users in Student Assessment in Social Work', *Journal of Practice Teaching in Health and Social Work*, 4(1): 27–43.

Thompson, N. (2006) *Anti-Discriminatory Practice*, 2nd edn. London: Palgrave Macmillan.

Thompson, N. (2006) *Promoting Workplace Learning* Bristol: Policy Press.

Thompson, N., Osada, M. and Anderson, B. (1994) *Practice Teaching in Social Work*, 2nd edn. Birmingham: PEPAR.

Topss/SfC (2002) *National Occupational Standards for Social Work*. Leeds: Topss. www.skillsforcare.org/files/cd

Topss/GSCC (2002) *Guidance on the Assessment of Practice in the Workplace*. London: GSCC.

Tsui, M.-S. (2005) *Social Work Supervision: Contexts and Supervision: Contexts and Concepts*. Thousand Oaks, CA: SAGE.

Walter, I., Nutley, S., Percy-Smith, J., McNeish, D. and Frost, S. (2004) *Knowledge Review No.7: Improving the Use of Research in Social Care Practice*. Bristol: The Policy Press.

Waters, B. (2001) 'Radical Action for Radical Plans', *British Journal of Occupational Therapy* 64(11): 557–8.

Wenger, E. (1998) *Communities of Practice: Learning, Meaning, and Identity*. Cambridge: Cambridge University Press.

Williams, S. and Rutter, L. (2007) *Enabling and Assessing Work-based Learning for Social Work: Supporting the Development of Professional Practice*. Birmingham: Learn to Care.

Yelloly, M. and Henkel, M. (eds) (1995) *Learning and Teaching in Social Work: Towards Reflective Practice*. London: Jessica Kingsley.

Young, P. (1967) *The Student and Supervision in Social Work Education*. London: Routledge and Kegan Paul.

Index

AASW *see* Advanced Award in Social Work
accountability 19, 137; GSCC *Codes of Practice* 137,
    138–9; *National Occupational Standards for Social
    Work* 27; supervision 102, 104, 106, 117
action plans 131, 132–3
active learning 44, 45
adult learning 38, 39–40, 121, 161, 164
Advanced Award in Social Work (AASW) 160, 169–70
Advanced level 5, 6, 10, 11, 141
advocacy 28
age 115, 117
agency capacity 121, 122, 123–4
andragogy 38–9
anti-discriminatory practice 11, 104, 157, 163, 164
anti-oppressive practice 29, 30, 83, 157; *Guidance on the
    Assessment of Practice in the Workplace* 11, 163, 164;
    supervision 102, 103, 104, 108, 110, 117; teaching
    strategies 63
Approved Social Workers (ASWs) 151, 168
assertiveness 150
assessment 2, 13, 63, 77–98, 104, 156–7; core
    characteristics and models of 80–2; definition of 78;
    *Guidance on the Assessment of Practice in the
    Workplace* 6, 7–9, 10, 11, 159–74; meanings of
    79–80; process of 89–93; reports 81, 92–3, 133–4,
    168, 169; *Requirements for Social Work Training* 25,
    86; research 82–5; self-efficacy model 93–7;
    supervision 109, 110; technical rational approach
    147
ASWs *see* Approved Social Workers
authority 113, 114–15
autonomy 19, 39, 107, 108

Bandura, Albert 42, 93, 94
behaviourist theories 41, 42, 55
beliefs 94, 108
boundaries 72
brain activity 47
bureaucratisation 18–19

carers 63, 156; assessment 79, 80, 84; feedback 85, 110;
    needs of 122; participation of 51, 124; practice
    curriculum 131

case notes 91
case study approach 68
Central Council for Education and Training in Social Work
    (CCETSW) 3, 4
Child Care Award 168
Children's Workforce Development Council (CWDC) 3, 4,
    23, 126
class 117, 164
collaboration 75
communication skills 25, 28
'communities of practice' 31, 54, 55, 56, 137, 151–3,
    154
competence 3, 15, 36, 156; assessment of 83, 93, 104,
    110, 159, 160, 165; *Guidance on the Assessment of
    Practice in the Workplace* 7–8, 11, 161, 163
confidence 94, 95–6, 107, 116–17
confidentiality 74, 106
consultation 18, 160, 161
continuing professional development 35, 138–41,
    152, 154, 159, 163, 172; *see also* professional
    development
critical incident analysis 68, 83, 91
critical pathway analysis 126, 127, 129
critical reflection 32–5, 37, 66, 70, 75–6, 138, 142, 145;
    Advanced Award in Social Work 169; anti-oppressive
    practice 103; contribution to the 'learning
    organisation' 158; experiential learning cycle 44;
    *Guidance on the Assessment of Practice in the
    Workplace* 163, 172; modelling 62; portfolios 85;
    post-qualifying framework 141; practice curriculum
    131; self-assessment 87; supervision 105, 117, 157;
    see also reflective practice
CWDC *see* Children's Workforce Development Council

data collection 85, 91, 93
deep learning 40–1, 57, 85
developmental approach 106–8
dialogue: assessment 92; critical reflection 85; reflective
    thinking 145
'didactic' approach 60
Diploma in Social Work 3, 167
disability 25, 74, 115, 117, 164
discovery 105, 117

discrimination 71, 72, 73, 102, 152, 164, 171; *see also* anti-discriminatory practice
discussion 67
diversity 72–4

emotions 48, 143
Employment National Training Organisation 160, 161, 173–4
empowerment: anti-oppressive practice 103; self-directed learning 75; service users 18, 156; social work definition 16; students 51, 76, 97
equality 72, 117
ethical issues 28
evidence for assessment 81, 91–2, 93, 97, 109
evidence-based practice 105, 147; assessment 82, 83; preparation 119; professional development 148
exclusion 17, 21, 73, 102
exercises 69
experiential learning 43–5, 75, 143, 144

facilitation theories 43, 60, 63
feedback 31, 144; assessment 84, 91, 92, 172; self-awareness 105; service users 85, 110, 124, 131; supervision 109
Freire, P. 76

GANTT charts 124–6, 129
gender 74, 115, 117, 164
General Social Care Council (GSCC) 1, 2, 23; *Codes of Practice* 4, 23, 30, 137, 138–9, 163, 164; *Guidance on the Assessment of Practice in the Workplace* 11, 160; Post Registration Training and Learning 139, 140; post-qualifying framework 4, 6, 141; principles of pedagogy 51; registration criteria 26; standards 10
goals 39, 85, 94; organisational objectives 114–15; planning 119, 120; practice curriculum 131; professional 154; supervision 110
GSCC *see* General Social Care Council
Guidance on the Assessment of Practice in the Workplace 6, 7–9, 10, 11, 159–74

Higher Specialist level 5, 6, 10, 11, 86, 141
Honey, Peter 45, 48
human rights 16, 17
humanist theories 42, 43, 55, 64

identity, professional 31, 71, 72
IFSW *see* International Federation of Social Work

ILT *see* Institute of Learning and Teaching
induction 126–8, 157
inequality 21, 103
information provision 58, 62
Institute of Learning and Teaching (ILT) 162, 163, 170–1
International Federation of Social Work (IFSW) 16
interviews 68

knowledge 28, 29, 30, 32, 37, 146–8; discovery process 105, 117; life experience 39; professional development 157; reflective thinking 66, 70; situational context 56; social mediation of 31; supervision 102, 113; tacit 139, 148; teaching strategies 63
Knowles, Malcolm 38–9, 65
Kolb, David 43–5, 48, 75, 143, 144

Lave, J. 54, 152
learning 1, 12, 36–52, 54–6, 156; agency capacity 123–4; assessment 80, 82, 90, 93; barriers to 49–50; behaviourist theories 41, 42, 55; collective 139, 151, 152, 153; deep 40–1, 57, 85; experiential 43–5, 75, 143, 144; *Guidance on the Assessment of Practice in the Workplace* 7–9, 162–3, 165–6, 168, 171, 172, 173, 173–4; humanist theories 42, 43, 55, 64; individualised learning agreements 90, 92, 93, 128–9, 130, 157; Institute of Learning and Teaching 170; planning 50–1, 120, 121; Post Registration Training and Learning 139, 140; post-qualifying framework 6, 10; practice curriculum 129–31; self-directed 39, 64–5, 75; situational 54, 55; social cognitive learning theories 42–3, 55; spiral of 38, 51; supervision 101, 109, 110, 111; surface 40, 41; time management 150; transfer of 57–9, 61, 105; whole brain 47; *see also* practice learning
learning agreements 90, 92, 93, 128–9, 130, 157
'learning organisations' 10, 158, 160
learning plans 131, 132–3
learning styles 45–6, 49, 50, 83
Learning Styles Inventory 45, 46
legislative requirements 104, 122, 159
life experience 39
lifelong learning 14, 35

managerialism 18, 19, 108, 113
mental health social work 17, 25, 71, 72, 168
metacognition 48
midwifery 162, 172–3
'modernisation' agenda 18
multi-agency working 139, 151
Mumford, Alan 45, 48

National Occupational Standards for Social Work 4, 24, 26–8, 30, 64, 87, 139; *Guidance on the Assessment of Practice in the Workplace* 161, 162; practice curriculum 129; *see also* standards

National Organisation for Practice Teaching (NOPT) 161, 163

National Vocational Qualifications (NVQs) 160, 161

NOPT *see* National Organisation for Practice Teaching

nursing 162, 172–3

NVQs *see* National Vocational Qualifications

observation 68–9, 91, 167

partnership working 25, 29, 103, 139, 157

pedagogy 11, 31–2, 38, 51

peer-assessment 85

personal capacity 121, 122, 124

physical environment 109, 123–4

placements 1, 3, 13, 28, 30–1; assessment 92; context 22; endings 111–12; *Guidance on the Assessment of Practice in the Workplace* 171; planning 119, 120, 121–6, 157; self-confidence 107; supervision 108–14; SWOT analysis 135; transfer of learning to practice 57

planning 50–1, 62–3, 119, 120, 121–6, 157; assessment 81, 89–90, 134; evaluation of plans 135–6

policy 17–18

portfolios 83, 85

Post-Qualifying (PQ) Framework for Social Work Education and Training 4–6, 10

Post Registration Training and Learning (PRTL) 138, 139, 140

Post-Qualifying Award in Social Work (PQSW) 3, 160, 169

post-qualifying education 3, 4–10, 35, 86, 141, 153

power 34, 56, 143; anti-oppressive practice 103; assessment 81–2; supervisory relationship 114–17, 157; types of 115, 116

PQSW *see* Post-Qualifying Award in Social Work

practice 33, 35, 37, 147, 156; assessment 83; practice curriculum 131; transfer of learning to 57–9; *see also* practice learning

practice assessors 2, 4, 10, 46, 160, 167, 168–9; *see also* assessment; work-based assessors

practice curriculum 62, 64, 90, 92, 93, 110, 129–31, 157

practice educators 1, 2, 29–32, 156, 158; assessment 79–80, 83–4, 87–8, 89–93; context of placements 22; development of role 3–4; knowledge-informed 146–8; role as a teacher 60–3; self-assessment 87; self-directed learning 64; supervision 102; support for 148–53; three-way relationship 57–9, 157; *see also* practice teachers

practice learning 2, 10, 13, 28–32, 156–8; assessment 86–7, 92, 93–7; centrality of 24–6; experiential learning cycle 45; *Guidance on the Assessment of Practice in the Workplace* 171; managing and developing learning experiences 118–36; power issues 82, 115; supervision 101, 102; *see also* learning

Practice Learning Self-Efficacy Scale 94, 95–6

Practice Teaching Award (PTA) 2, 3, 86–7, 160, 169, 171

practice teachers 2, 4, 79–80, 83–4, 167; *see also* practice educators

practice wisdom 107, 139, 148

practitioners 2, 19, 151

praxis 75–6

presentations 69

professional artistry view 33

professional development 14, 35, 137, 138–41, 154, 157; 'communities of practice' 152; *Guidance on the Assessment of Practice in the Workplace* 7–8, 11, 159, 163, 165–6, 172; spiral of 38; supervision 117; tacit knowledge 148

professional requirements 122; assessment 86–7, 160, 162; post-registration training 139, 140

programme providers 2, 25, 162

PRTL *see* Post Registration Training and Learning

PTA *see* Practice Teaching Award

qualifying for social work 23–8

questioning 60, 67

race 74, 115, 117, 164

reading 69

reflective journals 67, 83, 91, 143

reflective practice 14, 33–4, 62, 70, 139, 141–6; challenging organisational objectives 114–15; definition of reflection 142; *Guidance on the Assessment of Practice in the Workplace* 172; supervision 110, 150; tacit knowledge 148; teaching 66; *see also* critical reflection

reflexivity 34, 103, 139, 142–3, 148

Regional Planning Networks 4

Regulation of Care Services Award 168–9

relationships 16, 21, 22; ending 111, 112; supervisory 101, 109–10, 114–17

Requirements for Social Work Training 24, 25, 86

research 69, 82–5, 139, 147, 148, 153–4

resources 62, 65, 132

reviewing 110, 111

risk 18, 27

Rogers, Carl 43

role modelling 29, 62, 173
role-play 69, 72, 91, 145

SCIE see Social Care Institute for Excellence
self 13, 32, 75–6, 117, 137–55
self-assessment 82, 83, 85, 87, 91, 144–5
self-awareness 105, 112, 150
'self-care' 104
self-declaration 26
self-directed learning 39, 64–5, 75
self-efficacy 85, 93–7
self-esteem 94
service users 26, 63, 156; anti-oppressive practice 103;
    assessment 79, 80, 84; case studies 71, 72; ending
    relationships with 112; feedback 85, 110; needs of
    122; participation of 51, 124; practice curriculum 131
sexual orientation 115, 117, 164
SfC see Skills for Care
shadowing 26, 30, 60
situational learning 54, 55
skills 30, 63; skills rehearsal 69; supervision 102;
    'tuning-in' 110
Skills for Care (SfC) 3, 4, 23, 126
Skinner, B.F. 42
SMART planning 120–1
Social Care Institute for Excellence (SCIE) 23
social class 117, 164
social cognitive learning theories 42–3, 55
social context 52
social exclusion 17, 21, 73, 102
social justice 16, 17, 22, 103
social work: characteristics of good 21; context for social
    work practice 17–18; definitions of 16–17; practice of
    18–22; qualifying for 23–8; roles and tasks of 20
'Socratic' approach 60
Specialist level 5, 6, 10, 86, 141
Specialist Standards and Requirements for Post-Qualifying
    Education 10, 11
standards 10–11, 15, 36, 118–19; assessment 77–8;
    GSCC Codes of Practice 138; induction 126;
    professional development 137; supervision 99–100,
    103–4; teaching 53–4; see also National Occupational
    Standards for Social Work
'standpoint theory' 83
student-centred learning 43, 63
students 2, 24, 30–1, 157–8; assessment of 77–98,
    133–4, 156–7; diversity 73–4; empowerment 51, 76;
    needs and requirements 122; Requirements for Social
    Work Training 25; supervision of 99–117; three-way
    relationship 57–9, 157

'supercomplexity' 31–2
supervision 13, 31, 40, 62, 91, 99–117, 157; definitions
    of 100–2; developmental approach 106–8; functions
    of 102–5; Guidance on the Assessment of Practice in
    the Workplace 167; models of 105–8; power issues
    114–17; reflection 150; through the 'life' of the
    placement 108–14
support: practice assessor's role 169; for practice educators
    148–53; for students 58–9, 102, 104, 105, 157–8
surface learning 40, 41
SWOT analysis 135

tacit knowledge 139, 148
task-centred model 94, 97
teaching 12–13, 53–76; adapting to student
    characteristics 50; approaches to 60–1; diversity
    72–4; role as a teacher 61–3; self-reflection 75–6;
    strategies 63–72; transfer of learning to practice 57–9;
    work-based assessment 163
Teaching Circles 153
technical rational view 33, 147
theory 31, 33, 35, 37, 63, 131, 147
time management 134, 149, 150
Training Organisation for the Personal Social Services
    (Topss) 11, 23, 160
trust 65, 83, 110
'tuning-in skills' 110

uncertainty 31, 33, 34, 147
university requirements 87–8, 92–3, 122
university tutors 2, 26, 74, 110; individualised learning
    agreements 90; three-way relationship 57–9, 157

VAK see Visual-Auditory-Kinesthetic model
values 30, 35, 63, 156; Guidance on the Assessment of
    Practice in the Workplace 163, 164–5, 169, 170, 171;
    induction standards 126; National Occupational
    Standards for Social Work 28; reflective thinking 145,
    146; supervision 102, 106, 108
Visual-Auditory-Kinesthetic (VAK) model 46–7, 48
Vygotsky, L. 152

Wenger, E. 54, 151, 152
whole brain learning 47
work-based assessors 11, 120, 161, 162, 163, 164–7,
    169–71
work-based supervisors 2
workload 104, 148, 149, 150

Zone of Proximal Development (ZPD) 152